MY THANKS

...*to a hundred sweet souls, but* how do you send out a personal thank you when you're sharing insights from a twenty-plus year journey? So many dear precious family and friends have spoken into it. To keep from writing a chapter to itself in this tiny space, I am giving a heart-pierced thanks to all I have journeyed with in these circles. You'll forgive me, however, if I make an exception for my parents, children, and unbelievably beautiful writing partner and wife, Stephanie JoAnn Coleson Reid.

Mom and Dad, you are rocks of support and unconditional love. You listen to my dreams—as crazy as they often sound—while keeping me uniquely aware that all you really care about is *me*.

To Tsion, Salem, Bethlehem Hope, and Aiden Journey—every age and every phase has been my favorite. I would hold on to your past and gaze at it, but your character brimming with Holy Spirit-fruit ignites my heart to overwhelming joy for your future.

To Steph—there are no adequate words. My thoughts of you are a deafening chaotic heart-fluttering *other*. I try to grasp a thought, but none can come without all of the others rushing out with it. Everyday, I think to myself, "Someday, I'll be more like you." Life-companion, best friend—I'm loving life-living with you. xo

we also want to thank my sister, jen, for being the most conscientious and enthusiastically supportive editor ever. you gave this your time, your intellect, and so much of your enormous heart. we are forever grateful, sister.

CONTENTS

INTRO TO THE INTRO

jack found his pen on a leaf on the water while jill ran in circles around his kids (their kids)—and scrubbed dishes and threw laundry in and read a little of his writing when she could. then, because she was slightly more conscientious in grade school, they thought maybe it was a good idea for her to edit along the way. (i guess he just needed me like he needs the pen and the water.. .. ..)

so, hi. i'm jill, along for the journey—all the circles—and to add commentary, insights, and edits here and there, but also maybe a distraction from the hill-falling. the "jack and jill" thing came to us a couple of years back when all of life felt like a falldown. trudging up and falling down.. .. ..

the nursery rhyme hill has held some very appealing (and sometimes counterintuitive) imagery—as well as the pail they were fetching. like a bucket-list of midlife thinking—ya know—what has been and what is yet to be???? and this writing has become a healing place as jack has penned it all so carefully here.

since we started dreaming up the writing of this, we have known we were to write, but the outline was a little hazy at first. after scott opened the first document, typed the first sentences of the introduction, and began to give his heart voice, we have been figuring out what this book was to be—what we are communicating. so as the chapters and outline have fallen into place, we need to let you know what the title means: what and who this is for. (ya know, how you're supposed to tell what you are going to say, and then say it, and then tell what you said).

this is for someone who might be looking to find meaning in the happenings of life.

we go in circles. living out a chosen career or a job that chose us, traversing the hills and valleys of everything life throws our way: in work, in relationships, in all of life—our expectations seldom meeting reality. our experiences can sometimes make us feel stuck or maybe like we're spinning. this book is about seeking and finding meaning in the processes of God in it all. you'll read below that **God is doing something.**

so, here is the story jack (scott) tells from the beginning. to circles—never ending puddling, swirling, and rippling circles. to abraham. to joseph. to the wilderness and understanding. to JESUS—our way, truth, zoe life. to being a leaf on the water—finding rest in quiet moments and in the realization that He is making much of every circle.

INTRODUCTION

I am not quite sure where to begin. In some ways, I feel like Bilbo Baggins looking for *someplace quiet where I can finish my book.* [1] Before plunging into an introduction, I want to be sure to make it known that I am a person-in-process. Like anyone who may pick this up to read it, I am in the middle of the walking and living of life, which has come in ways I least expected and has often left me with more questions than answers. At any rate, please know that I am not writing this as one who has gone through the trial and is now writing victoriously from the other side. While I feel certain that I have known and been known by Jesus for nearly thirty-seven years, the past couple decades (the whole of my adult life so far) have been packed with unexpected journeys filled with happy surprises, great personal disappointments, and a few tragedies.

No doubt, many of you who will pick this up will have gone through much, much more. As I share some of my own story, the point will not be *my* story, but for you to see in *your* story a God at work that has not lost your way, who moves in concrete ways for the saving and restoring of your emotions, will, and intellect (the saving of your soul). In the mix of that, I believe with all of my heart that you can walk into a place where His will concerning these days can be made known to you and where you fit in it, and that you can experience an intimacy with Him that can carry you into *deep rest*, even as you are being poured out for Him. Essentially, I want to say, know it or not, ***God is doing a very practical and real thing in, around, and about you. You are now living a life in which God has yet to author an unproductive or useless moment! You may have wasted a few, but* He *has not.***

Please hear this again: the importance of this read you have in your hand is *your* story. In the writing and sharing of this work, I am confident that you very likely have felt the same things, maybe even reacted in some of the same ways in your own circumstances. In the living of those moments and seasons, you will find that much was revealed concerning your character and, if you were looking for it, the character of God. As we work our way

---

[1] J. R. R. Tolkien. *The Lord of The Rings* (New York: Houghton Mifflin Co., 1994), 32.

through the upcoming chapters, I want to share my understanding of how God may use moments and seasons in our lives (like character sandpaper), and about the great inheritance and richness that our life circumstances have, can, and *do* bring **in light of how we walk them out**. (with the hope that we can see them as He sees.)

IMPORTANT to NOTE:

As you read, you will find a dual imagery floating in and out of the conversation. The title of the book perhaps is the primary of these: that the Father *has us walking in circles and is intentionally taking us somewhere.* However, this rests upon the imagery which will be discussed in detail found in Isaiah 40:27-31. This is the life image of the *process* we will spend so much time with as we journey. Flying, running, and walking—flying, running, and walking—flying, running, and walking—again, again, and again—until our birthday suits fall off. We call it a process because *processes* are repeatable. It is intentional consistency which produces a *consistent* result.

The day-to-day living of this process can leave us feeling like *we're walking in circles.* To that end, we wanted to give you a heads up: as you find us discussing *circles* and/or *flying, running, and walking* that **these are one and the same**. It is hoped that as you work through this—when you see one, you see the other. My experience has been that it is immensely helpful to hold both images in my head as I have walked this out.

OUR CIRCLE JOURNEY

Looking back to my early years in ministry, like Paul, a "Jew among Jews," I was, in many ways, a "Christian among Christians." Nearly all of the great disciplines of Christ-followers were practices that I had adopted into a faithful daily routine. I had been reading my Bible every day from the age of sixteen. Also, a day had not gone by that I did not have a consistent time of prayer. I asked to know His will. Many and sincere prayers for my family's safety (including pets) were offered each night. I faithfully attended all services, went to Christian concerts, read inspiring books, and had served in the youth and collegiate pastorate for nearly eleven years before I began to realize that in the middle of my great "devotion," the amazing adventure of knowing Jesus had grown stale. Like many of you, there was no sermon point that I had not heard. No song, new or old, that rang with any chord of fresh revelation. No Bible passage was unfamiliar. Doctrines were rehearsed, and sadly, entrenched in a now somewhat bored mind.

As a youth pastor, the adventure had now become consumed with flavorful ways to present an all-too-familiar message. Please do not misunderstand; while I may have become accustomed to my religious habits, at no time did I doubt the validity of the gospel nor my belief in the exclusive call of Jesus upon the lives of men and women. I simply began to accept a very dangerous, and *embarrassingly ignorant notion* that I had gone as far as I could go, and now it was simply time to *keep* going while encouraging others to do the same. This is not to say that I thought I had arrived at a perfect experiential state of holiness. I knew all too well that I had not. I simply thought that everything there was to know about getting there was at least theoretically already known, and it was now time to live and hopefully *get better*, boot-strapping my way into the rest of whatever life-span that God would providentially give to me. **I was in need of an awakening.** I desperately (though I didn't know it at the time) needed a fresh confrontation with the Person of Truth that would place me in the winepress of life.

and the Lord was faithful to meet him at his need.

The beginning and end of 1999 would usher in what I have now come to recognize as a series of major *aha!* moments: seasons and revelations at some much-needed and necessary times in what has now become more than a seventeen-year journey. **They have altered and changed me.** Some of them are painful and even embarrassing (*humiliating!*) to look back on. Others stand as mountains of victory where significant life fence posts are firmly planted in undisturbed rock. With an honest heart, while I am not completely satisfied at all points with my current career "accomplishments," I can say that I am thankful for the journey and reluctant to even think about changing any of it. I am confident with a deep and abiding trust in the processes of God upon my life, past and present. In short, **He has been doing something!** Some of it, strikingly recognizable at first, and the rest —I am just now beginning to dimly see.

My hope is that as you read our circles that you will do so with a brutally honest heart: a heart that beats to know and see the face of God. A heart that will be granted a divinely-anointed courage to be revealed in the light of truth wielded by the skillful arm of the Holy Spirit who does not strike to wound the natural man but to *kill* it.[2] (*Yes, He is interested in re-birth in Him following a very real death to self!*) I hope that as you discover Christ in you, that you will begin to learn what it takes to discern His voice and that the sin entangled in your emotions, will, and intellect will be illuminated and confessed, and as you are brought to repentance, you will walk into a **freedom** with the Living Creative Christ that you had previously never known! I pray that in your divine freedom, you will find an expression in Him that brings the Maker's healing to your family, friends, and culture around you, and that "the eyes of your heart may be enlightened, so that you will know what is the hope of His calling, what are the riches of the glory of His inheritance in the saints and what is the surpassing greatness of His power toward us who believe" (Ephesians 1:18-19)!!

so, as jack begins this journey, sharing the only story he knows well enough to tell in these pages: **our walk** (which has often felt like an uphill-trudge!), we have to admit from the start—this: we **so** desire to make life happenings make sense. they do not always make sense. but there is **purpose!** we also have to share that we feel if someone doesn't learn something from our circles/our journey, we may very well feel the deep desire to grab a young friend or two and pour the bucket of water out onto their head(s)! friend, please, **please** catch the enormous grace we want to write as our story gives a picture of how God has moved us and how He has been in it all—and **how He is moving you and the circumstances around you.** read thirsty—expecting relief. He is **for you.** He meets you where you are, reader.

and side-note: i am typing in this quiet place with the thought—if only the sweet friends whom our lives have already touched and who are already a part of our story read all of this, it is worth the sitting and the writing. and if even one struggling friend is encouraged, or picked up or thirst-quenched—it is worth these early mornings and late nights of putting thoughts prayerfully to page. Jesus, use this.

---

[2] Watchman Nee. *The Release Of The Spirit* (New York: Christian Fellowship Publishers, 2000), 41.

PART ONE: OUR CIRCLES AND OUR PAIL

this is scott's story to tell. i am along for the circles and edits, but it's truly his message right now. as i sit in a quiet room, i have read and reread—and thought: these 237 pages took some time. years for him and many months following for me.

i am doing final edits in the early morning today, because we need to get this in print—we're in a hurry. certain haste and passion to share is burning in our hearts—and for jack, the circles have been intensely (everyday of the last twenty+ years) weighty. heaviness on his chest, and now: a lifting and sharing and relief in this. there's much to give and much to share from our journey—our circles.

as he's weaved in so much of our adult lives so far, it has been therapy. we talk a lot of processes and how God has walked us through some painful seasons, but this isn't about scott and steph. the Lord is close in this room right now. He wants to say to your heart: be quiet. sit quietly in this place. breathe in the idea that I can make much of what you have thought as time wasted and fumblings. My plan is intricate and redemptive. I redeem broken YOU. I repurpose. I want to.

our story is kind of embarrassing. it's ok if you blush for us. it doesn't hurt (like it did) anymore. the Promiser is our LOVE and the promise (the dream—our plans and hopes) pales in comparison. pales in our PAIL.

on the cover, jill holds a pail of water. Jesus told the woman at the well to drink and that He is Living Water. the other day, scott and i were praying, and i heard in my spirit, "drink Me."

as you read this third of our book, will you think of jill's pail not so much as the "bucket-list" pail mentioned earlier, but as a FULL pail of this Living Water—our Passion and Treasure. i imagine the ripples and circles as it has been filling up—symbolic of holding LIFE—carrying life with us on the journey and in every circle.

CHAPTER 1

in our early twenties/fresh out of college with youthful crazy enthusiasm, God opened a door of effective ministry to us...

OUR FIRST CIRCLE

Stephanie had just finished her undergraduate degree at a private university in Indiana. I had been serving as a youth pastor at a local church. These were very sweet days for Steph and me as we were coming up on two years of marital bliss. Our lead pastor and the congregation at the church we served had shown much grace in giving a very inexperienced young man an opportunity to get his feet wet in the river of youth ministry. Hardly a month or even a week goes by that I do not consider making the trip back to Marion, Indiana for the single purpose of saying, "Thank you, and please forgive me! Forgive me for knowing nothing when I thought I knew it all! I promise—I'm better at it now than I was then! So thank you, thank you, thank you!" Our pastor and the small Marion church truly cared for people, and Steph and I were two of them. We continue to be grateful to this day.

Upon Steph's graduation, we prepared to make the move back to North Carolina. It was home for us, and I was absolutely thrilled to be going home. At the time, I remember our Marion church family teasing us saying, "So you've had enough, and you're headed back to 'Mayberry!'"—to which I responded in fun that it was only because, "I could no longer survive the wilderness of 'Green Acres!'" Increasing my excitement was the very happy news that I would have the opportunity to accept an invitation to serve in another position in youth ministry. Looking back on it, the pay was strikingly minimal at this United Methodist two-church charge, but *I knew that I knew that I knew* what I wanted to do with my life. I wanted to be a youth pastor whose passion for Jesus reproduced itself in the lives of teenagers (who would, in turn, lead entire communities to Christ!) I burned with this passion, and if I'm honest with myself today—more than twenty years later—I still do, though it is not limited to a single age group anymore.

The church was a perfect fit for us. Though Stephanie had come from a distinctly Wesleyan background and my upbringing was highly conservative fundamentalist/Independent Baptist (both from protestant Christian theological roots—in case "wesleyan" is unfamiliar)—with no disrespect for our Methodist brothers and sisters, it seemed odd at the time to be serving outside our own denominational traditions. However, none of that really mattered, as we were about to meet a wonderful group of people who supported this young couple and my expanding vision, as you'll see, with faith in what God seemed to be doing. Even now as I write, it is a bit hard to hold back the tears that come forth for a people you have loved and whom you know returned your love and admiration.

Our new pastor had served these two small congregations faithfully for twenty years upon our arrival. With similar upbringings and ministry education, the pastor and I had a camaraderie and understanding that were beneficial, and I quickly gained helpful insight that these churches were full of remarkable Christ-followers who were living in our home community at the right places at the right time for something very special to begin to happen.

The first year and a half of our service to these congregations was spent implementing a consistent weekly meeting time with attention to the basics of the gospel and direct focus on the necessities of holiness and evangelism. They were good times, as friendships and trusts began to develop. However, whether by the Spirit or a young man's ambition, I saw much more in them and had a vision to match it.

On a hot Sunday afternoon in June, in the cool, slightly moldy basement of the church with roughly ten students present, I gave the "big reveal" of a vision and action-plan that I had been developing since my high school years. That afternoon, we determined that we would adopt this vision and commit ourselves to it. In many ways, it would be a youth worship format that would be ahead of its time. Foundational to the mechanical workings of this shift would be a sincere and realized belief in student leadership and responsibility. In essence, this small band of student leaders would be fully responsible for meeting weekly to write, rehearse, and produce a weekly worship gathering that was heavy on worship and production. To that end, we suspended all weekly youth activities for the next six months as we worked toward our opening date in November of 1997. Our goal was to have seventy-five in attendance for our opening night. While it may seem a meager number (in our small community, in a small rural UMC church), it would be quite special if it could be done. For good measure, we invited a well-known sportscaster from the local news channel. This local celebrity was famous in our area for his weekly sports segments. He would be our special "late night talk show" interview and special guest for the evening.

With much excitement, opening night came and went with *eighty-five* in attendance! Over the following months, we continued to see good fruit. By the middle of 1998, we were beyond the capacity of the fellowship hall in which we met. Somewhere along the line, a few neighboring churches had begun to forego their own youth activities and simply opted to join us. We were excited. Both churches that we served were excited. The local student ministries that had honored us with support were excited. Buoyed by the enthusiasm and boundless faith one might attribute to perceived success, I began to see an opportunity to take this ministry to what I thought to be *another level*. If the community and many local congregations were in support as they seemed to be, it only made sense to incorporate this ministry as a nonprofit organization with the hope to serve as a kind of *community youth group*. Therefore, with this thought in mind, and with the help of some very dear and special people (who served as the initial directors for this ministry), we incorporated as a nonprofit entity in January of 1999.

With this action came the hiring of a full-time partner and former college classmate, Mitch—as well as Jason, a young but particularly anointed worship leader. In addition, we were invited by another church to use their larger, more accommodating facilities for our weekly youth services. (This church body was the first of the community congregations to begin attending and participating in our youth gatherings.) Within two months of our move, we were averaging nearly two hundred students per week. It was, in many ways, a surreal time. With groups from all over the NC Triad and surrounding counties attending, we had become a ministry in our community that was very much in demand. From late 1998 to late 1999, we had seen hundreds move through this fledgling ministry. A great many of these students had made professions of faith during this span, and we were elated.

scott used the word 'surreal.' i remember the wonder at what God was doing, and that we had front row seats. it kept us awake at night and had us living for wednesday nights!

By November of 1999, however, something disquieting was beginning to happen. Looking back on it, the thought of supporting two full-time staff positions along with a part-time worship director seems laughable. While we had certainly enjoyed some enthusiastic financial support at the beginning of our first year, by late summer, we were already having difficulty making ends meet. By the time August came around, Jason was feeling a call to step away into a time of preparation. It was a departure I felt deeply. Even though I tried to support him verbally, my heart anxiously wanted to find a way for him to stay. While those who came after him in the following months did well, the anointing and gifting upon Jason's life proved irreplaceable in many ways. As October and November rolled around, our numbers, though still good, had leveled off. While the nineties and low one hundreds would have been something to write home about a few months before, it was a noticeable drop that had us very concerned.

At first, it merely seemed a leadership void as our juniors and seniors who served as student-leaders had begun to graduate and to move on to their college careers. We simply hoped to identify new and upcoming students to fill their shoes and to continue to press on. With this hope and desire in mind, Mitch and I launched preparations for what we dreamed would be a large scale community youth revival. For three months, everything we had (financially and otherwise), was poured into this event. We booked the Dove Award nominated band *The Waiting*, and rented out a spacious auditorium, thinking it would be the perfect venue. (Finch Auditorium— remember this place as it will come back later!) We built sets, did radio and television advertising, traveled to community churches pleading for their support and participation. Everything we could think to do, we did—and then some.

In the midst of our frenzied activity, Steph and I were about to receive news of the first real tragedy that we would experience together. Approximately twenty days before the event was to be held, we received a late evening call. As has become a fairly regular event, we were giving the living room of our home a new paint scheme, and as Steph was preparing to roll the first strips of paint, I was answering the phone. It was Steve, Steph's dad. His voice sounded brave and calm, but something in it seemed to say far more. Steve said, "Hey, I need to talk to Steph. Vangie has been in an accident, and it's pretty serious." Without questioning, I put my hand over the phone receiver, and calmly relayed the message to Steph, "It's your dad. Your mom has been in a car accident." She immediately grabbed the phone and began to pace as Steve shared what he could about the accident and Vangie's current condition. Her car had hit a slick spot in the curve of the road which caused her to skid, spin around, and hit a tree. She had sustained a broken leg and a very serious head injury. By the time she had arrived at the hospital, Vangie had slipped into a coma from which she would never recover. However, for the time-being, there was hope. As the phone conversation came to a close, we immediately made plans for Steph to make the trip to Kansas City, MO to see her mom.

Early the next morning, Steph was on the plane to KC, and I was left to finish the living room and to get ready for our big event. It was quickly approaching, and a difficult thought began to come to the forefront. Neither Mitch nor I had ever planned anything of this kind. As we began to track the ticket sales, or *lack* of sales, the thought that we were about to lose our shirts began to firmly root itself in our minds. For the first time in my ministry life, I was beginning to catch a glimpse of prayer that can be birthed out of desperation. With my mother-in-law stable but in a coma, a beloved wife pleading for the return of her mentor, friend, counselor—and a ministry dream and career seemingly in the balance, I had begun to plead with the Lord as never before.

In the mix of the panic and pleading, there was plenty of confused and frantic work to go around. Realizing that we might be hosting an evening for which we would not be able to pay, we began calling and inviting anyone who would listen. As the day of the youth event came, I was somewhat comforted to have Steph back home. Stephanie Reid is a support and companion like none other. She has that rare quality to be able to watch her husband walk straight off a cliff, over and over again—loving me all the way. you're pretty lovable, even in the panicking and pleading, confused and frantic times.

Our team of students and volunteers were ecstatic. The Finch Auditorium looked as good as we could make it. We had rehearsed, and we were ready for everything that would happen on that platform. *The Waiting* was there. Professional sound and AV companies were there. Our support and hospitality teams were there. Everything was there—except for an audience large enough to cover the cost. As the night wore on, Mitch and I sat dejected at the side of the stage as months of work and investment seemed to crumble into ruin. As an emergency measure, Mitch had given from his personal savings account to pay the contract of the band for the evening. The proceeds from the ticket sales were given that night directly to the auditorium to cover rental and city usage fees. The sound and AV companies graciously agreed to give us two months in which to pay them our agreed-upon amounts. As the dust settled and Monday morning came around, we were sitting in a veritable mess.

As Mitch and I spoke that morning, he graciously told me that he would need to seek work with his father and asked about the timing of reimbursing his savings account. We agreed that all pledge support and charitable gifts that were received by the ministry at that time would go directly to pay this debt before moving forward to pay any others. A few short weeks later, we did what we could to honor Mitch and his lovely wife for their service and heart at their last weekly youth meeting. It was a bittersweet night. Mitch is an amazing man of God. His integrity is impeccable; his heart is giving and resolute to worship and holiness. There are few brothers that I respect more. Hardly a week goes by that I do not wish to call him up to ask his forgiveness for ever inviting him along. To my mind, he deserved better, and his graciousness through it all continues to be an inspiration and heartbreak to me.

With Mitch gone and freed, I sat alone in our ministry office left to ponder and to search for a way out. The next six months were spent with no salary while incoming funds went toward debt reduction... and my heart sorted direction.

By then, 150 in our weekly meetings had turned to seventy-five and seventy-five had turned to thirty. On a warm spring day, the youth director at our host church (who had served as one of our directors) asked if he could meet with me. I was somewhat relieved. For weeks, I had been contemplating a time to discontinue our weekly gatherings. With the numbers significantly low versus the amount of time and energy we put into each week, this seemed like the right opportunity to broach the subject. As we sat in the fellowship hall where our worship services had been held, Mike beat me to the punch. A new pastor had come to the church, who, while friendly to us, did not share the passion and support of the previous pastor. With the numbers dwindling and the community support gone, a decision was made to "better use the space." So, with grace given and received, it was agreed that we would be out by the end of March. Without fanfare or much ado, that season of our ministry in our small community was over.

•

and the door was quietly closed.

---

as i read and edit—this is a bit crazy. going into "Another Go Around" which jack had originally entitled "A New Work Begins," there is not much pause as he looks to what is next. but then, life did that too. the memorial service for the dream-realized-faded-died never happened, and closure felt like a million prayer-thoughts, "Lord, we don't understand. give understanding. feed our hope, because we really don't get this failure or what to do with it."

so, jack jumps into our next...

ANOTHER GO AROUND

Clear the way for the Lord in the wilderness and make smooth in the desert a highway for our God. Isaiah 40:3

It was during this time that a long-held, yet quiet dream began to amplify in me. By spring, I had reached a certainty in my mind that it was time. The dream was to create a live talk/variety show designed for Christian television. (Translation: "rebound" to success!) Essentially, we would take our worship format and tweak it to accommodate an hour-long TV show layout.

With much excitement, I, along with eight others, sat in the modest little rented office. It was at this time that we unveiled a new name for this ministry: *140v3 Productions.* We knew (or at least *thought* that we knew) that we were embarking on something special and very hard. The dream to produce a weekly television show was precisely that: *a dream!* Apart from a few conversations with a talented local producer, I knew *nothing.* This gifted friend had a rich history in the television and entertainment industry: at one time, a sound-technician for the *Eagles*— eventually redeemed and settled in our community—he was a long-time veteran in the Christian media world with the added bonus of having a relative who did work for the legendary *Saturday Night Live!* In this knowledgable friend, I felt like I had received my confirmation and divine command to proceed with all speed and diligence. Why else would some-one with his skill and experience be available to us? All through that spring and summer, we began to work on scripts and formats along with embarking on a search for a place to host this endeavor. As the months wore on and my pockets remained empty, pressure grew to find income and provision for my home.

In September of 2000, Stephanie's mother continued to convalesce at a rehab facility in Kansas City, MO. she had spent a few weeks in the hospital but had not recovered to any sort of normal. She was still in a non-communicative, comatose-like state, but we continued to have hope for her recovery. Family friends of Steph's parents, who had served in medical missions for years, felt certain that Vangie could receive better care at a facility near us in the Triad of North Carolina. With their help and remarkable connections, we were able to have Vangie moved by private jet to Winston-Salem, NC. The connection was a Nascar driver whose name you would recognize. (Yeah, I'm not making this up!) it was a crazy time as we held onto hope.

Our hopes for Vangie, however, at this new facility, were soon dimmed as the medical staff deemed her physically unable to benefit from their services. She ended up being placed at a local rehab center which served primarily to give life-sustaining care and day-to-day service. In essence, it was a place for her to lie while we waited to see if she would ever "wake up." With Vangie's move to NC and Steve, Stephanie's father, unemployed yet determined to care daily for the needs of his bride, it was decided that he would simply move in with us. In this way, Steve could give Vangie all the time she needed without the pressures of a day-to-day job. However, as fall turned to winter, it was apparent that we both needed one.

I needed income, and Steve needed to "get out" and to put his hands and mind to work. In many ways, I was in denial. **My dream of a burgeoning youth ministry had collapsed into nothing.** I was now entangled in an endeavor for which I had no experience and seemed to be going nowhere fast. While some financial support continued to trickle in, it was not enough. From the age of eighteen, all I had ever known was youth ministry. Vocational ministry was all I ever wanted. I was mortally afraid of anything else. My pride in what I did was conquering my vision and emotional stability. I was bordering on depression and internal panic.

In late December of 2000, Steve's medical missionary friends approached Steve with a unique opportunity. A widowed friend of theirs was hoping to restore and remodel an early 1900's two-story farmhouse which had belonged to her late husband. It would be a big job, but one that could be done as time allowed which would enable Steve to continue to care for Vangie. Immediately, Steph and I felt that this was exactly what he needed. At first, he was reluctant, as he was faithful to spend sun-up to sun-down with Vangie at the rehab center. However, to relieve his doubts, Steph, seeing an opportunity to bring in some additional income, convinced me to temporarily accompany him in this work. Up until his agreeing to move in with us, we had spoken less than a combined 150 words to one another over an eleven-year span. Other than an adoration for his intensely gorgeous red-headed daughter and a very strong shared faith, we had absolutely nothing in common. To Steve, I had always been the kid who needed to grow up and get a real job. I remain convinced to this day that this was his opportunity to see to it that I did—under his supervision. He said yes.

So on a very cold January morning at approximately five a.m., Steve and a very miserable son-in-law set off in his Chevy S10. With the *Gaither Vocal Band* screaming *Oh My Lord, What a Time*—a somewhat too *vigorous song* before the sun has shown its face (no disrespect for the Gaithers) —we were on our way. I distinctly remember thinking that morning as we made the thirty-minute drive over: *It's dark. It's going to be dark for the next hour and a half. This place has no electricity and no generator. What exactly is he planning to do??* Upon making our way into the house via flashlight, it soon became apparent, he had no idea! Steve was so stoked to go to work on something—anything—that small details like *light to work by* were completely beside the point. For the next half hour, I was charged with lighting a portable kerosene heater which we found sitting in the middle of the downstairs hallway. If we were going to be there in the dark for the next hour, we could at least have a place to warm our hands while doing it. After thirty minutes of my abject failure at kerosene heater lighting, Steve made the executive decision that it was going to be a bit hard to know what to tear out if we couldn't see our hands in front of our frozen faces. He therefore decided that breakfast at a somewhat near Waffle House was in order. Later that evening, having arrived back home in much the same way I had left it that morning (in the dark), I was completely convinced of what I already thoroughly *knew*: I hated, absolutely despised, and detested this kind of work. And three months later, I hated it more than ever.

my dad was an excellent carpenter but often worked alone. he wasn't used to having an apprentice alongside, and scottie ended up with the odd jobs and some back-breaking ones. i remember one particularly undesirable and lengthy assignment: the clean-out of an old shed crammed full, with loads of sorting and trips to the dump. scottie was the lowest of low, feeling pulled away from fruitfully using his gifts in ministry and watching teens come to Christ on a weekly basis to back-breaking trips to the landfill and feelings of despair in this work he so disliked.

but all was not lost. this closed door and time of testing would lead us to understanding. God moved us immediately to a place where we would learn how to process this failure. a new way of thinking that gave soul-strengthening help in our processing...

CHAPTER 2

STRENGTH NEEDED TO KEEP CIRCLING

Upon the incorporation of our nonprofit organization, I had given my resignation to the two churches we had served, and a very dear pastor friend and mentor from my youth advised us to connect with a larger church body. His thinking was that significant connections might be found that could help an endeavor such as ours. So, we began attending a very large Baptist church that had a wonderful impact on our community. It was certainly large enough, with nearly 7,000 in attendance through three services on Sunday mornings. After spending the past seven years on a church ministry staff, it was beyond refreshing to be in a place where we could be unknown and from beneath the microscope of small church politics, as well as a place to breathe a bit.

While we had taken the advice to find a worshiping body of this kind, we did little to make ourselves or our television dream known. We were simply content to worship unhindered and unnoticed. The pastor of this large Baptist church was Dr. Mark Corts. His preaching and teaching were like rivers upon dry land, and Steph and I drank like stranded wanderers in the desert! As the finances and students of our failed ministry began to disappear, our time at Calvary became more of a comfort and rope to hold on to than I can relate or explain. As I began the dreaded carpentry work with Steve, Dr. Corts began a sermon series which in no uncertain terms *altered the course and direction of my life and ministry.* His text was Isaiah 40:27-31. The sermon titles were: "Looking for Strength?" and "From Filling to Power." The text reads:

Why do you say, O Jacob, and assert, O Israel, "My way is hidden from the Lord, and the justice due me escapes the notice of my God"? Do you not know? Have you not heard? The Everlasting God, the Lord, the Creator of the ends of the earth does not become weary or tired. His understanding is inscrutable. He gives strength to the weary, and to him who lacks might He increases power. Though youths grow weary and tired, and vigorous young men stumble badly, yet those who wait for the Lord will gain new strength; They will mount up with wings like eagles, they will run and not get tired, they will walk and not become weary.

Certainly, I could relate to the house of Jacob. I was *tired*. The Jewish people, who would be coming to the end of a seventy-year exile from home and heritage in this passage, were exhausted, disillusioned, and *forgetful*. None now in living memory knew the blessings of *the land*. Only those whose fathers had been exiled as children could report *living experience* during those days. They were a people living under the judgment brought on by generations past and now living for the dream of deliverance from it. Much like our generation today—*longing for an awakening*—they looked to the promises of Abraham and the works of Moses, yearning to see God move on their behalf as He had done long ago.

However, as the great football coaching legend, Vince Lombardi, famously said, "Fatigue will make cowards of us all." Hence, we hear the voice of God confronting the exhausted heart, "Why do you say, O Jacob, and assert, O Israel, 'My way is hidden from the Lord, and the justice due me escapes the notice of my God'?" My heart, as Dr. Corts began to break open this passage, was *in this place*. The dreams of expanded ministry were fast becoming an illusion. As I labored day-by-day at the old homeplace remodel, my hope began to fade. Subtly—almost without my recognizing it—the uncompromising optimism which once exuded from me was turning to an internal pessimism that hoped in nothing. It had turned to a false hope that seemingly found itself waiting for the "other shoe to drop" at any sign of blessing or light. For the first time in my young life, I found myself afraid. Tired, angry, confused, and very afraid. I needed it all to make sense. I needed to know that God had not "lost my way."

God knew his need. that's why He led us to calvary baptist in His perfect timing.

Isaiah 40:28 confronted me to the core. In answer to the questioning heart, the Living God responds with a question in kind: "Do you not know? Have you not heard? The everlasting God, the Lord, the Creator of the ends of the earth does not become weary or tired." (Is. 40:28)

Before continuing on with Dr. Corts' thoughts, it would be good to record a few of my own. I am struck that God begins the word of encouragement not with a promise or counsel, but with a reminder. Almost as if to say to His people: *I've heard you. I'm going to help you. However, before I move on your behalf and before I can do anything that will be a rescue that you can grab, you will have to remember Who I am. It's been awhile. Everything you know about me, you've either heard read from a scroll or heard at the evening meal or from old men who heard of me from old men. To walk out of this, you will need to remember as a people and as individuals Who I am. If you get that, the rest of this will come into place for you.*

Reader, if you find yourself in these days walking in the shadows and in darkness that seems to have no end with no perceived visage of purpose in it all, consider the thought as if for the first time: *Who is this God?*

this section is so important. the most important of the book.

WHO IS THIS GOD?

I would first remind you that *His name is significant.* He reveals the fullest sense of it for the first time to Moses as He is tasking him with the adventure and mission of both declaring and leading the long-awaited freedom of the Jewish people from Egyptian bondage. The conversation takes place like this: "Then Moses said to God, 'If I come to the people of Israel and say to them, 'The God of your fathers has sent me to you, and they ask me, 'What is His name?' what shall I say to them?' God said to Moses, 'I AM WHO I AM.' And He said, 'Say this to the people of Israel, 'I AM has sent me to you.'" (Ex. 3:13-14) In some respects, this could be reflected upon as an almost comical scene. Moses, already desperately looking for an *out*, launches one out there: *"So, when I get there, do you have a name I can give?"*

The answer couldn't have been larger in meaning. It is a name that points you in the direction of everything you will need or want to know about God. No doubt for Moses, an awkward and possibly sarcastic-sounding introduction to give to the Pharaoh, the supreme leader in human government at that time. *I have this picture in my head of Pharaoh asking, "So—who sent you?" with Moses responding, "Uh—I AM." And Pharaoh (looking rather perturbed and slightly confused): "Who?"—Moses replying again, "I AM THAT I AM." Then Pharaoh demanding, "You are what?" with Moses, feeling his face begin to flush, "No, not me, you know, I AM."* And continuing—awkwardly seeming to pave the way for what would eventually become Abbot and Costello's *Who's on First.*

However, what other Name could an Infinite-Being give to Himself? In stepping back to remember who He is, we will need to wrap our minds around the concept of His infinity. It starts there. We are dealing with a Being that doesn't have a birthday. He simply IS. All of His essence IS. All of His abilities ARE. All of His attributes ARE. Let's take a moment here to bullet point several of these:

- Love
- Mercy
- Justice
- Jealousy
- Kindness
- Omniscience
- Omnipotence
- Patience
- Goodness
- Faithfulness
- Truth
- Wisdom
- Immutability

And the list goes on. In each of these, we do not find something God simply *does* (although He certainly does them all with pristine perfection); we see who *He IS*. He IS love, kindness, justice, mercy, etc. He can be no other than that which He is, and each of these—He is *infinitely*. The implications for us, then, are immense!

The writers of the Psalms seem to grasp this concept. Listen to these thoughts as they roll out through the book of poetry/worship:

Who is like the Lord our God, Who is enthroned on high. (Ps. 113:5)

The heavens will praise Your wonders, O Lord; Your faithfulness also in the assembly of the holy ones. For who in the skies is comparable to the Lord? Who among the sons of the mighty is like the Lord, A God greatly feared in the council of the holy ones, And awesome above all those who are around Him? O Lord God of hosts, who is like You, O mighty Lord? Your faithfulness also surrounds You. You rule the swelling of the sea; When its waves rise, You still them. You Yourself crushed Rahab like one who is slain; You scattered Your enemies with Your mighty arm. The heavens are Yours, the earth also is Yours; The world and all it contains, You have founded them. The north and the south, You have created them; Tabor and Hermon shout for joy at Your name. You have a strong arm; Your hand is mighty, Your right hand is exalted. Righteousness and justice are the foundation of Your throne; Lovingkindness and truth go before You. How blessed are the people who know the joyful sound! O Lord, they walk in the light of Your countenance. (Ps. 89:5-15)

The earth is the Lord's, and all it contains, the world, and those who dwell in it. For He has founded it upon the seas and established it upon the rivers. Who may ascend into the hill of the Lord? And who may stand in His holy place? He who has clean hands and a pure heart, who has not lifted up his soul to falsehood and has not sworn deceitfully. He shall receive a blessing from the Lord and righteousness from the God of his salvation. This is the generation of those who seek Him, who seek Your face—*even* Jacob. *Selah.* Lift up your heads, O gates, and be lifted up, O ancient doors, that the King of glory may come in! Who is the King of glory? The Lord strong and mighty, the Lord mighty in battle. Lift up your heads, O gates, and lift *them* up, O ancient doors, that the King of glory may come in! Who is this King of glory? The Lord of hosts, He is the King of glory. *Selah* (Ps. 24:1-10)

Isaiah captures a similar thought when he writes:

Who has measured the waters in the hollow of His hand, And marked off the heavens by the span, And calculated the dust of the earth by the measure, And weighed the mountains in a balance And the hills in a pair of scales? Who has directed the Spirit of the LORD, Or as His counselor has informed Him? With whom did He consult and *who* gave Him understanding? And *who* taught Him in the path of justice and taught Him knowledge And informed Him of the way of understanding? (Isaiah 40:12-14)

And so for these exiles, stripped of *all*—save memory—God says to them, *Would you please remember who I AM?* If you want renewal, strength, vision, healing—a way out—or a way to *live* in the midst of it all, it is the infinite God to whom you must go.

there's more to dr. corts' message, but first some more of jack's thoughts here with illustration:

THERE ALL ALONG

In the early spring of 1995 *(quick flashback to college days)*, I was serving out my last few months at the church in Marion, Indiana. On one particular day, for whatever reason, the church offices and building were empty, which gave me time all to myself to work uninterruptedly. As my office was far separated from the youth classrooms, I had spent quite a bit of my time in various parts of the building. With time drawing near to "call it a day," I began to gather my things to hastily head out the door.

With everything in hand, I was puzzled to find that I didn't see my keys sitting on my desk. I remember moving my chair back to see if they had fallen to the floor. Not there either. I then proceeded to look at the windowsill and bookshelves lining my office walls. Still, no keys were to be found. I checked my left pant and coat pockets; I checked my right pant and coat pockets, along with my back pockets. Still, I could not find my keys.

I was beginning to get frustrated. I had things to do. It had been a turbulent time. Steph was on her way to graduating. I was walking through my first ministry transition while preparing for my "next place." At this stage of my young life, I was more than a little distracted and preoccupied. Well, I thought to myself, "This is a large place, but they've got to be here somewhere." So, out the door I went, in search of the keys. I searched down the halls, along the floors, on my way to the fellowship hall. There, I searched under tables and chairs. For good measure, I made my way to the kitchen, searching each cabinet and drawer—fumbling through the contents inside. I even searched the refrigerator! (You may laugh, but it's happened before.) As one might imagine, at this point, I had become more than a bit frustrated. I had begun to say things aloud like, "Really.... Seriously.... Come on!"

I headed to the Sunday school classrooms upstairs. From there, I proceeded to literally tear the rooms apart. Couch cushions were strewn about the rooms, buckets of pencils and desk drawers were overturned; no nook or cranny was overlooked. At this point in the search, it had gotten personal. As I stomped back down the stairs, I began to challenge the church building at the top of my lungs. "I Will Find My Keys And There Is Nothing You Can Do About It!" A few moments later, having exhausted my expansive hoard of *angry words,* I shouted, "I will not leave you in peace until my keys are back in my hand! I will stay here forever!" It was an empty threat, as Steph and I only had one car, and it wasn't as if she could bring me her keys from twenty minutes away at the drop of hat.

Even as I shouted my threats, my spirit raged all the more as I knew that *it* knew I was at its mercy. So, without choice or remedy for the circumstance, I continued on. I had been in search of my keys for a good forty-five minutes when finally—broken, and in despair—standing in an upstairs hallway, I stopped. My rage grew; my limbs were shaking. A primal scream roared from the deepest parts of my chest and throat as I hurled my twirling keys. Soaring downward through the hall, bouncing off the far wall with a *chink,* they fell to the carpeted floor.

And then—completely stunned—squinting to see if it could be true, **I beheld my keys.** In that moment, I was conflicted. There were both joy and relief rising up in my soul even as I paused to look down at my hands in disbelief. HOW IN THE WORLD?! Could it really be true that I had just spent forty-five raging minutes searching for the very things that were **in my hand?!**

i would comment here, but i might get myself in trouble. (at least he was a really cute still blonde-then twenty-something. wink. wink.)

I want to say to you, friend, if you find yourself questioning or even declaring the perceived absence of the manifestation of the living God in your circumstances and days, perhaps you might consider what the journey has driven from your mind. **Life-living has a way of filling our days, hours, minutes and moments with much that is bad, much that is good, much that *seems* good or innocuous—that is simply not of Him. In the mix of these times, we become a forgetful and distracted people. We can become stressed, depressed, and even angry in our circumstance. In a word: *consumed.*** Our circumstance may become all that we can see, even as we wonder "from where does my help come?" (Ps. 121) We begin to think the Lord has "lost our way." (Is. 40:27) **All the while—in the midst of it all—*He is near.*** Isaiah says to us, "Seek the Lord while He may be found; Call upon Him while He is near." (Is 55:6) Before moving forward, you would do well to ask the Lord to remind you once again of who He is. The marvel of this is that *He wants to, friend.*

yes, He wants to remind you!! don't be embarrassed by the need.

His declaration over you is: **I Am Sufficient.** Charlie Hall penned it well in his song from *The Bright Sadness:*

SCENES
Chill and cold and flakes of snow
Ice and sleet, and frost and cold
Each storm cloud and thunderbolt
Lifts my mind to You

Every work and every power
Every second of every hour

Fall of dew in sweet rain showers
Lifts my mind to You

The summer wind, fire and heat
Autumn leaves and blooms of spring
Ocean waves and mountain streams
Lifts my mind to you

As I lay me down to sleep
As I walk on city streets
As I laugh with friends and feast
It lifts my mind to you

As my children play and run
In the news with wars and guns
In the church where songs are sung
It lifts my mind to you

Deep inside the beggar's eyes
As for sweet love I fight
On the radio at night
It lifts my mind to you

Painting pictures of your love
You lift my mind up
Reminding me of you
My heart comes alive

I see you in every scene
I bet you are thinking about me
I have such a short memory
So you keep reminding me of you[3]

---

[3] Charlie Hall. *The Bright Sadness.* Sparrow Records, Sixstep Records
5099952222221, 2008, compact disc.

Yes, You remind me in the midst of my circumstance—my wilderness—that you are *"the creator of the ends of the earth that does not become weary or tired. That your understanding is inscrutable..."* Is. 40:28.

"i have such a short memory. you keep reminding me of You."

my short-term memory is stellar. i could cram the night before the test in high school and make a perfect score every time. however, my long-term memory can have its glitches. it isn't in my nature to replay scenes in my head. i definitely do not live in the past, and things don't always stick. and—i need a lot of reminders. so grateful that He graciously gives them.

the idea in the next chapter of an exchange of strength blows my mind. back to calvary and dr. corts—keep reading, friend.

CHAPTER 3

THE EXCHANGE

If you are at a place where the Spirit is reminding you of Him, you will be able to hear the power of what comes next. "He gives strength to the weary, and to him who lacks might He increases power." (Is. 40:29) With the Infinite God in view, we find Him an endless and All-sufficient Fountain.

As we consider this, there are principles in view that need to be understood. Coming back to Dr. Corts' message, the following statement continues to sit in a very prominent place in my thinking as it relates to the rigors of everyday life-living: "Life and its exigencies require strength."[4]

I remember hearing that and thinking to myself, "Wow. Yeah, wow—that's so obvious, but incredibly true." Up to this time, I had lived my life as if the energy I had for it was an assumed-given. The thought that living was slowly exhausting me had never come to mind. I suspect that this is a subtle thought many readers may miss as well.

The certain veracity of this statement is found in the fourth commandment that we should *keep the sabbath day Holy.*(Ex. 20:8) "For in six days the LORD made the heavens and the earth, the sea and all that is in them, and rested on the seventh day; therefore the LORD blessed the sabbath day and made it holy." (Ex. 20:11) In my studies through the years concerning the levitical laws—including the Ten Commandments—I have found that these were far from arbitrary statutes. Each carries the benefit of either provision or protection for its keeper. Properly understood, it displays a profound grace—a grace now that has come through the cross. Even before the cross, it was an amazing instrument of grace *in and of itself.* If kept—much health, peace, provision, and relational richness are to be found.

In this fourth commandment, however, we find the mirrored reality that we are created, time-bound beings for the *present.* As such, we do not possess in-and-of-*ourselves* an infinite supply of strength. Rest, therefore—for the purpose of replenishment—is *commanded.* As the Lord addresses these Jewish exiles, He hears their cry: *Father, we are exhausted. We can't do it*

---

[4] Dr. Mark Corts. *Looking for Strength.* Audio sermon on cassette.

anymore. Where are You?!... In this desperate cry, we need to hear exhaustion clearly. While certainly, there was physical exhaustion, what was depleted was their *zeal*, their *hope*, their *energy*—to grab and hold Him and His promises close—to have and hold hope that He will do something regarding their circumstance.

He continues His answer to them: *You are tired, but I am not. I don't get tired. You are desperately wanting to understand what this time has been about for you. You don't get it.* **I do.** *My understanding of all things is infinite. Hey, good news for you:* **I give strength and understanding. I've got what you need, and I give it!**

So, Dr. Corts referred to this as **the principle of exchange.** In this concept, he suggested that we bring our weakness to Him, and He takes it from us. Like a burden carried until our arms and back are numb and cramped into position, **He seeks a transaction in which we are not only given strength, but that our current burden would be taken from us in the exchange.**[5]

this is life-giving. do you see it??

NEWLY FOUND STRENGTH

This principle brings to mind my final visit to the doctor to have the hard cast removed from my broken right arm. For six weeks, white plaster had encased it. As the doctor's saw cut through and the cast was removed, I marveled at my struggle to maintain control over the movements of my arm. Without the weight of the cast, it seemingly wanted to float above my shoulders, out of my control. Oddly enough, the carrying of the cast had made my arm stronger, and (now with the cast removed) I would have to learn to operate with this newly found strength!

We get a picture of this *exchange* as Jesus says, "Come to Me, all who are weary and heavy-laden, and I will give you rest. Take My yoke upon you and learn from Me, for I am gentle and humble in heart, and you will find rest for your souls. For My yoke is easy and My burden is light." (Matt. 11:28-30) An alternate rendering in verse twenty-nine is "come to Me all *who work to exhaustion,"* which can be found in the NASB side notes. The exchange is evident as our burden is *exchanged* for a new one. **Those who have "worked to exhaustion" have remedy for their souls.**

---

[5] Dr. Mark Corts. *Looking for Strength*. Audio sermon on cassette.

Peter, in the midst of much exhortation, also seems to note the idea as he says, "casting all your anxiety on Him, because He cares for you." (1 Pet. 5:7) Again, the idea central here is a **removal of our burden—of our weakness—for in a grace of graces we embrace the Father's heart, learning that He cares for us!** Additionally Paul writes, "Be anxious for nothing, but in everything by prayer and supplication with thanksgiving let your requests be made known to God. And the peace of God, which surpasses all comprehension, will guard your hearts and your minds in Christ Jesus." (Phil. 4:6-7) The theme carries here as well, with a path and platform for which to hand over—or once again—**exchange** our burden. In doing so, it is taken from us and replaced with peace.

Of special note is the consistency of the weight of **anxiety.** Webster defines it as: *1) a: painful or apprehensive uneasiness of mind usually over an impending or anticipated ill b: fearful concern or interest c: a cause of anxiety and 2) an abnormal and overwhelming sense of apprehension and fear often marked by physiological signs (as sweating, tension, and increased pulse), by doubt concerning the reality and nature of the threat, and by self-doubt about one's capacity to cope with it.* [6]

Perhaps nothing causes greater exhaustion than that of the anxiety of the unanswered questions we carry. For the Jewish exiles, it is: will He ever have favor over us again? Will we ever know home and blessing again? For us: perhaps it's a failing relationship, an illness (perhaps fatal). It could be a dream, a hope of career in which we've invested everything that now seems on the precipice of failure or doomed all together. Regardless, *we carry these to exhaustion.* We carry these to a place that eventually may break us, leading to a place where only divine rescue will remedy. Hear these words again, paraphrased: *come to Me all you who are weary—who work to exhaustion—casting all your cares on Me, and I will give you rest... an 'exchange' of peace that passes all understanding, giving strength to replace your weariness and **might** to replace your weakness* (Matthew 11:28-30; 1 Pet 5:7; Phil. 4:6-7; Is. 40:29).

So, ok, that sounds pleasant. Be honest. You're asking the question, perhaps even sarcastically or maybe despondently, "How exactly do I exchange my exhaustion for strength and rest?" If you're asking in a negative tone, I would advise you to take another look at the *seeing God* **thoughts written**

---

[6] Webster's. *Webster's New Encyclopedic Dictionary* (New York, NY: BD&L, 1993), 44.

about earlier. Before starting chapter four, hear this: **HE wants to renew your strength far more than you want it to be renewed yourself.** But, there is a secret involved.

CHAPTER 4

THE SECRET

immediate spoiler!: WAITING WITH HOPE

My grandmother has two specialties that remain in high demand to this day among my extended family and home church family of Samaritan Baptist Church. If you are from North Carolina or possibly anywhere in the deep South, you may guess one of them—that's right, banana pudding!—the other (not so obvious) is homemade macaroni and cheese. Any church potluck or family gathering that is devoid of either of these dishes will consist of a crestfallen crowd murmuring their displeasure. I do believe that they may devise annual plots to coax this otherwise-amiable woman into divulging the closely guarded secret of her personal recipes. To be sure, imitations have been offered. Each has been met with soured, pitiful faces. A resignation has settled over family and friends alike: *There's a secret to it.* And like it or not, we're simply going to have to wait and hope for it.

i actually did get her to tell me the ingredients to her banana pudding. (i think she likes me.) so, you definitely do not use artificial banana flavored pudding. ewww! it is vanilla, for sure—but the kind that you have to cook according to the packaged directions. vanilla wafers. bananas. and whipped cream. that is all, ladies and gentlemen, but mine does not quite taste like grandma peggy's. what is up with that??

however, the secret to waiting for this beautiful exchange of strength will work! we have experienced it and believe...

Knowing that *youths grow weary and tired, and vigorous young men stumble badly* (Is. 40:30), there is a secret, a "catch" if you will, to obtaining the "exchange" of strength that the Father offers. Indeed, *He gives strength to the weary,* and the key to receiving it is counterintuitive to our nature. Isaiah reveals this secret with a really, really big transitional *yet!* "Yet those who wait for the Lord will gain new strength...." (Is. 40:31a) Other translations render the verse, "Yet those who *hope* in the Lord..." (italics mine).

41

Upon closer inspection of this particular word, you will find that both ideas are carried here. The word in question, translated *wait* or *hope*, is found as the Hebrew word *qavah* in verse thirty-one. Its figurative definition is *to wait, to hope, to expect intently*. Its literal definition is that of a many-stranded rope—one that can be held and will not break. It will not allow separation to happen, because it is a rope of many cords.

However, the word has a root of sorts which is rendered as *qaveh*. Again, it carries the idea of a cord—not only for binding—but also for measuring. It measures *around*. Because it has a marked beginning and a marked ending, it is not indefinite.[7] It is not forever!

With these thoughts in view, perhaps we can paraphrase verse 31a as follows: *Yet those who wait **(with an intent hope—holding on to Him—expecting His intervention and presence—understanding that the wait is not forever—that it will have an end)** will gain new strength!* Perhaps now, His admonition to remember Him takes on new meaning. He wanted them to remember His power and His character attributes—not the least of which was/IS *His faithfulness.* Faithfulness to act, to restore, to rescue, to hold, to comfort, to provide, to save. Regardless, the *secret* to receiving any of it, is a **patient, expectant heart.**

when our youngest son was a toddler, he had this quirky awesome response to waiting. this is bizarre, because as we are writing this, he is eight and still does not completely understand that the day before this day is called 'yesterday.'

so, when he asked for something—anything—that he really wanted, if i said two magic words: NOT YET, he was GOOD. the kid interpreted this in his little brain to mean, i DO get the thing i want. just not at this moment, and i am okay with it.

this is my blog post from march 11, 2012: he has somehow figured out that "not yet" could mean that it will happen later. (he used to think "tomorrow night" meant maybe it will happen soon...sometime in the future.) but it's been simplified to an expectation of "not yet."

---

[7] James Strong. *The New Strong's Dictionary of Bible Words* (Nashville, TN: Thomas Nelson, 2001), 780.

ahhh***i love it. but! the cutest of cuteness of it all is the beautiful. adorable. patience—of this three-yr-old!!! if he sees the plate of cookies on the counter and he reaches for one and i say no—and he says, "not yet?" and i say "not yet," he immediately echoes, "ok, not yet." with the most content look and patience. what in the world?

so, i've been thinking about how i could be more like aiden journey. when i am hopeful for something, when i ask God for something, and i hear "no" or "not right now" or "not yet..." i want that look on my face!!!! i can't even explain it...it's just the most adorable, peaceful, trusting—quietly-waiting—contentment.

Father, make me content like my three-yr-old when he says, "ok, not yet."

(((don't get me wrong: we did not have perfect toddlers, nor perfect kids. i'm actually thinking now that the "not yet" phase would be welcomed back five years later! i still love the memory of his face and the reminder to be content and patiently expectant in the waiting.)))

WAITING IN THE CURRENCY OF GOD

If you are the short-cutting type—you know, the one who uses the car pool lane in heavy traffic when it's only you in the car. The one who cooks your bacon in the microwave instead of the frying pan (a.k.a. the bacon flavor-neutralizing device!) You might—in the personal corners of your heart—be asking, "So—just how important is this *waiting* that you speak of? Are you absolutely certain that there is no other way?"

Let me share it with you in terms of currency. To my knowledge, the highest US currency note ever printed by the US treasury was a $100,000 bill issued in 1934 for President Franklin D. Roosevelt. It was printed as a gold certificate. In the currency of God, this would be the currency value of *love*. See any production of character traits (that the Spirit of God produces in you)—with the foundation of it representing fulfillment—will be the production of His *love* in you. (see 11 Pet. 1:5-7 and James 1:3-4). Following this was the $10,000 bill, first printed in 1861 and discontinued in 1969.

This bill would represent *godliness* in divine currency. You've heard it said that *cleanliness is next to godliness.* I would paraphrase: *love* is next to godliness, as it seems to be the final fruit of godliness.

so, love=really enormous value and godliness=still a really, really large amount of value.

Next in line, and still a ridiculous amount to be printed all on one piece of paper, would be the $5,000 bill. This bill, also first printed in 1861 and discontinued in 1969 would later bear the image of James Madison.[8] To this bill would be attached the extreme value of *perseverance*. Hear James 1:2-4, "Consider it all joy, my brethren, when you encounter various trials, knowing that the testing of your faith produces endurance. And let endurance have its perfect result, so that you may be perfect and complete, lacking in nothing." Notice the location in these verses of endurance to completion. We will come back to these words a little later, but the value of perseverance is noted in the admonition to consider suffering and trial *joy* in light of the treasures they bring. If you begin to read through the Petrine and Pauline epistles, this theme will become evident. Check out a few:

So, as those who have been chosen of God, holy and beloved, put on a heart of compassion, kindness, humility, gentleness and *patience*; bearing with one another, and forgiving each other, whoever has a complaint against anyone; just as the Lord forgave you, so also should you. Beyond all these things *put on* love, which is the perfect bond of unity. (Col . 3:12-14 italics mine).

Now may the God who gives *perseverance* and encouragement grant you to be of the same mind with one another according to Christ Jesus, so that with one accord you may with one voice glorify the God and Father of our Lord Jesus Christ. (Romans 15:5-6 italics mine).

Now may the Lord direct your hearts into the love of God and into the *patience* of Christ. (2 Thess. 3:5 italics mine).

While what must first be recognized—the end products of *godliness* and *love* as the ends to all His means—the linchpin of patience/perseverance cannot be understated (*not sure what a linchpin is exactly*). Its *value* in what He seeks to accomplish in your life and days is of such preeminence, that

---

[8] Arther L. & Ira S. Friedberg. *A Guide Book of United States Paper Money* (Atlanta, GA: Whitman Publishing, 2016), 334-344.

in today's US currency, it (like the $5,000 dollar bill now) seems ridiculous to print. At a closer view, it may be said that without the cultivation of *perseverance* in you, His greatest hope and divine destiny for you will not be accomplished in your earthly life-living.

so, the currency of God is the great VALUE of love, godliness, and perseverance in the waiting.

If you're weary, beat up, lonely, questioning, disillusioned—the secret to moving out of it is in the *waiting*. However, please grasp this! It is, in large part, the *perseverance* produced by the grind of the circumstances found in the waiting that He, in a seemingly hidden grace (*i love this, scott!*), insists and ensures that you will acquire and must hold on to tightly. It's something, in the nagging middle places of the mind, that pleads for an answer to the question, "What is this all about?"

No doubt, many of you are at this place now. Some, like me, are holding broken and seemingly-derailed dreams, wondering if their origins weren't really from the enemy in the first place as a sadistic ploy to torment your hope and sanity. Even worse, there may be some who have fallen into the snare of placing cruel aspirations at the feet and motive of God in His dealings with you. Somewhere along the way, your excitement to move on a "*God-given" assignment* went sour, was delayed, or failed all together, and no acceptable reason other than a perceived lack of self-worth, competence, or simple disfavor with your God, now accounts for it in your recriminations of this season or seasons of your life. You are now watching others around you pass through the ranks into the fruitfulness you've dreamed of your whole life.

For what it's worth, I think Jesus wants to scream into your soul (your emotion, intellect, and will) PEACE! BE STILL.

As I sat and listened to Dr. Corts break the secret of waiting open, like a sliver of sunlight streaking through a pinhole in a dark storm cloud, a picture that held hope began to form in my clouded spirit. (*you should be an author, jack. this imagery is publishable!*)

"Yet those who wait on the Lord will gain new strength." (Is. 40:31) I had to admit, it sounded good—ethereal even. However, just how do you go about *"doing"* this waiting? Heck—I was broken and empty. I literally felt I had nothing to lose (a dumb thought by the way, as it is rarely true).

dr. corts shared an amazing illustration of HOW to wait...

WAITING ON THE CATCHER

I will never forget Dr. Corts' picture of waiting through an interview of the *"Flying Rodleigh's,"* penned by author Henry Nouwen. According to Mr. Rodleigh (the patriarch of this family of acrobats), the relationship between the flyer and catcher is a special one, and there are certain rules of the trapeze that must be observed.

In the conversation, Nouwen is given the names and definitions of the principle-players involved in the trapeze. The acrobat who hangs from his knees with outstretched-hands is simply named the "catcher." The one who launches out from the platform, swinging by his hands in a graceful fall, is appropriately called the "flyer." The most important rule in this dramatic act: as the flyer simply lets go and the catcher prepares to receive him—the acrobat leaves the platform, gathers speed and momentum, and soon reaches a point where he must let go, launching his body into the air. While in flight, at the beginning of its speed and thrust—flips, twists, and contortions can be executed, however, each flyer is inevitably met with the pull of gravity. Momentum ceases, and—there is nothing left but to wait for the catcher. Concerning this exhilarating moment, Mr. Rodleigh shares with Nouwen: **"The flyer must never try to catch the catcher." The flyer's job is to wait in absolute *trust*. The catcher will catch him, but he must wait with his hands perfectly outstretched and still.**[9]

Interested in the imagery of this story for the past fifteen years, I caught a break in the most serendipitous of ways during the summer of 2014.

In July of the previous year, while in Venice, Florida, I "happened" across a fully-functioning *legit!* trapeze while on a random errand. It was located on what looked like an abandoned parking lot, surrounded by very aged steel-beamed structures. Nothing remained of these but bare/unsided support

---

[9] Henri J. M. Nouwen. *Sabbatical Journey* (New York, NY: The Cross Road Publishing Co., 1998), viii.

beams. The sign on the fence read, "Trapeze Park—Open to the Public." I made a note in my phone so that I would not forget the place. My hope was to return in the next day or so before we left town.

That time did not come, but in August of 2014, Steph and I were back in Venice celebrating our twentieth year of marriage. I had told her that, if it were at all possible, an absolute *must* was to take a moment to pay the trapeze park a visit while we were in town.

On the last day of our stay, we made my long-awaited stop at the park. Approaching the entrance, we passed a memorial marker for Barnum and Bailey's *Ringling Brothers' Circus*. According to the marker, the structures noted in my phone the year before were all that remained of Ringling Brothers' winter training quarters which they had used in the 1950's and 60's.

Just a few moments later, we were parking in a sand field nearly conquered by grass up against a chain-link fence. A fading vinyl sign advertising a summer trapeze camp—*open to the public*—hung by the gate.

Apparently, we had arrived at the perfect time. A few young girls (probably between the ages of nine and ten), with a young boy and teenager, were preparing to climb the ladder to the elevated platform. A dozen yards or so from the actual trapeze was an aging enclosed trailer (the kind you see at the fair in which the side has a large opening that props up, acting as a sort of canopy). Across the counter were posters and memorabilia showcasing the Gaona Family and the Barnum and Bailey's *Ringling Brothers' Circus*. In particular, a rather small and athletic man was specifically featured on many of the items on hand. His name was Tito Gaona. In the middle of being *wowed* (there was a picture of Tito and Paul McCartney together!), a very graceful and beautiful lady, looking to be in her forties (whom we would be introduced to as Tito's wife, Renata), stepped into the merchandise trailer and jumped directly into introductions about the trapeze summer camp that she and her husband ran.

At my first opportunity, I told Renata of my writing and fascination with the trapeze and asked if she could confirm Mr. Rodleigh's *secret*. Without pause, Renata's eyes glinted with pleasure as she immediately grabbed Stephanie's forearms, and (speaking in her passionate South American accent) proclaimed, "YES! The secret is to keep your hands absolutely still until the catcher catches you. If you do this, you will not fall!"

To our amazement, Tito was a particularly outstanding member of the "Flying Gaonas." Having performed with *Ringling Brothers Circus, Scott Betrum Mills Circus* (Note: while with Bertrum, his family performed for Queen Elizabeth II!!), *Big Apple Circus*, and *Beatty-Cole Brothers*—to name a few, they won the circus world's highest honor: the "Gold Clown."

All of that to say, on this barren patch of worn concrete, in the middle of Venice and in Florida's oppressive August heat, Steph and I were about to have the mystery of the trapeze unfolded by perhaps the most honored trapeze families of ALL TIME! If you ever get the chance, you would do well to do a Google search on Tito Gaona, and you will not be disappointed. The man who perfected the *triple* and managed to get caught is worth a moment of your time!!

Aside: During the summer of 2015, we were privileged to bring a mission team to the Gaona's for a day of trapeze camp. (Tito had just returned from Budapest designing the world's first four-way trapeze show!) For us, the day and the experience were nothing short of spectacular! (the scariest part of trapeze camp for each of us, i think, was looking down 30-40 feet to the ground below and stepping off the itty-bitty ledge!! but it was AWESOME!!! scott's mom was with us on the trip, and she even braved it gracefully!!)

With all of that said, and from all that I can gather through internet searches and simply watching the very act of the trapeze, *Dr. Corts' illustration of the Rodleigh family is confirmed.* If the flyer, toward the end of the flight, begins to doubt and to attempt to catch the catcher, they will miss each other nearly 100 percent of the time. The flyer's only hope is to wait—*with hands outstretched.* **Nearly all drops are related to the flyer's failure to remain patient and still.**

Even as I write this, I think of those moments when I panicked—when I became frustrated and took matters into my own hands—*only to fall.* I recount the gradual decline of our nonprofit youth ministry and responding with the big event that we planned to try to redeem it. The result: crushing abject failure. In the flailing of that, the I40v3 television show resulted in two years of what seemed pitiful waste. Exhausted effort that left me falling through the air—disillusioned, bitter, angry, and lost—wondering, "Papa, have you lost my way?"

I do not doubt that many who are reading this may be or have been at this place. You launched out on a dream—what seemed to you a *divine call.* As time passed, place markers here and there went unmet. Expectations began to be manipulated to fit the reality on the ground. You had to keep the team, the family, the organization behind it all *energized.* Before you knew it, nothing was where you thought it would be, and you were flailing for solutions, groping for answers. God, where are you? In the mix of that, some of you (like me) felt as if you simply fell—hard. Now, you find yourself working through it—recriminating it—trying to piece it back together.

If I can, I want to share with you a very important thought:

Friend, *the fall was not fatal.*

Yes, if you're still here, reading this now, *the fall was not the end.*

And—I have encouragement for you: "The Lord will accomplish what concerns you; His lovingkindness is everlasting." (Ps.138:8) "For I am confident of this very thing, that He who began a good work in you will perfect it until the day of Christ Jesus." (Phil. 1:6)

failure is a tricky thing. it feels like IT won and YOU are alone in a crumpled mess in the bouncy rope-net below. but if—IF—you can let the pride of humiliation fall away and look to the Catcher, He is there to stand you back on your feet and tell you to march right back to that tall skinny ladder and try again (and to hold still this time!!)—and He will catch you with His strong arms and perfectly-timed grip.

jack has one more meaningful illustration in this chapter on waiting and perseverance and trust.

THE FALL IS NOT FATAL

To catch this idea that *the fall is not fatal*, I would like to share with you one of the many mating habits of the American Bald Eagle. Phil Driscoll (the great trumpet player), during a concert which Steph and I attended, spoke of this—and keenly sparked my interest in the subject.

Bald eagles are monogamous in their relations. What is even more interesting is one of the remarkable ways in which they choose to commit to one another. As each reaches sexual maturity (typically at or around four to six years of age), they begin the search for their lifelong mate. Whether in air, nearby eyries (nests), or landing places, the male and female eagle inevitably meet.

If the female is interested, she takes a small twig up into the air with the male suitor following closely behind. At a time of her choosing, she releases the twig and watches. At this, the male eagle drops through the sky, catching the twig before it reaches the ground. If the female eagle is satisfied, she goes back to the ground for a larger twig (usually a stick) and leaps back into the sky, getting her suitor's attention once more before dropping it. Again, the male eagle soars through the air and retrieves the stick before it can make landfall.

Over and over, this is repeated with larger and still larger sticks. Each time, the male eagle has the opportunity to prove his skill and speed, which are considerable. (It has been noted that the bald eagle can dive at speeds of seventy-five to a hundred miles per hour!) It is a unique courtship to be sure, even if parts of it seem a bit familiar to the adolescent dating scene. *too funny, jack!* However, if the male eagle is able to succeed on each attempt without failure of any kind, and in so doing satisfies her desire, they are then mated for *life*.

The preparations for the making of a new generation of bald eagles begins to take shape, and the nest of the female bald eagle is prepared for this eventuality. It is typically a flat-topped bed, roughly seven to eight feet in width—lined with rushes, mosses, and grass. Usually located in trees ten to 150 feet from the ground, this little eagle family is birthed and nurtured by the mother eagle, reaching the ability to fly at approximately twelve weeks of age. Papa eagle does not nest with the family but stays some place close, often bringing a variety of twigs, branches, and food. As the eaglets' down gives way to feathers capable of flight, the mother eagle begins to make the nest an uncomfortable place. Soft layers are removed, and food becomes a little scarce, making the outside world seem more desirable.

When mama eagle deems the time to be right, she begins the process of teaching the eaglets—one by one—to fly. Craftily enticing an eaglet onto her back, she quietly drops from the nest with baby eagle clinging for dear life. She and baby are soaring when mama levels off her flight, giving the tiny passenger a chance to acclimate to the open sky. Eventually, the eaglet relaxes its life-grip upon its mother. As mama eagle feels the release, she "bumps" or makes a sudden drop, causing the eaglet to hover momentarily in the air, only to catch baby as it reaches for her back.

For hours, this process can play out between mother and eaglet. Each time, the baby eagle gains confidence as its wings allow it to hover upon the air for brief intervals. As the baby eagle becomes accustomed to these patterns, mother eagle—at last—does something completely unexpected. Climbing further and higher up into the air (whether by dropping or turning over)— *baby eagle is given over wholly to the sky.*

It is now time for baby eagle to fly.

Though not observed in all instances, for this first test, papa eagle has been circling in the sky, watching. He is waiting to see how the flight will turn out. Most likely, as he has watched the hours of training with its mother, papa eagle already knows the outcome. He is simply there to ensure that *the fall will not be fatal.* Pinning its wings back, diving at speeds of up to a hundred miles per hour, papa soars to the rescue. **Baby eagle will have the opportunity to fly again.**

I remember standing in the Tampa convention center, listening to this account of nature at work, holding Stephanie in my arms and thinking, *I'm still here. I missed the Catcher, but HE, my Abba Father, somehow made sure the fall wasn't fatal. I'm alive.*

Since that time, David Crowder's *You Alone* has followed me into deep declaration and a screaming heart that often needs to shout forth: *I am alive!* After all—sun and rain, cloud and storm—I AM ALIVE.

if you don't know the song, find it, and listen as you read. and breathe. if you FEEL FAILURE right now, FEEL still ALIVE. you're still here. your fall wasn't fatal.

YOU ALONE

You are the only one I need
I bow all of me at Your feet
I worship You alone

You have given me more than
I could ever have wanted
And I want to give You my heart and my soul

You are the only one I need
I bow all of me at Your feet
I worship You alone

You have given me more than
I could have ever wanted
And I want to give You my heart and my soul

And You alone are Father
And You alone are good
You are alone are Savior
And You alone are God

'Cause I'm alive, I'm alive
I'm alive, I'm alive
I'm alive, I'm alive
I'm alive, I'm alive

I'm alive, I'm alive
I'm alive, I'm alive
I'm alive, I'm alive
I'm so alive
I'm alive, I'm alive

And You alone are Father
And You alone are good
And You are alone are Savior

And You alone are God[10]

FALLS AND CIRCLES AND WAITING (AND MEANING IN IT ALL)

If you're in that place of waiting with your arms stretched out, hoping and praying for a rescue—or quite possibly fresh off a nasty fall with emotional scars and bruises—I want to help you see an answer to the macro "why" or "what" of it all.

Praying for you now, friend.

No doubt, if you're honest, it is a question you're asking—maybe even screaming—at God right now. While it is my hope to help you come to a place where you can have the necessary tools to search out the specific circumstantial *whys* of His working in your days, here we want to start with the overarching macro-question of "What is He doing?" or more specifically for some of us, "What is He doing *to me?*!" As we get ready to move to the next chapter, we're going to take a shot at that, and—in the mix—possibly grant you a "wow" moment and a divine patience with a firm knowledge that: No, *you have not been forgotten.* **Better yet, a very intimate thing is happening in and around you.**

---

[10] David Crowder Band. *The Lime CD.* Sparrow Records, Sixstep Records B0001KL4VS, 2004. Compact disc.

CHAPTER 5

THE PROCESS: *Purpose in the Circles!*

They will mount up with wings like eagles, they will run and not get tired, they will walk and not become weary.

Isaiah 40:31

Lately (seems like the last few years), I've found myself in a cycle which has me losing my car in Walmart parking lots. I don't lose my car in really large mall parking lots, theme park lots, or even enormous sporting arena parking lots—just Walmart parking lots. My personal best car search currently sits at forty-five minutes. The most *disconcerting* was an excursion with two large flat screen televisions purchased that evening for the church I was serving (the twenty-five minute search for my vehicle in a theft-proned parking lot was certainly the most frustrating to date).

At any rate, at present, it seems to be a trial I face with no remedy in sight. Much akin to being lost and going in circles, I feel like I'm getting nowhere. Maybe this is why, even while living in the heart of the Nascar world, I've yet to find any real excitement for a race that encompasses 500 miles of left hand turns and ends in the same place it starts.

The thought of going in circles as a pattern of life is not one that conjures up inspirational thoughts of hope and future. Like a sufferer of vertigo on a carnival merry-go-round, my initial reactive thought is sickness. Sickness of heart.

I want to embark on a journey, have a little bit of adventure, and arrive. I want to look back over the distance traveled and say, "Wow! That was awesome, terrible, amazing, but worth it—and now, here I am!" I then want to look ahead with vision and hope to a new journey, to a new place, and embark (insert instrumental western traveling adventure music here).

Perhaps it's that natural inclination that caused me to miss Isaiah 40:31 for so long: "They will mount up with wings like eagles, they will run and not get tired, they will walk and not become weary." It was not strange to me. I had long held it as a promise.

Maybe you've heard it in your thinking the way I had: *I'm young in my faith now, and if I'm honest, next door to a perfectly functioning heathen in my thought-life and imaginations. There's so much I simply don't get or catch in the Spirit...or flesh. I am definitely walking right now. However, my heart and goal is to come to a place where I can run. I want to build up that endurance James is speaking of in chapter one of his letter. I want to be consistent. I want my language cleaned up. I want to recognize the needs around me. I want to be in the game and contributing, etc. Eventually, I'm holding an even greater hope that a day will come when I will become Billy Graham (insert hero of the faith here) super-professional Christian. I will mount up with wings like an eagle and fly off to an endless sunset of near sinless bliss and fruitfulness until my birthday suit falls off-continuing my flight to elevations of **infinity and beyond!*** (his favorite expression again: "until my birthday suit falls off." hopefully you've caught jack's description of a human passing into eternity. it's perfect.)

i had always thought of the isaiah eagle passage that way as well.

one day, i will be strong and fly. one glorious day, i will mature to that awesomeness.

This thinking had relegated this passage to a wistful and abstract promise for *some day* which lined up beautifully with my linear desires and thoughts concerning my progressions with the ever Living Creative Christ. However, as Dr. Corts pointed out, that is not what the passage says. Not even close. It says first (following an encouragement for those exhausted and spent, waiting for strength): "They will mount up with wings like eagles." Counterintuitive here is that *flying happens first*. The eagle comes into view again. If you can catch the imagery of its flight cycle, perhaps you'll guess where we're going before we get there.

so grateful for isaiah's imagery and for these close looks at the eagle. another one:

From all I can find on the molting cycle of the eagle, it appears to be a process that can take up to 150 days to complete. The feather of the eagle is a hardened dead structure, and as such, it has a shelf-life of sorts (which is largely determined by usage and other varying circumstances). Over time, as the flight feathers become worn, the eagle begins to lose its speed.

While it never loses the ability to fly, its effectiveness for the hunt and *extended* flight are diminished, until it becomes necessary for those feathers to be molted (removed). As the feathers fall off—and recover in patches—over the 150 day span, it once again reaches a place of peak performance. What is caught here again is a process—a cycle of life-living. Hear again Dr. Corts' thought: "life and its exigencies (stuff) require strength."[11] (parentheses mine).

You might want to take a moment to remember those first days when you had gone from death to life in Christ. The *rescue of Jesus* was fresh in you. Do you remember a light heart and step to match? Do you remember an unlooked-for hope and passion to engage cause and mission? You were *flying*. Emotion, intellect, and will—**in flight**. But then something happened. You weren't exactly sure how or when, but ethereal excitement was no longer an expression you would use to describe your daily pursuit. You still had passion for the journey with an unquestioned will to run with it. Then—a day came when your thought had a chance to accept it: "Um. I'm exhausted. I've got nothing. What's happened to me?" Hear this. Underline it: *Life-living happened to you and did to you what God intended for it to do.*

Coming back to James 1:2-4 and the value of perseverance and waiting!: "Consider it all joy, my brethren, when you encounter various trials, knowing that the testing of your faith produces endurance." What we are seeing in Isaiah 40:31 is *process for life*. Receive it in paraphrase: *I know you are exhausted; life has done to you exactly what I allowed it to do. I'm coming to renew your strength, and yes, you are going to fly again. However, various trials are coming your way (James 1:2-4), and it won't be long before the best you're going to be able to do is run.* **So run.** *Run hard and run fast while you can. Why? Because more life is coming. Broken promises, derailed dreams, conflicted relationships—and yet amazing adventures too—(but all of these things can exhaust heart and mind) and eventually, the best you can do is walk. And when you get to that place,* **simply walk.** *It's ok. As far as I'm concerned, it's the most fruitful place for you, because I'm doing something crazy-big then. Walk and wait. Because I'm going to come again, and I'm going to renew your strength again.* **You're going to fly again,** *run again, walk again, fly again, run again, walk again. Again and again and again. I'm going to walk you into a lifetime of circles, and*

---

[11] Dr. Mark Corts. *Looking for Strength.* Audio sermon on cassette.

*in the end, you're going to look up and find that you're nowhere near where you started. **You will have walked in circles and gotten somewhere.***

CONSIDERING IT JOY?

To better understand how exactly He's getting us there by way of a *process*, we need to bring James 1:2-4 to the forefront. Let's take a look at it: "Consider it all joy, my brethren, when you encounter various trials knowing that the testing of your faith produces endurance. And let endurance have *its* perfect result, so that you may be perfect and complete, lacking in nothing" (italics mine).

These verses are taken from James' letter to those among the Diaspora: in short, to Jewish believers who have been scattered. Many conservative scholars agree that it is most likely addressed to members of the Jerusalem church who have been driven out due to the persecutions that had recently arisen against them in particular. As such, it is possible that many receiving this letter are believers who had been personally nurtured and discipled by James. We can, therefore, guess that these are people who are already familiar with *trial*. It is likely that James knows or guesses that more is to come, and his heart in writing is to give them perspective and purpose in it.

In light of what has happened and what is to come, he writes, "Consider it all joy, my brothers, when you encounter various trials...." Some translations render *trials* as "temptations." Most scholars agree that both are acceptable in the context. Either way, I must confess that this wording had been a puzzle to me for years. While I could imagine a glorious and resolute heart to endure such, I could not in honesty and sincerity imagine *feeling* joy at the prospect of trial and trouble. Mostly because, up to that point, I had not. Watchman Nee had described me very well. (and sadly, me as well): "Yet here is our difficulty—we fret over trifles, we murmur at small losses, and we complain about insignificant things. The Lord is ever finding and preparing a way in order to use us. Yet when His hand slightly touches us, we begin to feel unhappy—even to the extent of quarreling with God and having a negative attitude."[12]

---

[12] Watchman Nee. *The Release of The Spirit* (New York, NY: Christian Fellowship Publishers, 2000), 15.

JOY IN PAIN: (CRAZY GYM GUY)

However, it is right here, in the middle of the "life-living" and all that can come with it (trial, trouble, and temptation), that God is most at work in you. Yet, it still begs the question, "How do you consider these times of testing, *joy*?" I would liken it to the following:

Coming up through high school sports, I was never a fan of the weight room. I was 5'11" and weighed a very unimpressive 135 pounds. My passion was basketball. However, due to my neglect of lifting, the moment I stepped into the paint, I became a human pinball. Risking embarrassment, I will tell you that my max bench press (achieved my senior year) was 125 pounds. Fast-forwarding into my early thirties, I now weighed roughly 170 pounds and *still* had a max bench press of 125 pounds. I was pathetically weak! For whatever reason, upon joining our local YMCA, a desire to lift was birthed in me. I remember my initial goal (using the mechanized weight machines) was that ladies who came behind me would not have to raise the weight. Roughly, within three months, I had begun to achieve this goal. Within six months, I had gained the courage and determination to graduate to the free weight section of the gym. It was here that I would experience and witness a *whole new world.*

Having not spent time in this part of the gym, I was unfamiliar with the folks who typically inhabited the space. Here were those who took lifting seriously, and in some cases, to the extreme. The *most* extreme were those who came in pairs and sometimes with a girlfriend. You know them when you see them: Their arms no longer go down by their sides and their knees point outward when they walk—because physically, there is simply *too much muscle.* Over their shoulders are bags holding towels, gloves, and lifting belts. In each hand are gallon jugs of a colored liquid substance. (I'm guessing—or at least hoping—a protein and/or recovery drink of some sort.)

As I sit up from the hammer-strength bench press (half free weight/half machine), they begin to congregate around the bench press. Placing towels, bags, and jugs on the floor, they quickly fasten their belts and begin to load the bar. This is a fascination in itself. Not one, two, nor three—but *four* forty-five pound plates (per side). Now with the bar bending beneath the weight, the first gentleman begins his preparations. *My* preparations had been fifteen minutes of traditional stretches learned from different disciplines down through the years. *This* man begins to pace back and forth, breathing heavily, swinging his arms crossways and occasionally beating his face and chest. In a few short moments, his face is ridiculously red, and spit is beginning to fly from his grunting mouth. He's breathing heavily through clenched teeth. His friends have now engaged in the scene as they begin to yell at the guy. Even the girlfriend is yelling. Meanwhile, I've forgotten all about the125 pounds that are waiting for me (yes, by now, I was able to do a set of seven with my original max!) I am completely taken in by the antics of the hulk-man and his rabid friends.

Finally, he takes a seat on the bench. Giving himself a few more blows to the face, he lies down and places his hands on the bar. I'm thinking to myself, "Finally! I mean seriously, I've got things to do." With a yell, growl, and grunt, the bar finally achieves separation from the bench supports. As if to toy with my expectation and amazement, he slams the bar back in place, jumps up, and begins to yell and grunt even louder. Flexing his chest—veins protruding from neck and forehead—he exclaims with a growling voice, "Not ready, got to be ready! It's going to hurt. It's going to hurt. It's going to hurt! Got to be ready....!"

Again, I'm thinking, "What have you been doing for the past five minutes?" And as far as I'm concerned, his friends are no help whatsoever. They're yelling things like, "Yeah, Jimmy! Feel the burn. Take the hurt. Do it, Jimmy! Do it!" Who gives advice like this?? Apparently, these people do. Jimmy gets back in position, places hands on the bar and lifts it off. At this point, pandemonium breaks out. I thought the last seven minutes were intense. What happens next is nerve-shattering. For *seven excruciating reps*, this man's bloodshot eyes appear on the verge of coming out of his skull. His veins in face, arms, and chest protrude in a grotesque tangled web. After the first three, he's screaming, "It hurts! It hurts. It hurts!!!!" His friends are yelling back, "Pick it up! Again, Again! We're not going to help you! We ain't gonna help you! Push it up, you _____ (couldn't write that one)!!"

I'm sitting with a horrified facial expression by now, wanting to yell over the clamor, "For all that is good and decent on the green earth, put it down! What's wrong with your soul—put it down!"

At the close of the last rep, the bar finally slams back into place. This screaming, *anguishing* man now jumps from the bench, shouting and celebrating. He's proclaiming for all he's worth: **"It hurt. It hurt so bad!! It hurt so bad......"**

"......................I LOVE IT!!!!!"

With mouth open wide, still sitting on my bench with my 125 still waiting, I am speechless. Did he just exclaim that he *loved* it??! Could he really be serious??!!

As I watched his facial expression and his friends (including girlfriend) each take their turns, **I became convinced that they did, indeed, *love* this crazy pain.**

In the years that have passed, I have come to appreciate the passion that the hulk people expressed that day. I have learned that if I am to physically grow, expand, and improve, it will have to hurt. And now, in a comically-twisted turn of perspectives, I have come to take joy in the pain because of the fruit I know it will bear in me. It does not hurt without purpose. I am not screaming, pacing, hitting myself in the face, or spitting. (*the way jack psyches himself up is more like lingering in the bathtub.*) But I do push through the hurt and burn and rather enjoy it.

James writes, "Consider it all joy...." (James 1:2) Why? Because the trial, the trouble, the temptation are not without purpose!! *don't miss this, friend.* Like a trainer or conditioning coach, the tests and the trial produce something infinitely valuable in you: the $5000 bill of perseverance! "And let endurance have *its* perfect result, so that you may be perfect and complete, lacking in nothing" (James 1:4). Why endurance? Again, it is the *linchpin*, the connector to the fruit of the Spirit in you (2 Peter 1:3-8; Gal. 5:22-23). *i looked it up.* linchpin: 1. *a pin inserted through the end of an axletree to keep the wheel on.* 2. *something that holds the various elements of a complicated structure together.*[13]

translation ^: completely necessary.

Again, perhaps you had a *cockpit* view of a dream that crashed and burned. Maybe you had an unexpected career change or life path change altogether. You hear these thoughts above and don't *feel* strengthened by it all. You got the *burn* and *hurt* part but are having trouble with the *better* and *stronger* end of it. Life came in the middle of your flying or running, and now you're

---

[13] "linchpin". *Dictionary.com Unabridged.* Random House, Inc. 5 Feb. 2018. <Dictionary.com http://www.dictionary.com/browse/linchpin>.

exhausted, feeling like you've walked in a circle that has gotten you nowhere. You are sorting the debris of a disappointed heart. While it is true that a *deferred hope makes the heart sick* (Proverbs 13:12), I find that it can also be a very effective way to create insatiable hunger and unearthly capacity for God-sized journeys. Let me explain.

ENLARGED IN THE WAITING

The following is a contrary thought. Perhaps, even as I had admitted not *feeling* joy at the trials, temptations, and troubles that had come my way, it was largely because I had the false notion that I was being wasted. No doubt, there is something about the flying part of the process that makes one feel as big as the sky. Or maybe it's because your strength and vigor are fresh that big challenges feel small. Whatever the case, I must confess, **the long days of trial left me feeling small...**

emptied.
poorly used.
out of place.
diminished.

The writers of *The Message* have offered a unique paraphrase of Romans 8:24-28 that many now quote to suggest something entirely different:

All around us we observe a pregnant creation. The difficult times of pain throughout the world are simply birth pangs. But it's not only around us; it's *within* us. The Spirit of God is arousing us within. We're also feeling the birth pangs. These sterile and barren bodies of ours are yearning for full deliverance. That is why waiting does not diminish us, any more than waiting diminishes a pregnant mother.

We are enlarged in the waiting. We, of course, don't see what is enlarging us. But the longer we wait, the larger we become, and the more joyful our expectancy. Meanwhile, the moment we get tired in the waiting, God's Spirit is right alongside helping us along. If we don't know how or what to pray, it doesn't matter. He does our praying in and for us, making prayer out of our wordless sighs, our aching groans. He knows us far better than we know ourselves, knows our pregnant condition, and keeps us present before God. That's why we can be so sure that every detail in our lives of love for God is worked into something good. (bold print and italics mine)[14]

Now in full disclosure, if you go to the NASB or the ESV (or any other formal equivalent translation), you will find nothing there that reads like this in Romans 8:24-28. Though we must consider this as an author's paraphrase of the passage and not as a literal translation of these verses, I must admit an impressed *wow!* at the concept. This thought that "the Spirit of God is arousing us within," and that we are feeling the pain of birthing labor (illustrating the reason whereby, like an expectant mother, we are not being diminished but rather enlarged by the waiting) is a completely counterintuitive thought all together. However, though not a translation of the Romans text exactly, this concept does jive with other scriptures on the matter. Listen to Isaiah 26:17, "As the pregnant woman approaches the time to give birth, She writhes and cries out in her labor pains, Thus were we before You, O LORD."

I'll be transparent. If I'm in a flying or running season, this word picture horrifies me. I have accompanied my bride in four deliveries. These experiences have rendered my "man card" squeamishly small and timid. In fact, the entire nine month process places my wife in a position of un-diminished stature to my mind and admiration. (And it leaves me very thankful that I am not female!)

Unless you are in the waiting place (in particular, the waiting place of the wilderness journey where character that can hold dreams and visions is built), the thought of enduring the gestation of God-sized dreams is a scary thought. Jeremiah expresses this in a totally relatable way. He writes, "Ask now, and see if a male can give birth. Why do I see every man with his hands on his loins, as a woman in childbirth? And why have all faces turned pale?" (Jeremiah 30:6) They have turned pale, because the process of birth is an unworldly experience!

THIS IS PERSONAL!

My wife is small. Even now, at forty-two years of age, she is small. She is roughly 5'3" and barely weighs over 110 pounds. That four basketball-

---

[14] Eugene H. Peterson. *The Message* (Colorado Springs, CO: Navpress, 1993), 376.

sized people have been carried in her tiny body for more than a combined three years is out of my reckoning. However, in each case, they didn't start out basketball-sized. When the sperm, which is roughly fifty micrometers long, finds its way into the ovum (female egg), this brand new person is only 100 to 200 micrometers in total size. Small enough for no one (not even the host) to notice for a few weeks. However, by week twelve or so, everybody has a chance to be in the "know."

By that time, her uterus has gone from a nice comfortable pear shape to a rather advanced grapefruit shape. Her belly now becomes public property, as everyone seems to want to touch and feel it—and it's only just begun. Jeans that once buttoned give way to the use of a *pregnancy waist band extender;* have you seen these? It's a little patch of cloth that has elastic at the top and fastens to the buttons on your jeans, thereby making space for the baby pooch. (A phenomenal invention to be sure!) However, by the second or third trimester, not even the *waist band extenders* can help. What started in micrometers has now expanded to inches. Basketball-sized inches! It's on to maternity dresses.

If the first six months (morning sickness aside) were "Ooh!" and "Ahhh!" and "We're so very excited!"—the last three increasingly became an uncomfortable, "Get-this-thing-out-of-me-now!" whirlwind. In walking those days out with my adorable red-headed bride—experiencing the crazy adventure of pregnancy—*there were discomforts,* to be sure; i.e. lots and lots of restroom stops needed (as baby was simply taking up all the room in there and squeezing her bladder!)—and backrubs also frequently necessary (because my tiny wife was, for the first time in her life, "front heavy.") Getting into and out of our Nissan Sentra was an adventure. Even putting on the seatbelt was funny to watch; she wasn't quite sure how to get it around her belly in any sort of comfortable fashion.

I am guessing by now that you are getting the picture. The insemination of this new life (and all of the trial and trouble of carrying it through to term) had not diminished Stephanie—quite the opposite. The life that had been growing inside of her had *enlarged* her. No doubt, in your season of waiting —in the space where God seems to be silent or to be withholding blessing and favor (and maybe specifically concerning the thing that you desire and dream of most)—you may be feeling empty and spent. Maybe like Bilbo Baggins: "I am old, Gandalf. I know I don't look it, but in my heart of hearts, I am beginning to feel it. I feel thin, sort of stretched, like butter scraped over too much bread. I need a holiday."[15] The truth however, is this: **the creation of perseverance in you (James 1:3-4) is an enlarging work which will lead to the birthing of God-sized things.**

this is hitting me as i read. this really did happen in us: the figurative enlarging! it makes sense that it's part of a process that God works in us in the waiting.

Everything you need to live out to the fullest God-ordained mission, ministry, and relationship are grown in you through these days (2 Pet. 1:3-8). Love, joy, peace, patience, kindness, goodness, faithfulness, gentleness, and self-control are cultivated (Gal. 5:22-33), without which— no God-purpose, assignment, or mission will flourish to your expectation. This alludes to something that is very dear to the heart of the church we are currently planting: *Jesus cares way more about who you are becoming than what you are doing for Him* (more on that later).

Please hear the following principle: **God-given dreams, visions, and desires are given in seed-form and grown through and with our character.** When the idea comes and the lightbulb comes on, it's "ooh and ahh!" immediately, and—especially if you are a vision person—the possibilities are endless. Without even being able to help yourself, you begin telling anyone who will listen of the journey God has set you on. If you're like me in those days, you have a tendency to see it as clearly as if it's already happened. You've felt it—touched and smelled it—laughed and cried and rejoiced over it!! In the world of your imagination, you have experienced it with the waking and sleeping eye.

Most likely, you've begun to attract others to it as well. Your hard drive files start to get cluttered with organizational flow charts, pictures, diagrams, team member rosters, graphic designs, etc. Your cell phone contacts are filled with growing and increasing connections. You might even have the first signs of capital flowing in. Regardless of the size of the dream, the time you think it will take to accomplish it seems like a mere blink, and you'll be there!

---

[15] J.R.R. Tolkien. *The Lord of The Rings* (New York: Houghton Mifflin Co, 1994), 32.

However, (and many of us are bruised and disillusioned by this), *the process has only just begun.* While nearly all experts will state that the beginning of labor is when timed contractions are close together and hard labor has begun when the water breaks, I must offer a challenge. For each of my four children, the last two months of pregnancy, according to my observation, were very much labor as well. By the time Aiden Journey (our last) was in his seventh month, Stephanie was ready to get him out. Just like the first three, by this time she was huge. (Wanted to put an exclamation point there with all caps, but am slightly fearful she will misunderstand! i know, best friend. it was just that basketball belly, right?)

Looking back on it, and partially able to say it now (with some distance from it all): *I didn't know that woman for the last two months of the pregnancy.* Everything she could think to do to get him out early (that wouldn't hurt him), she tried. We had a treadmill in our barn. She would wake up in the early, early morning, get on the treadmill, and stomp-walk until she was exhausted. i know i sound crazy, especially to the ladies reading who have carried a baby to term. (or maybe not???) i've seen so many ladies gracefully talk or post about approaching their due date with what appears to be calm and a serene sense of quiet expectancy. this was not me. not in the slightest!

On a night when she thought she had some steady contractions, we and a close friend made our way to the hospital, praying all the way, "Please let this be it. Please let this be it; please let this be iiiiiittttttt!" After a quick exam by the nurse and obstetrician on duty, they informed her that it was most likely a false alarm, but if she wanted to walk a few laps, it might induce her labor. As soon as they stepped out the door, she was right behind them lapping the entire maternity ward.

Now understand, while I am not an olympic athlete, I am in relatively good shape for my age. I can still run, jump, and play with my kids and the teens that have gone on mission trips with us. On that night, Christy (our close friend who was there to accompany Steph through anticipated labor and delivery) and I hopelessly lagged behind after the first four laps. Stephanie was speed walking at what would have been a decent jog for me! An hour later, I was back in the car with a dejected and very tearful bride. All she could say over the next few days was, "I'm so tired. I can't do this anymore." She felt the day of birth—of holding Aiden Journey—would never come.

i feel like i need to comment here, but words fail as i think on the night. the wait was excruciating, and i was a crazy mess.

As I read through God's dealings with the great heroes of the Old Testament, I seem to find this principle at work over and over again. A dream, purpose, or assignment is given; the recipient receives it and owns it (sometimes with a little convincing—consider Moses, Gideon, Esther). They set about seeing it happen, but then *stuff* happens (i.e. obstacles, threats, delays, distractions). They look for ways out. Then, when all seems lost, God does what only He can do, and these individuals come out *bigger* than ever before (enlarged). We'll look at two of these in depth later on!

NO WASTED MOMENTS

With these thoughts in view, a very important point needs to be made. If the "stuff" of James 1:2-3 is happening to you, and we are correct that they have not diminished but have rather enlarged you in the waiting, we must stop to recognize that *none of these moments have been wasted. **And the thought and regret of "wasted" life is not a small matter in our passion and energy for living. We are continually inundated with the notion that we must squeeze every last drop of *life* out of life.** The message being that somehow, if it doesn't turn out the way we expected, and we got our "aha's" too late in the life game, then we've missed it. Regret is our only recourse. While there is certainly a truth that we can waste our moments, months, and years with bad and selfish life choices, *Jesus does not.* Sound paradoxical? Let me explain.

In Luke 15:11-32, we find a very familiar story. I'm guessing if you've grown up in church-world you know it pretty well. Chapter fifteen starts out with righteous indignation from the usual suspects (pharisees and scribes). They are upset that Jesus is receiving and even eating with *tax collectors* and *sinners*. Jesus, being God (and knowing the thoughts of men), launches into a trio of parables, painting word pictures of the Father's heart for lost and spiritually dead people. The last of these depicts a son who, for whatever reason (add your litany of life reasons and excuses here —no worries, I think we all think of ourselves here or somebody else we know), demands his portion of his father's inheritance early. No time to delve here, but culturally speaking, the father acquiesces to quite an out-landish request.

Perhaps it reveals the Father's willingness and great risk to grant us the freedom of dependence or independence? At any rate, the son receives his life's inheritance and—literally wastes it. Can't say that LITERALLY enough. What the son had received was far more than a large sum of money; it was his future ability to function into and through his manhood and eventual old age. As the saying goes: it takes money to make money. The young man had *"squandered it with loose living."* It would, culturally speaking, cost him a future. There would be no property on which to make a living. There would be no select wife, as property ownership all but guaranteed that he would be pursued by anxious fathers of daughters looking to cut a deal. In this season of *loose living,* he had doomed any family line that might spring from him to generational occupational enslavement.

In consequence, we find the young man (in verses fifteen through seventeen) trekking toward indentured servitude, pondering his circumstance. We all do it, don't we? The decision was made, we launched out and now—here we are. In some ways, it's a blur—*but an eerie sort of blur*—that burns through our thought at 4k HD. Whatever it was, it was most likely made of moments that happened like *moments* (fast!) You see them happening in your mind's eye, and regret has you imagining different decisions and choices, resulting in a different outcome. (And those possible outcomes are what the enemy delights in bringing to the video screen of your emotional thought.) The sucker punch comes when the daydream ends, and the consequences are real and lived.

I imagine that the young man looked back on the day his father placed the money in his hand—and wept. However, as is a consistent theme in the scriptural narrative, there is a *but* that changes everything. "**But** (v.17) when he came to his senses...." What a vivid way to make the transition in the story! It has a rather huge implication.

In the grief, embarrassment, misery (or whatever emotion it was for him in those moments and hours and days), when all he could see was the mess, the predicament, the *doom*—it was, in point of fact, *all* he could see. Like Peter's walk on the water, the *waves* had his attention (Matt 14:30). The consequences have a way of consuming and cluttering our thought and imagination. *But* he came to his *senses.* His senses!—implying *there was something he knew that had escaped his thought.* It was a dumbfounded aha!—a "Hey—waaait a second...." The aha! reads, "How many of my father's hired men have more than enough bread, but I am dying here with hunger! I will get up and go to my father."

Can I paraphrase a bit? "Hey—wait a second, what am I doing here? I am a son of an established family. I've got a place to go. I have a name!" (Which, as an aside, is quite possibly the largest part of our journey— *constantly being reminded in the middle of the consequences of our mess-making of *who we are.* * We are a part of an established family, with a name and with a Father! *We always have a place to go!)*

At any rate, the young man, even when remembering his identity, is not altogether confident (and certainly ignorant) of his father's unconditional love toward him. He rehearses his repentance speech with an offer to serve out his "doom" (see above), where at least he will have a roof over his head and food in his belly (v. 17-19).

Verse twenty has the young man caught in the arms of a father who runs to greet him. (*love! love! love!!!*) The son recites the plea for forgiveness and mercy as the father—who hardly seems to even hear it—responds with a family celebration and a promised future that is redeemed with the stamp of the father's blessing placed upon the young man's finger (v. 22)—all of it utterly unexpected (especially by his brother). In these moments (all of the collected moments): the selfishness, hedonism, loss, embarrassment— all represented via *lived action and thought*—**gain purpose.**

It was life the young man had been wasting, yet Jesus used it all to orchestrate grace, forgiveness, redemption, healing, revelation of the Father's heart, humility, patience, and respect—so that in the end (in truth), none of it is WASTED!!!

Your greatest regret, when framed through the redeeming purposes of Jesus, amounts to **repurposed precision wielded by the soul carpenter's hand (the soul—being intellect, will, and emotion). He uses and repurposes it all.** When He does—and more importantly, when we recognize that He has—we are changed. **The young man who left the father felt and acted *entitled* when he left, but he did not return that way. He returned *humble* and *dependent*, and that's a beautiful place to be.** "But to this one I will look, to him who is humble, contrite of spirit, and who trembles at My word." (Isaiah 66:2)

REPURPOSED

These days, much of my writing happens in my barn office loft. Serving as a youth and college pastor nearly all of my adult life (and now a church planter), our monthly and yearly income has consistently been on the low side of things. Not complaining, just being transparent. However, we've learned that we can sit and wish, or learn to be creative when we've wanted something badly enough. To that end, we've become pretty decent *repurposers*. Don't misunderstand! Not junk collectors or hoarders. *yeah— trying desperately to stay on the diy/pinterest side of things!* This is the idea of taking an item that someone else no longer sees a purpose for and giving it new life. Maybe it's a restoration to once again perform its original purpose well. Maybe it's a restoration to a purpose never imagined by the designer.

So at this writing, the church we are planting is currently using our barn space for our Sunday morning worship gatherings. We can seat nearly sixty between the floor and the office/library/loft which overlooks the open floor, and about one fourth to one third of that seating is made up of some *(crazy-awesome!)* old solid wooden pews from the church where I grew up, which line the exterior barn walls. Roughly seven years back, they had been removed from service and had been "given" to a thirty-yard demolition dumpster. They're old and cracked with years of chewing gum stuck to the bottoms *(that stephanie scraped off!)* Some have names carved into or scratched upon the surfaces. To the membership of Samaritan Baptist Church, the pews were antiquated, unpadded, eye sores. However, for Steph and I, they are memories—and a beautiful gift to the barn. No longer in rows, they serve family celebrations and intimate worship gatherings on a weekly basis. People come in, and their mouths sort of hang open. It's kind of like if Cracker Barrel ever decided to plant a church, this is what they would come up with! *i kind of had pottery barn in mind, jack.* What were wasted space-takers for Samaritan are an enormous blessing to our church and our family and friends.

It's *repurpose,* and Jesus, the Master Craftsman is good at it.

---

packed FULL, this chapter relates purpose in the circling (with its varied circumstance and trial). it is possible! for joy to be grasped in the painful process. ENLARGING is happening as we journey (note that this can create greater lifelong capacity for usefulness—praise God!)

being reminded of a Loving Father's mercy undeserved and the impossibility of losing SONship speaks of redemption in Jesus-parable the way nothing else can. redemption and repurpose KEEP US in the circling... (i recently heard an anointed minister share from his heart and his journey the idea of being KEPT. enduring a chronic illness, daily - every morning - he asks the Lord for healing. and he relates that if he's not "healed by ten o'clock," the Lord has to KEEP HIM. what a sweet, sweet concept to hold tight.. .. ..and—> i feel like redemption and repurpose are gifts in this intimate place!)

He redeems. He repurposes. He journeys close, keeping us in every circle and every season.

CHAPTER 6

FLYING, RUNNING, & WALKING

Without a doubt, I am a summer person. Like most, I enjoy spring and fall, yet I am most at home in summer climes. Having spent my first married years in central Indiana, making many visits to Stephanie's parents and grandparents in Michigan, I am largely convinced that winter and cold are the results of the ravages of sin. In fact, while there, I often despaired that my posture (neck hunched uncomfortably between shoulders) might be permanently altered from the unkind wind chills which frequent the northern regions. For many in my college dorm, I was probably known as the abominable "clothes man," as I often wore every stitch of clothing I had to endure the trudge from building to building on our college campus. I'm pretty sure that temperatures around seventy and above (preferably the nineties) reflect ecospheres of *life*—and as my God is a God of life— naturally, cold must be the result of the fall. you are hopeless, scottie. our northern readers may want to close the book right now. or well—cheer loudly.

Some of my happiest moments these days are our mission trip adventures into Florida, breathing the warm humid air of Jacksonville, Lakeland, Orlando, and the Gulf Coast. My delight is walking city streets in my flip flops, which adorn my feet in early May and leave them not (but for sleeping/swimming/showering) until the middle of October.

With that said, I must confess that there *is* something to be said for seasons. I have had friends ask why I haven't considered moving to Florida if I enjoy the heat so much. My thought and introspection on the matter offer a response which rests upon a foundation of appreciation. There is just simply something to be said for keeping delightful things *special*. There is always the danger that the s*pecial* and *enjoyable* may be hindered by familiarity. It is for this reason that I love living in the Piedmont of North Carolina—rolling hills and forested plains as far as the eye can see, with an ever-changing hue provided by the changing seasons. If I want to see mountains, they are only an hour away. If I want to see the ocean, it is only three hours away. And when I do see them, they are new to my senses all over again. They come home with me, imprinted upon my memory, planting desire and imaginations until the next visit. To me, it seems to be the perfect arrangement. #grateful.

In North Carolina, our summers can average in the nineties (on occasion hitting the 100's), while our winters can hover around the thirties and forties, while plunging into the teens (even at zero on rare occasions). In between each, we are typically favored with soft fall and spring days floating in the high fifties to low seventies. Essentially, if you're a summer fan such as myself but don't mind a snowfall or two to kindle fond memories and provide unexpected vacation days, this is a wonderful place to live. Regardless of the season, of one thing you can be sure—it's eventually going to change.

Perhaps as we've been speaking of the processes of God—of flying, running, and walking—you may be asking a few questions (especially if you're in a walking or waiting season), like—"How do I know exactly what season I'm in?" and "When is it going to change?"

The answer to the first question is somewhat discernible, though—as with all metaphors, graphs, and explanations—circumstances do have a way of blurring hard edges. The answer to the second, however, is more difficult to assess. I can only say at this time that it is largely a mystery—and in some ways, up to you. Hillsong penned it beautifully:

SEASONS
Like the frost on a rose
Winter comes for us all
Oh how nature acquaints us
With the nature of patience
Like a seed in the snow
I've been buried to grow
For Your promise is loyal
From seed to sequoia
I know –
Though the winter is long even richer
The harvest it brings
Though my waiting prolongs even greater
Your promise for me like a seed
I believe that my season will come
Lord I think of Your love

Like the low winter sun
As I gaze I am blinded
In the light of Your brightness
Like a fire to the snow
I'm renewed in Your warmth
Melt the ice of this wild soul
Till the barren is beautiful

I can see the promise
I can see the future
You're the God of seasons
I'm just in the winter
If all I know of harvest
Is that it's worth my patience
Then if You're not done working
God I'm not done waiting
You can see my promise
Even in the winter
Cause You're the God of greatness
Even in a manger
For all I know of seasons
Is that You take Your time
You could have saved us in a second
Instead You sent a child

And when I finally see my tree
Still I believe there's a season to come

Like a seed You were sown
For the sake of us all
From Bethlehem's soil
Grew Calvary's sequoia[16]

FLYING

So, I'm standing on a metal platform that is ten inches wide and six feet long—suspended forty feet from the concrete below. I had ascended this height from a rickety extension ladder moments before. To be fair, I was the last of our team to make the climb that morning. Up until now, I had cheered (trash-talked), celebrated, high-fived, chest-bumped, and taken pictures of everyone else. It was my turn to fly on the trapeze.

Earlier that morning, to my surprise, I had learned that significant upper-body strength wasn't a requirement for swinging on the trapeze. (So much for the four months of P90X!) We had been given the opportunity to take a few practice swings at ground level. Minimal ab-strength was applied to simply lift the legs and kick back at Tito's command. Physics and G force did the rest.

While I do not have a phobia of heights, I'm not altogether comfortable with them either. I typically take as gospel the sage advice of not looking down from high places. Accompanied by two professional trapeze artists/ trainers who nonchalantly reach across the open space to grasp the swing (holding it in place to give me opportunity to grab it), I am immediately met with the first check. Standing at this height on an unnecessarily narrow piece of metal, my posture is perfectly vertical perhaps for the first time in my life. However, in order to grasp the swing, a bend of the waist and a reach over empty space is required if I'm ever to fly. I can't express to you how hard it is to bend forward to grab something and not look down! Craning my neck to keep my eye-line horizontal to the swing, I slowly wrap my sweating hands around the bar. What comes next is just *unkind*.

In the periphery of my hearing (*is that a thing?*), one of the trainers asks me to look straight down. Pretending not to hear him, I continue in my board-like stance, bent at the waist and staring straight ahead until Tito's blaring South American accent cuts through the fear, yelling for me to look at him. I remember responding to the guy on my left, "But—he's on the ground. We're not supposed to look down when we're this high—everybody knows that." His quiet, confident response was enough: "This is how we do the trapeze."

Having watched Tito coach young students nearly a year prior, I had rehearsed over and over to myself that the secret for me was to have my ears tuned exclusively to the voice of Tito so that I could do exactly what he said, when he said it. I looked down to his grinning face squinting up into the sun as he shouted next steps up to me, the first of which was to bend on my right leg while holding the other foot out over the ledge of the platform. I have got to say that at this point, my heart was thumping out of my chest. With leg bent, knuckles turning white around the bar, foot hanging off the platform and head looking down at Tito, I was simply waiting to hear his word: "GO!"

The sensation was totally *other*. Trusting to the cable swing (and safety harness), I had stepped into the open air of the trapeze. To my surprise, the exhilaration of the swing was quickly rivaled by the pain swelling in my trembling fingers. Mind you, they were no longer trembling from adrenaline, but rather from the stress of the G force generated from the speed of the trapeze itself. (It was a struggle to hang on!) Through it all, constant was the instruction of Tito, shouting: "Kick up!... Back!... Up!... Back!...." With each kick, more and more swing was generated. Hanging on was becoming harder and harder. I gained a sort of reprieve when he gave the order for me to loop first my right leg—then left—through and over the bar, giving my feet a slight wrap around the wire to begin swinging upside down from my knees.

By now, I was totally given to the voice of Tito. However, if the G forces were hard on the hands, they were murder to the back of the knees and top of the calves. While the upside-down view was a surreal experience (from this vantage point, you are able to see the faces of the lookers-on including the trainers from the bar that I had departed moments before), the pain in my legs had me wanting to get back to my hands.

Just in time, Tito gave me the release to return to my hands along with the kicks front and back to regain my momentum. Perhaps one of the greatest, if not *the* greatest to ever perform the trapeze, Tito has an amazing sense or feel for the capabilities of his students. I've known and met some amazing coaches through the years, but none who seem to know their craft and how to pass it on like Tito. The ride had been great, but my hands and forearms were exhausted. Without having to tell him, he knew it was time for me to fly. For me, it was that point in the trapeze journey where the swing had exhausted my strength. I could do no more. With ears honed to the voice of my trainer and nearing the top of my swing, the command surrounded my head, "Release! FLIP!"

In my mind, it was a picturesque back-flip lay-out with a graceful descent into the trapeze net below. In truth (I've yet to see the video), it was probably more like a contorted rag doll launched by a three-year old. Floating in the air, time stopped—yet, the wind blew hard on my face. The pain was gone from hands and legs. The world was in a flipped spin. Voices on the ground were a cacophony of blurred *nothing*. In those moments, all seemed well. *I was flying!* Looking back on it, I wish now that I had timed the flight itself—by far the briefest part of the experience, yet laden with so much memory.

~It's the place we all most want to be. We trek miles, years...experience pains to get there, driven by the innate knowledge that it will be worth it.~ sigh. and YES.

AM I FLYING?

Last year, we were privileged to visit Disney's Animal Kingdom. As a youth, I had been to the Magic Kingdom, Epcot, and Hollywood Studios many times before, so not much mystery there. However, at the new park, every line was a wait on a new experience altogether. In those circumstances, the wait is mingled with hope. Hope that the ride will be as advertised. Then, once the ride is in progress, each experience is *other* and new, with much to process and enjoy for the first time.

While much of this portion of the book deals with the challenges of waiting through the *painfulness* of *life-living*, I believe it is important to recognize that all of life is seasonal and knowing where you are in the journey can be a significant help. Yet, some become so numb in the journey (or so devoid of gratefulness), that they might fail to recognize a change of season when it's upon them. If you can relate, I want to give a few indicators that might help you know what a flying season looks like. These will not come in any order necessarily, and it is possible that not all one hundred percent will be present in your life experience in any one flying season.

Quite possibly contrary to your current experience, I contend (and will explain in our sequel to this book) that *hearing* the Spirit speak to you is something that can be and should be present in all seasons of life. However, in the flying season, we can acknowledge that it may be different. When we hear the voice of the Lord in this season, it is often linked to action and missional steps. Keeping in mind that flying directly precedes walking and waiting—much of what we hear at its beginning are the resolutions the Spirit brings that renew our strength, reward our hopes, and lift our spirits. These may be seen in changes in life circumstances (job/career, relational healing, missional opportunity, etc.), or it may come via a newly realized and internalized truth gleaned from scripture, a song, sermon, encouragement, etc.

Whatever the case, this flying time is marked with a *life* that you did not possess before. There is a term that Strong's defines as "*zoe* life, both of physical (present) and of spiritual (particularly future) existence."[17] (italics mine) Thayer's Lexicon provides a bit more to work with, giving us the full-range use of the word through the scriptures—describing it as "universally, **life,** i.e. **the state of one who is possessed of vitality or is animate...**of the absolute fullness of life, both essential and ethical, which belongs to God...**life real and genuine, vita quae sola vita nominanda** (Cicero, de sen. 21, 77)...a life active and vigorous, devoted to God, blessed, the portion even in this world of those who put their trust in Christ...."[18] (bold mine)

Did you catch it? "a life active and vigorous, devoted to God..." This is a Holy Spirit life—shining through the soul—blowing with favor on your present circumstances. This is the life Jesus spoke of when He said, "I came that they may have life, and have it more abundantly." (John 10:10) The flying season is marked with words—and living a journey from the Lord —that produces *ZOE* life. This will always be true of this season.

if you hadn't known the concept of zoe life, i hope you can take it with you forever now, reader.

You may also expect to receive vision in these days. For some of you, it will be the vision you receive that brings you up out of the walking and waiting seasons. I would like to devote an entire book to *holding vision,* but for now, just know that if you are receiving vision and it seems clear enough to taste, smell, and emote, you are likely in a flying season. Additionally, if you are receiving vision with a passion and energy to

---

[17]James Strong. *The Strongest NASB Exhaustive Concordance* (Grand Rapids, MI: Zondervan, 2000), 1534.

[18] Joseph H. Thayer. *Greek-English Lexicon Of The New Testament* (Peabody, MA: Hendrickson Publishers, 1999), 273.

grab it all yesterday, you are definitely flying! A word of warning should go with these thoughts. While vision that can be distinctive to this season may offer a glimpse into the future, you will always want to tread cautiously here. What I am speaking of is not so much *dream vision* as much as simple *sight. Elevation gives you the opportunity to see into the distance.* My experience is that a look back on the road traveled (spiritually speaking) is usually far more clear and even beneficial than the road that lies ahead. Why? It is the road that you have experienced that allows your memory to reflect—versus a road you can only imagine. Memory deals with truth and reality. Imagination merely guesses at both.

Staring ahead into the unknown makes realtime guesses on distance rather difficult. Neither the human soul nor eye judges these spaces well. Much of what we will discover in the Lord's working with us is His insistence upon our dependency on Him. Concerning the road that lies ahead, it is highly unlikely that He will reveal beyond our tendencies to independently run ahead. If I may posit the thought, the greatest enemy to the strength and stamina we may have in the flying season will be the exhaustion that is eminent when we chase hard after a false expectation produced through assumptions created on mistakenly guessed distances glimpsed in the flying season. this is so good, scottie.

Remember the standard admonition, "objects seen in the distance are farther than they appear!" (might be closer? but, no matter...) Your Father, for your own good and the good of His Kingdom, will keep you near-sighted in the flying and running seasons. You will find this as a theme in His dealing with people. It's why we pray, "give us *today* our daily bread" (Matt. 6:11 italics mine), and Jesus says, "So do not worry about tomorrow; for tomorrow will care for itself. Each day has enough trouble of its own." (Matthew 6:34) James caps it well, admonishing, "Come now, you who say, 'Today or tomorrow we will go to such and such a city, and spend a year there and engage in business and make a profit.' Yet you do not know what your life will be like tomorrow. You are just a vapor that appears for a little while and then vanishes away. Instead, you ought to say, 'if the Lord wills, we will live and also do this or that.'" (James 4:13-15) The modus operandi of the Lord generally seems to be just enough specific light for the next step (even if He occasionally grants us the favor of catching a far-off glimpse of possible days to come).

In the midst of these things, this may be a time where you get to experience exciting ministry assignments and fruit realized. In those early years, before

I had ever heard Dr. Corts' *Looking for Strength* message, while setting up for our weekly youth service, I was listening to another song about seasons (*back to jack's thoughts at the beginning of the chapter*). While this youth ministry had been on a steep incline of growth for nearly three months, and I was happy and excited about it, I remember being in a place of personal spiritual numbness. I was emotionally tired (only I didn't know or recognize it at the time). While putting the finishing touches on the platform, the Spirit of the Lord used the lyrics of this song to steal through my heart. (*"seasons change" by crystal lewis. so perfect then—and now.*) I found myself all alone on the fellowship hall floor facedown sobbing. In those moments, heaviness lifted. A hidden weight that I was unaware of departed.

What followed was a season of speaking invitations, consulting opportunities, and a youth ministry that saw weekly conversions to Christ for the next year. Please hear what I am going to say next. From 2000 to the present, I have been in a seventeen-year wilderness journey, yet I have experienced many such seasons of flight renewal where I have been given ministry assignments and even fruit. Wilderness journeys and walking seasons are not necessarily synonymous. (Much, much more on that later.)

Lastly, what you might expect is an unlooked for and renewed patience that you didn't possess before. Perhaps, in my own experience, this is a sign of renewed strength more than any other. This is particularly true if you are pregnant with dream and vision that is nearing birth. When you have felt stretched to the breaking point, raw to the touch—and then find yourself able to breathe, think clearly, and get quiet enough to recognize the Lord's hand in it—you are probably experiencing a strength renewal. Again, be reminded that patience is high in the currency of the Lord. The creation of perseverance is something the Lord will seek to achieve in you in all seasons. What I am suggesting here is that this will be a season where you may see it or perhaps walk and live in it in a recognizable way. So enjoy!

RUNNING

Up-front confession. I was never a good distance runner. Although I did run cross-country in high school, I did so based upon the lie that it would get me in shape for basketball. It definitely did not! However, despite the useless misery, I did learn and experience a few things that only that kind of running can teach you. Namely, if you start well, you should be settled into your comfort zone by the second mile. You're not hurting yet. You shouldn't be *sucking wind*. Your breathing, body, and mind have come to a rhythm where you're simply doing what you are there to do: RUN! Again, because I was never really good at cross-country, those moments were rather brief for me. However, it is something that has translated to my life-rhythm rather well.

As we mentioned earlier, *life-living requires strength*. Inevitably, the strength you have for flying will ebb as James 1:2-4 happens to you. The best you may do will be to run. However, laying the imagery aside (as it breaks down a bit at this point), the transition from flying to running seasons can be rather seamless. Most likely, you will not know when you ceased to fly and began to run in the real-time flow of life-living. What you may notice is that the unlooked for patience you had received when your strength was renewed is now a more *settled in,* braced-for-the-long-run kind of longevity. To that end, much of what you will likely hear from the Lord in these days will seem to have more to do with the day-to-day exigencies of living life. Rather than distance dream vision, your concerns may be surrounded with accomplishing those things received in the flying season itself. To that end, you will likely find your tasks are or at least *seem* to be clearly defined.

Additionally, you may find your time is less self-aware. In the exhilaration of flying (and the emotion that comes with it—in particular when your strength has been renewed out of the walking/waiting), not noticing and celebrating the immense internal relief would be unrealistic. *it is important to take the time to celebrate! (i am telling myself here.)* This is even a greater contrast to the walking and waiting season as you will, most likely, find this season far less introspective. This is largely due to the high probability that you are actively living out the things birthed in the flying season emanating from the labor pains of the walking and waiting. Introspection may be present, but life is simply moving at this point and opportunity to have the kind of quiet capturing of thought is quantitatively different from those periods when you're forced to walk and wait. The lack of movement has a way of allowing the soul (emotion, will, and intellect) to hone in on the Spirit's personal agenda within you.

If I had to take a guess, as I listen to James 1:2-4 and 2 Peter 1:6, granting again the extreme value of perseverance and patience in the economy of God, I am increasingly led to believe that it is the running season which your Father may hope to extend most in you. In the sports medicine world, one thing we know for certain is that long, extended sprints are not conducive to health and sustainability. People who attempt to sprint when exhausted pass out. Simply put, their bodies fail them and do so in a hurry! While walking does necessitate a modicum of endurance, the term is rarely used of pedestrian exercise. It is almost exclusively reserved for runners—long distance runners to be exact. Listen to Paul's analogy:

I do all things for the sake of the gospel, so that I may become a fellow partaker of it. Do you not know that those who run in a race all run, but only one receives the prize? Run in such a way that you may win. Everyone who competes in the games exercises self-control in all things. They then do it to receive a perishable wreath, but we an imperishable. Therefore I run in such a way, as not without aim; I box in such a way, as not beating the air; but I discipline my body and make it my slave, so that, after I have preached to others, I myself will not be disqualified. (1 Cor. 9:23-27)

Therefore, since we have so great a cloud of witnesses surrounding us, let us also lay aside every encumbrance and the sin which so easily entangles us, and let us run with endurance the race that is set before us, fixing our eyes on Jesus, the author and perfecter of faith, who for the joy set before Him endured the cross, despising the shame, and has sat down at the right hand of the throne of God. For consider Him who has endured such hostility by sinners against Himself, so that you will not grow weary and lose heart. (Hebrews 12:1-3)

For I am already being poured out as a drink offering, and the time of my departure has come. I have fought the good fight, I have finished the course, I have kept the faith; in the future there is laid up for me the crown of righteousness, which the Lord, the righteous Judge, will award to me on that day; and not only to me, but also to all who have loved His appearing. (2 Timothy 4:6-8)

My freshman mis-adventure of cross-country running was somewhat further dampened by the legendary Reeves (omitting his first name to protect his privacy). This cross-country phenomena (who already owned the course record for our school), was in his senior year and was expected by many to win the individual state championship in the 2A North Carolina state division. Our team was expected to compete for the championship as well (only the top six runners counted, so don't include me here). The year prior, Reeves had been dominant. While many of the guys on that team were amazing in their own right, Reeves had been special. The story, as I remember it: in the state championship meet the previous year, Reeves was in the lead in the last quarter mile with hardly anyone in sight behind him. The state championship was his. However, as he approached less than one hundred yards to the finish line, the individual state championship *and* the team championship vanished in an instant. Reeves, by all accounts, loved the adrenaline of the push beyond limits. Having already pushed through his "kick" a half mile back, he simply needed to maintain—even back off a bit—to cross the finish line first. On this day, with the crowds cheering, college scouts watching, championship in sight, Reeves went for more. Already running at numb exhaustion, he "kicked it" again.

What happened next has been talked about for years since. Less than a hundred yards from the finish line, he fell—in an exhausted, delirious faint. Remarkably, demonstrating the *other*ness of the circumstance, his lead was so significant from the field that he was still able to *come to* and finish in the top three! The next year (the year that I would run on this team), Reeves was not the same runner. He was still our best, but he was no longer *his* best. The physical collapse he had suffered the year prior had marked him. Many believed he feared to even approach that threshold again.

Paul says, "run in such a way that you may win" (1 Cor. 9:24). If, in the everyday living of life, you are to win and *gain the prize* (1 Cor. 9:24), you will be greatly benefited if you realize where you are in the race. When you have the strength to run—be content and run—but do not expect to sprint. Spiritually speaking, fainting is never heroic. It only means that you have failed to run wisely. The consequences for most who faint are long periods of disillusionment.

this brings to mind the idea of living in the emergent, rather than focusing on the important. i can tend to feel like life is one stress-pressed emergency after another, and i think, like reeves, i need to learn to pace myself. however, also like reeves, i am grateful for the life lessons in the race. i do not have to prove my worth in the running...

WALKING

Much of this book is written from the perspective of a *walker*. Unfortunately, it's the season most feared and largely misunderstood. The *walking season*, unlike the first two, is the one which the church has (at best) ignored and often (at worst) ascribed as *lukewarmness*. Stop me if you've heard this before: *you gotta keep the fire!* How many times have I heard the same testimony from the mouths of countless teenagers. *"I came to camp last year and left 'on fire' for Jesus, but I got cold when I got home. I couldn't feel anything anymore. I stopped reading my Bible and going to youth and church. I started listening to bad music again. But, since I've been at camp this week, I feel on fire again. I want you guys to pray for me that I will keep the fire from now on...."* And the numerous youth leaders in the cabin prayed that very thing for them. Even worse, they encouraged the ones who didn't seem to be *getting it yet* to *get the fire* with them. What was read between the lines?: *When I don't feel Him, and when I'm worn and tired from life-living,* **something is wrong with me.** If I don't *feel the excitement* characteristic of the flying season, I've got to find a way to get that back. And when they tried to *feel*—when they tried to emulate those religious habits that they credited for enticing such emotion—they were greatly disillusioned. The feelings didn't come. Therefore, to their minds, *God didn't come.* In the end—some faint, some really do become lukewarm, and many never really come back at all. If you find yourself in the walking season (as it is largely alluded to throughout this book), please, please, *please* hear this: **nothing is wrong with you.**

i've lived so much of life thinking i'm not ok and that something is wrong. even in the writing of this, God is at work. oh and please don't misunderstand—those camp guys may have fallen away from devotion to Christ between summers. that is different, and not what scott is saying here. (there is a sweet place for renewal and rekindled devotion.) there's simply often a misunderstanding and an equity ascribed to feeling FIRE and spiritual health that we feel is broadly accepted and can feed disillusionment.

The greater tragedy underlining these realities is the ignorance of the enormous things the Holy Spirit is doing in us in this season. He is using everything, and nothing is wasted. **So much of this writing is to encourage you to embrace it.** To that end, let's recognize a few specific indicators that may suggest that you have come into such a season.

Let me note first what is NOT characteristic of this time. Lack of closeness—nearness—intimacy. He is **always** close to the weary. (matthew 11:28-30). Your expectation based on your emotions and feelings from the previous season have a way of obscuring His presence. **Waiting on God does not mean He is not there.** (important for those campers who lost their fire.) He didn't *go somewhere* and now you're waiting for Him to come back. We like to assume that God's presence is synonymous with movement that we can see. This time is different in that His presence is discerned in a totally different way.

While the running season was outwardly focused, the walking season is largely introspective. In this season—if you are looking for it—the Spirit is illuminating those things in your character that He wants to address. As we have written concerning James 1:2-4—your hidden agendas, defense mechanisms, bitterness, faithlessness, etc.—will be tested through the trying of your patience. When you find yourself lacking the stamina for personal relationships, lacking desire for fellowship with the body because of the emotional energy it demands, lacking zeal for mission—you will know that you are coming into or are already in the walking season. At first glance, because we equate closeness with movement, it may feel that God is distant. He isn't. He's close.

i think it is important to note here that this season is not to be confused with that falling away from devotion to Christ that i mentioned a minute ago. when we become fatigued, there is always the temptation to allow negativity a place (and even depression which can be a downward spiral) and to neglect prayer, the encouragement and instruction of His Word, being with faithful friends who edify and build us up in our faith. in walking times, be reminded, that this is MOST needed and that we would do well to keep doing what we were doing when we were flying and running.

When you come to this place, any human strength you may have had will be found woefully inadequate. You may feel hopeless. Nothing seems to work as it did before, but *nothing is wrong.* The season has simply changed. You are asking for His hand—which may have been rather generous when you were flying and running—but now, *He is showing you His face.*

His face is full of light and truth. His face will first show you your sin—because light. does. that. This will likely become the primary focus of your praying in these days. As you're asking the Spirit, *What's happening?*— the reply will most likely be: *Look at Me. See Me—so you can see where I'm taking you. Not the vocational destination, but the "becoming of you" destination. The journey thus far is doing what I've intended for it to do. It's revealing your weakness, your brokenness, your inadequacy. I'm going to address those now. The deeper you let Me in, the further I'll go, and the further I go, the truer you will become, because it will be the "you" I had perfectly ordained from the beginning of time.*

When you can recognize that this kind of movement is every bit as glorious as the movement of your dreams and promises, then you will recognize that this season, more than any other, is moving you the furthest along. Dear friend, if you really want to get somewhere as these seasons progress, you will learn to embrace the walking season. It is the walking season which traverses the most ground when it comes to *who you are becoming.* However, because we instinctively believe that the revelation of our sin and inadequacy are a form of punishment rather than a grace-door to freedom, we tend to shun such seasons. Satan is super crafty in this way. **When you understand that** *all sin* **carries** *real pain,* **you will understand that having it revealed and removed from your life is perhaps the most beautiful of graces bestowed on us by a loving Father.** *The walking season, for that reason, is the most powerful of all!*

my biggest takeaway from these isaiah 40 thoughts is the idea that the seasons are to be expected. they are normal and purposeful and come and go with the intentionality of the Lord's interest in us and in what He is making of us. (and that when we are in the walking season—with the waiting and delays we all "walk" as well—there is nothing wrong. we are not being punished nor pressed down. as we "qavah," He comes to renew our strength.)

if you're walking and your gait has slowed (scott often quips, "like an old man with his shoes tied together")—take heart. QAVAH. wait with hope, friend. He will keep you until the next season.

---

part two is my favorite now after reading and re-reading through to the end lots of times (writing this blurb for our second printing).. .. ..

the old testament narratives become more and more meaningful to me as i grow in understanding. i am prayerful now that this one will be as meaningful to you.

PART TWO: THE GENESIS STORY OF PROMISE

when scott first brought me chapter seven—in parts, (there were lots of days in a row of chapter seven and still writing about abraham). i felt tired and listless—and almost (I AM SOOO SORRY) bored and worn from the wait and **weight**—and the wait and **length** of the story. THEN, i read it yesterday from beginning to end, adding subheadings and LIVING with abram and sarai for a few hours, and i held our pail a bit tighter and let my grip on the promise come a bit looser.

and—i am still sitting still, the next morning, thinking of the way God COVENANTS. and it is personal.

CHAPTER 7

*a chapter of LENGTH — intentionally·

ABRAHAM CIRCLING

I am firmly convinced that unless we can see the processes written of so far at work in the stories of Abraham, Joseph, Peter, and others, then much of what is written here may be little more than well-intentioned presumption and one author's ideation of the way God works in our lives.

Hebrews twelve speaks inspirationally of an Old Testament cloud of witnesses that has gone before us. Within this cloud are the legends of the Torah and Prophets—stories that not only seem outrageous in the reading but *are* in **reality.** Most of these are people who *journeyed long with God.* Sometimes that is missed, as it's hard to *feel* a life *lived* in a span of three to fifteen pages. For us, the story is over in one sitting. But for the one who "journeyed long" (as for us), it was full of the anxiety, joy, fear, peace, anger, rage, doubt, happiness, and sadness of *moments*—with no real knowledge of the end in sight! Perhaps, this is why I am often intrigued and most benefited from *life* studies of the Bible heroes.

Let's spend awhile with Abraham.

When Abraham is introduced into the story of God, we find him taking his place as the head of an established family tribe in the making. His father, Terah (already in his late hundreds), was looking to take the extended family into the lands of Canaan but had settled in Haran before completing the journey. Even when reading the text closely, it's hard to see what kind of relationship Abram (as he was known then) had with the God of Creation at this time. Whatever it was, he was apparently a man with a heart that God could grant grace to move, and we know He spoke with Abram directly. Unlike Moses and a burning bush—Paul and a blinding light—God seemed to have given a simple and straight-forward, unadorned and unaccompanied (no miraculous confirmation for the message) directive. Listen to it:

> Go forth from your country,
> And from your relatives

And from your father's house,
To the land which I will show you;
And I will make you a great nation,
And I will bless you,
And make your name great;
And so you shall be a blessing;
And I will bless those who bless you,
And the one who curses you I will curse.
And in you all the families of the earth will be
blessed.

Genesis 12:1-3

A quick *time-out* is in order. The more I see of my country and the world, and the more I read of people past and present, I find that people are *people*. We feel many of the same things—with some cultural variance. Yet, at the core, the remnant of the Creator's DNA rings true across time and space. Abram and Sarai have *felt needs and wants* which include significance, provisional security, and belonging. What we learn of Abram's family history is that they are a people without a land to call ancestrally home. (this reminds me of the dwarves in tolkien's *the hobbit*.) There is a formed world power to the South in Egypt and a forming power to the East in the Assyrian tribes (in modern day Iran and Iraq). There are city states forming in Canaan, yet Abram and his clan are a people without the status and protection that comes with belonging to a place and larger people. I believe this may be a felt need in Abram's heart.

Secondly, we know that Abram is without a son. Any basic survey of the culture of the times will reveal the immense burden, pressure, and humiliation this would have been to both Abram and Sarai. When we find Abram and Sarai in the story, the clock isn't just ticking, the family is likely chanting down the remaining seconds! 10, 9, 8.... You get the idea. Much like a failed NFL first round draft pick, they aren't far from being labeled a family *bust*. Again, when we pick up the story, Abram and Sarai are a couple in *need*.

And isn't that usually where the Lord finds us?! At the point of need. Needing an answer to hard circumstances that has the added benefit of engaging or giving us purpose. my need, bringing Him close. everything about this is personal.

The invitation to Abram, as given above, must have been a life dream come true. When we pay attention to Abram's story, God's command is not *hard* at all, but rather the *miraculous break* for which he had been waiting. In his father's house, he was becoming a failure in the generational sense, and now he was to be made the titular head of a nation. In his father's house, he was a nomad among nomads. Now, he was being picked by the Creator to birth a nation which would not only rival, but someday subdue the powers to the East and South. In his father's house, he was becoming a man whose name would die with him—now, his name would be eternally blessed! It couldn't get any better than that.

I would humbly suggest that Genesis 12:4 reveals Abram's state of mind upon receiving the invitation. Unlike Moses and Gideon who want to think the matter over, verse four finds Abram picking up the family and belongings and striking out in the general direction of Canaan. He and Sarai are on their way! There is no conversation recorded or ever alluded to between Abram and God with any sort of hesitation on Abram's part. We only read that he didn't stop to *look the gift horse in the mouth*. He saw the opportunity and went with it. Simply said, Abram—because of his obedience—is **flying**!!!

At Shechem, Abram again receives a word from the Lord with another direct promise saying (in verse seven), "To your descendants I will give this land." It is in this season that we see Abram building his first altar to the Lord. *It is an intimate time, an adventurous time. God is speaking of direction and blessing, and Abram is listening.* From there, Abram continues to journey until he comes to a mountain that rests between Bethel and Ai. In this place, Abram builds his second altar, and we read for the first time that Abram "called on the name of the Lord" (Gen. 12:8).

Here, I want to be careful not to fall into the trap of presumption or emotional projection, but I am curious as to the timing of Abram's seemingly deliberate stop to address God. Up until now in the story, God has initiated the contact. Now—Abram is doing the initiating. The 400 mile journey (on foot) from Haran to Shechem is not a short one. It would be especially challenging with a wife, livestock, life possessions, and "acquired" persons, along with Lot's entourage of the same (found in verse five). We're potentially looking at a traveling party of 600+.

I would remind you of what we said in chapter one that *life-living and its exigencies require strength.* While we know that Abram becomes wealthy before the journey is over, it seems safe to say that if he is traveling with *acquired persons* (noted in verse five), he is relatively well-off at the start. Moving this many people with livestock would require traveling close to water and pasture (water and pasture that is available in lieu of occupying peoples). Possibly at times, he would have needed to barter for these as well as food stocks. It also means traveling with large tents, cooking gear, clothing, carpets, curtains—all of the necessities and comforts of "home" that a lifelong nomad would take on the journey. Regardless, traveling 400 miles in this fashion is an adventure potentially years in the making. (Let us not forget that God has not given Abram a specific destination as much as a general vicinity to which he will travel.) Abram is *wandering*—with everything that he and Lot own.

How much time has elapsed from the word Abram receives in 12:1 and his arrival in Shechem in 12:6, we simply do not know. However, we can make a safe bet that it's more than a few months, if not a year. Without specific dates, it's hard to do the math, but it's been some time since Abraham has heard from the Lord. I would imagine that after the achingly long journey, he was ready for it.

From my own experience, and I do conjecture a bit here: was Abram beginning to question? Was the message months (possibly a year) before delusions of grandeur or really a divine *Go?* Most likely now in a running season with strength ebbing from the toil of living place-to-place (and with no son, as of yet), this word seems a reassurance to confirm to Abram that he is trekking in the right direction. However, this brings us to verse eight. Again, how much time expires between Shechem and this mountain between Bethel and Ai, we do not know. But here, Abram builds another altar and calls on the Lord. *Why??* Is it in response to the promise given in Shechem? Did he travel to this hill for a better vantage point—and upon seeing what the eye could see—feel the need to build an altar and worship? I've often thought this in my summary reading of the chapter. However, when considering the time and distance traveled and the everyday living of life that happens between, I'm not so sure. Again, what we read in approximately three minutes takes Abram and Sarai months or years to live. I feel convinced that we human-types fail to possess that kind of memory for divine moments.

The Lord explodes on our scene—rocking relationships, healing bodies and finances, and two weeks later we're calling out to Him, "Where are You???!" Is it possible that on this mountain, we are watching Abram move into his first walking season? By now, he's traveled over 425 miles most likely "knowing" Sarai at every opportunity and still—*no child.* No one to whom he would pass the blessing. No seed for a promised nation.

What's more, by now, as you may have noticed in 12:6, the Canaanite is in the land. Abram's not getting any younger, and there is already a burgeoning people established in this land. Somebody's living in his *promised land* (and they have a large head-start on baby-making)!

NEED AND SILENCE

Because of what follows in verses nine through twenty, I would begin to wonder if Abram's calling on the Lord at Shechem has more to do with a growing impatience (which is often the fruit of delayed hope and fatigue from waiting) than celebrating the promise. I'm not suggesting here that he is angry, irreverent, or panicked. We don't know his emotional state during this time of sacrifice. However, it's completely within the realm of possibility that (at the very least), he has questioned, felt heart need, and simply needed the Lord to come close. Quite possibly, what had come easy in his *heart strength* is now becoming hard. Life may have absorbed Abram's strength for living it, and now he is discovering something God must reveal in all human vessels: NEED.

The response Abram receives from the Lord after calling upon Him is something we very often overlook. Perhaps this is because it's the response many of us are accustomed to or even numbed to expect. God's reply is— SILENCE. How often have I launched out on a Divine directive: flying then running, and then—winded, on the precipice of walking, calling out to the Lord—*What next? Where to? What now?*—and the answer was the **non-answer.** So Abram (according to 12:9) simply continues to journey, making his way into the South of Canaan to a region known as the Negev. Here, in Abram's first real walking season, the real work of a God *who delights to teach His kids to trust* begins.

Verse ten opens: "Now there was a famine in the land; so Abram went down to Egypt to sojourn there..." Let's stop there for a moment. If you'll remember, the last word or directive Abram received from the Lord was to go to a *land* that He would show him (which was confirmed in Shechem when the Lord told him that everything he had just walked through was to be given to his descendants). Nowhere in that message was there given a permission or command to go outside of this land. The blessing was in the *land.* Henceforth for the Jewish people, the blessings have always been connected to the land. Even today, there is still promise for the Jewish people connected to the land.

95

Let's keep in mind that famines don't happen overnight. Weeks and then months pass before being recognized as drought and before the condition *famine* is recognized. In famine, the land no longer supports life. Day by day, Abram is hit with the pressures of making life work in an environment that seems to be abandoning it—striving to make life work for Sarai, Lot, their servants, livestock, THE PROMISE.

Walking seasons can feel like that. All of *life* may seem still and desolate. Everything that could produce fruit and progress in life and dream—withered in Divine silence. **We'll know we've grown in these seasons when we learn to *remember* the promises and commands received in the flying and running seasons.** *Do you not know? Have you not heard? The Lord...* (Is. 40:28).

Abram, in his first go-round in the process, has forgotten the word of the Lord in lieu of the immediate pressures of life-living. **Consequently, an attempt to avoid the trial of faith has nearly disastrous consequences for Abram and Sarai.** In verses ten through sixteen, Abram, nearing the borders of Egypt, is in complete survival mode. how often have i found myself here—living in the emergency of life?

SURVIVAL MODE

Having lived as a nomad in Ur and likely familiar with the peoples and culture of Egypt, Abram becomes keenly aware of the attractiveness of his wife! Keep in mind, Abram crossing the borders into Egypt with his wife and nephew and looking to settle in a quiet suburb is not what we're looking at here. Abram coming into town is more likely to look like a small scale invasion than a visit. (Remember, he is coming with everything he owns and with all that travels with him: nephew and children, servants and their children, donkeys, cattle, etc.) In brief, Pharaoh is not only going to notice a *bedouin tribe* coming to live off of his land; *he's going to care.* All the more, because you could be sure that Abram and company are not the only ones making their way into the Fertile Crescent of the Nile.

Abram has good reason to fear that his wife is going to be noticed by people that will desire her (and have the power to take her). For that reason, Abram concocts a rather shrewd, self-serving plan. He has Sarai tell a half-truth: that she is Abram's sister (true) and that yes, he would be happy to give her hand in marriage to Pharaoh (false)! The plan was for Sarai to put in a good word for Abram, thereby assuring that Abram wouldn't be killed for having the audacity to cross into Pharaoh's land uninvited. Remarkably, it actually works. Word of Sarai's beauty does reach Pharaoh. Pharaoh does indeed ask for Sarai to join his *stable* of wives. Abram and Lot *don't die* and not only get to keep what is theirs, but Pharaoh also loads them down with sheep, donkeys, oxen, and camels. I hope you catch the gravity of what has happened in this five-minute story.

Abram—in his exhaustion, disillusionment, despair, and panic—has *fainted* in his spirit. Abram has quit on the promise, quit on the journey, quit on the vision—even quit on his wife! While I am well aware of the sad devaluing of women in Abram's time and culture, I find it hard to swallow that Abram is not experiencing a heart-death in these moments. Remember that it is with Sarai that he was to bear a son. I want to keep this *PG*, but it needs to be pointed out that it is likely these two had quite an active sex-life (they have been trying for decades to have a son)! Later on in the story we get to see Sarai interact and converse with Abram, and it's *not* a master-servant relationship. They sound very much like couples in modern culture. *He procrastinates—she nags—it eventually gets done.*

By verse fifteen, Abram is sitting in his tent bed alone, stewing on where his wife might be and what she may be doing with whom at that moment. While he may be rich, he remains a life and world away from everything his heart desired. What happens next is not a word from the Lord to Abram. No "buck up little camper," but rather a show of gravity via an end-run communication to Pharaoh himself.

God strikes Pharaoh's house with multiple plagues, while at the same time, keeping both Pharaoh and Sarai from engaging in adultery. Somehow (we're not told how), Pharaoh is made aware of the real relationship that exists between Sarai and Abram and promptly sends her back (and sends them packing across the northern borders). So unnerved is Pharaoh that he provides a personal escort to make sure they leave, and it even looks as if Abram gets to leave with everything he brought along (as well as with what he was given!) Shortly thereafter, Abram is right back at his altar between Bethel and Ai. Again, he calls on the name of the Lord.

abram's emergency living wasn't a fatal fall:

While I would argue that this does not represent a renewal of strength for Abram, it does illustrate the grace we spoke of earlier in reference to the rescuing nature of papa eagles: God providentially ensures Abram's fall in this season *is not fatal.* It's a grace that Abram appreciates, which is reflected in his once again *calling upon the Lord.*

Even so, God remains silent, and life pressures continue to come at Abram. Having survived Pharaoh and Egypt, Lot and Abram are now struggling to survive in a land that is in a famine recovery. However, because of the gifts of Pharaoh, they now have way more mouths to feed! The consequence is stress and competition between the servants of Abram and Lot. *This will very shortly reveal something we all need to catch as it concerns the Father's goals for us.*

COMPLETE OBEDIENCE

The story, as it's recorded in Chapter 13:1-13, shows Abram's humility and wisdom in proposing to Lot that he simply pick a direction for his clan to settle. Lot shows a bit of his nature by selecting the side that looks best. Abram, without pulling rank and reminding Lot of the promise (or whose land this would all be someday), simply went with it.

Something fascinating happens in verse fourteen. It reads, "The Lord said to Abram, after Lot had separated from him..." If you have a Bible on hand, you might want to look at this passage for yourself. Do you see it? It is subtle, yet really needs to be caught. Go back to 12:1, and read carefully: "Now the Lord said to Abram, 'Go forth from your country, and from your relatives and from your father's house..." But what do we see in 12:4? It reads, "So Abram went forth as the Lord had spoken to him; and Lot went with him..."

Who is Lot exactly? According to Genesis 11: 27-31, he is Abram's nephew. The directive of the Lord was for Abram to not only leave his Father's house, but to leave his relatives as well. I'm no genealogy expert; not even a pre-Judaic culture expert, but I'm pretty sure that Lot is excluded on both counts. He is the son of Abram's brother of the house of Terah and Abram's nephew. From the outset (before Abram has set his first foot on the divinely-ordained journey to Canaan), he has failed to walk in complete obedience.

I believe we can make an observation here that reflects the idea and the title of this book. The Father is gracious to His children. I will say this again later, but hear it now for the first time: *I am immensely grateful that God does not show all of my sin to me at once. Depression and despair would swallow me!* **The good Father deals with it in His time, on His terms, and at the right seasons and places of life.** At the outset of the journey, the primary obedience factor was for Abram to depart. That Abram fails to comply fully in the details while undertaking the larger and more difficult part of the command by leaving his father's house shows the patience of God. **Abram's attempt at obedience is rewarded** (with the voice of God upon his arrival to Shechem). **However, what is revealed in between the lines of the story is a God who walks His kids into detailed-oriented obedience.** The specifics matter. The Abram that *generally* obeyed is about to experience *another place of obedience.* Twice now, Abram has called on the name of the Lord and received silence. But now, when Lot is separated from Abram, the word of the Lord comes to Abram again. Genesis 13:14 states, "The Lord said to Abram, after Lot had separated from him...." after Lot left, He spoke.

Having walked a complete circle since hearing from the Lord at Shechem, Abram hears the voice he so much desires (and so needs to hear)—but not until the demands of Genesis 12:1 are fully met. **After full obedience to what was revealed in 12:1 is completed, we see the greater revelation Abram receives in 13:14-17:**

"Now lift up your eyes and look from the place where you are, northward and southward and eastward and westward; for all the land which you see, I will give it to you and to your descendants forever. I will make your descendants as the dust of the earth, so that if anyone can number the dust of the earth, then your descendants can also be numbered. Arise, walk about the land through its length and breadth; for I will give it to you."

I think I can almost hear the Father say, *"Ah, sheesh, thought that guy would never leave...I can finally tell you what I wanted to tell you between Bethel and Ai!"* Yes, I'm kidding, but in some way, I would contend that this is not very far removed from the truth. (and though we do infer here that God's speaking is consequential of abram's full obedience, the circumstances and timing offer compelling evidence that this the case.) What's more, what Abram receives is continued confirmation for what his heart wants most: the fruition of the dream. It's no longer a general direction, but a specific initiative to tour the future borders. It's one thing to say: *Hey, I'm going to give you that place someday.* It's quite another to say: *Walk and explore it as if it's yours already.*

Abram's response is telling. He moves his tent to Hebron by the oaks of Mamre and there builds yet another altar to the Lord. Two things: (1) Abram doesn't stick around to mull it over. He's on the move again. (I would remind you that it is no small thing to travel like this.) Chapter fourteen of Genesis is going to reveal that Abram is traveling with at least 318 fighting men which are part of his household. (This does not include their wives and children!) Picking up and committing to move about in this way is a large endeavor. (2) Abram builds another altar, but this time something is notably missing. Abram is neither receiving words nor *calling on the name of the Lord.* **He's getting nothing, and he's asking for nothing. He's simply offering a sacrifice and making the heart of God happy.**

I once overheard my father-in-law counsel a young, ambitious college student after a church service one evening with the thought:

We spend too much time seeking the hand of God, rather than His face.

This is not the same Abram that started the journey from Haran. **He's gone in a circle and actually gotten somewhere.** Abram, it appears, is flying again.

DETOUR FROM THE PROMISE

So what happens next? More life-living. Abram is about to get a belly full of it. Steph recently passed the following thought from C. S. Lewis to me: "The great thing, if one can, is to stop regarding all the unpleasant things as interruptions of one's 'own,' or 'real' life. The truth is of course that what one calls the interruptions are precisely one's real life – the life God is sending one day by day."[19] If you can believe it, smack dab in the cresting brilliance of Abram's long-awaited flying season comes the dreaded tragic, urgent, life-altering *interruption.*

You'll remember we mentioned at the beginning of Abram's story that the land he has been promised is not an uninhabited one. As you read

---

[19]Wayne Martindale & Jerry Root. *The Quotable Lewis* (Carol Stream, IL: Tyndale House Publishers, 1990), 335.

through the stories of the Patriarchs—on into the histories of the kings—you'll note some of these peoples repeatedly: folks like the Amorites, Horites, Amalekites, and more. Something has happened in the region, and now these kingdoms and tribes are picking sides. Lot happens to be residing in the valleys encompassing the territorial rights of Sodom and Gomorrah, which for many reasons—their renowned wickedness not withstanding—turns out NOT to be the best side.

Abram, having come off his first genuine worship experience in Hebron, is swiftly greeted with the news that his nephew and family have been taken captive along with all they own (livestock and servants; i.e. people). I wonder if he said to himself, "This is the devil's work. I'm supposed to be taking a tour of the land, and my idiot nephew and family are captured. I don't have time for this!!!" Whatever his emotion, he doesn't waste time in assembling his men (318 to be exact) to pursue Lot's captors. Before the incident is over, Abram defeats the captor and his allies. He rescues Lot and recovers everything that was taken: women, children, surviving men, livestock, and monies. Abram's growing character is revealed in what he does next.

Melchizedek, the honorable king and priest of Salem, along with the king of Sodom, who had fled (leaving folks like Lot and family at risk), now come to Abram to express thanks and to seek a politically advantageous relationship. Melchizedek, the high priest, sees the call and favor of the Lord upon Abram. Abram, after receiving Melchizedek's blessing, gives a tenth of all he recovers to him as an offering. The king of Sodom (likely sensing an opportunity), offers Abram all of the financial spoils taken in the battle, yet Abram will have none of it. (He knows trouble when he sees it.) *He also has come to fear the Lord and have respect for His Glory. Abram, with honor, restores to others what was taken from them, while only keeping his own.*

Hear it again: *Life living requires strength.* While Abram was flying before he received news of Lot's captivity, it is highly unlikely that he is still flying by the end of it. His earnest heart desire is to run after the dream. His *life* circumstance is to rescue his nephew. **Few things exhaust strength more than those things we perceive to be distracted pursuits.** Moving is a stressful activity. Moving with 318 into battle with the knowledge and belief that not all will come back is sleep-stealing, emotion-grinding, intellect-draining angst, accompanied by a very real fear that the promise is at risk. **The energy the heart expends in holding and protecting**

dream and vision in tragic adventures cannot be missed. The word of the Lord comes to Abram again at the start of chapter fifteen. His weariness is evident in the conversation.

It begins, "after these things the word of the Lord came to Abram in a vision..." Mind you, these were no small things for Abram: distraction, battle, (no offspring!), and now having had to fight in a land where he is currently a traveling guest. In noting the transition, I have to wonder at the timing. Harkening back to the Lord's response to the exiles, "Why do you say oh Jacob, and assert oh Israel, that the Lord has lost my way...." (Is. 40:27).

My guess is that God wants Abram to know—to have assurance—that He *sees* him, and that He *has not lost his way*. Certainly, Abram would need such an encouragement. I would! The opening of the word confirms this: "Do not fear Abram, I am a shield to you; Your reward shall be very great." Paraphrasing: *Abram, I saw it all. I was there. I was and will be a shield to you. There is no need to fear the tribal peoples in the land. They will not hurt you. I won't let them...and about the offer you turned down from the King of Sodom and the tenth...you honored Me with Melchizedek; I saw that too. I'm going to reward you for it.*

A big reveal comes next. The gut-level bottom comes right out of Abram. Not to make light of his fear of neighbors; I'm sure it was real. Not to make light of the monetary sacrifice; I'm sure it was significant. **At the raw core of Abram's being is the dream planted at Haran: a promised son and exploding heritage. A heart cry question comes forth.** Almost sarcastic, some might say, but I would caution against it. I would venture more a question from a disillusioned heart—frustrated, yet not proud. It's a question on the edge, perhaps, but not lacking in reverence. It's a heart and mind at a sincere loss for what to feel or think. Much like we discussed earlier, Abram is pregnant with expectation. Directly in the middle of being *enlarged* for the God-sized dream, **he's not sure his soul can contain anxiety of desire any longer.** So he asks: "Oh Lord God, what will You give me, since I am childless, and the heir of my house is Eliezer of Damascus...Since You have given no offspring to me, one born in my house is my heir?" (Gen. 15:2-3)

Friend, GOD COMES to hearts with honest questions and honest hurts.

Does Abram have *hidden agendas?* Most likely, yes. However, I would differentiate and perhaps call them *false expectations.* **So much of the circle process is learning to hear and discern the voice of the Shepherd above our imaginations and delusions of grandeur and hopes for significance.**

On a particularly difficult multi-day stretch of my own personal frustration in the waiting, the Lord once gave me the following word: **Do not allow your hope to surround a word and take it into reception without confirmation of its origin. Be sure! False hope and false expectation are the fruit of this.** Something we will cover thoroughly in a book we hope to write as a sequel to this will be the hard-to-learn truth that *hearing the Lord and understanding Him are two totally separate things.* When we receive a vision or dream from Him, it is so easy for our minds to set to work on how it can or *will* be accomplished. We are ripe for presumption in this place; we think He means the destination is NOW. Our imaginations are good at constructing the circumstances by which it can happen. These imaginations then become our false expectation.

The fruit of false expectation is disappointed hope, because it is a hope in something the Lord has not purposed to do. *It is chasing wind.* That is why we have weapons that are strong for pulling down such *imaginations* (2 Cor. 10:5). When viewing Abram's story, factoring in time-elapse between reception and fruition, it becomes crystal clear that Abram's expectation, after each encounter with the Lord is: *Ok, now it's going to happen.* If he was like any human, he probably has a picture in his head of how it can or could work out. Each time, when it doesn't, Abram is in danger of the fruits of *disappointed hope.* The questioning of Abram in verses two through eight reflect the honest heart of a searcher who simply wants to understand, *to know,* to have it *make sense.*

A GOOD FATHER SPEAKS
(AND WANTS TO BE BELIEVED)

After addressing Abram's immediate fears stemming from the freshly fought battle, God confronts Abram's most likely point of potential failure: Plan B. He tells Abram that Eliezer will not be his heir. John Davis, in his *Paradise to Prison,* writes that Abram's proposal isn't nearly as crazy as it seems. The culture of Ur—what is now modern-day Iraq—had a custom whereby wealthy couples with large servant populations could legally adopt the child of a slave girl of their household, making him the heir of their possessions. That Abram knows the child by name shows that it's likely more than a casual idea on their minds. Again, the Lord comes with specifics. This child is going to come from your body, Abram. Paraphrasing here, God says: "Abram, step outside, I want you to see something. Look up at the night sky."

I have not seen this for myself, yet those who have often marvel at the clarity of the stars in this region. Unobscured by modern light pollution, the view had to be breath-taking. "Abram, can you count the stars? You can't?! —Yeah, your personal bloodline descendants will be beyond count." Verse six is foundational to everything we know about the salvation of a man: "Then he believed in the Lord; and He reckoned it to him as righteousness." (Gen. 15:6)

The Father wants to be believed. The Father wants to be trusted. The Father's heart is for those whose confidence rests at peace in Him. When we trust (like the drowning victim who ceases to flail and lies limp in the arms of his rescuer), we are drawn close and secure into the arms of the saving Father. The storm rages. The story seems to lack a satisfactory ending. The loose ends dangle hopelessly—and—**we breathe easy on the chest of a Father who is good and can be trusted with *all* of it. He lets His heart beat deep into our ears, pounding peace and rest. And when we rest in that place, His heart is most happy—and we are most safe.**

---

this is a story of length. is it ok to pause here for a minute at this beautiful thought, jack?———

as i am reading, i keep hearing the word trust. and scott just nailed it. i wanted to say in chapter five when he was defining the flying, running, and walking seasons, that the patience and perseverance needed when we face trials is related to how. we. see. God. IS HE TRUSTWORTHY? do we believe He is benevolent even when things go wrong? really wrong sometimes...? [as abram did when life had to (violently) pause for him to rescue lot, when sarai was taken into pharoah's house—in all of the travel, in famine, in the years of waiting for a son!]

2 chronicles 16:9 says, "for the eyes of the Lord move to and fro throughout the earth that He may strongly support those whose heart is completely His." is my heart completely His when my circumstances feel upside-down and i am broken open?

do i trust Him?

proverbs 3:5-6. trusting is: not leaning on my understanding, acknowledging Him. do i build altars along the way, as abram did?

BELIEVING GOD WAS AT WORK ALL ALONG

God's conversation with Abram continues in verse seven. What He reveals next causes a rather large leap in my heart. **When I read it, I have to catch my breath a bit. Partly because of what God will do next, but also because it remixes the entire journey for Abram up to this point.** God says, "I am the Lord who brought you out of Ur of the Chaldeans, to give you this land to possess it." (Gen. 15:7) Chances are, unless you're an Old Testament scholar who delights in discovering nuances in ancient biblical manuscripts, you may have missed it. If you'll remember, verse one of chapter twelve begins: "Now the Lord said to Abram..." This happened while Abram and Lot—with their fathers' houses—were staying in Haran.

A face value reading of Gen. 11:31 makes it pretty clear that it was Terah's idea to take the family clan into Canaan. There is no mention in this passage that Terah had a conversation with God about the matter. In fact, it may be highly unlikely that the convo took place, as Terah *very* likely worshiped— or at least paid some reverence—to the moon god associated with the peoples of Ur in modern day Iraq. Yet, the scripture records in Gen. 15:7 that it was God who initiated the move to Canaan.

So, what are we looking at here? I would like to take a stab at it. Nearly every commentary I have consulted, both hard copy and internet search, either hints at or directly suggests that a previous conversation between God and Abram is most likely omitted in the telling of the story. According to these scholars, the word which comes from the Lord to Abram in Haran should be considered a confirmation of an earlier, unrecorded encounter. I would like to suggest an alternate solution. Primarily, the word of the Lord, as we have received it, can be trusted at face value and may disclose a theme God is revealing to Abram at this time. This may not be the result of an unrecorded conversation, but rather, the Father opening Abram's eyes to the fact that *He* is doing this. Maybe if I can state it in a paraphrase, it will help:

Abram, before I ever shared the first word with you about Canaan and your promised son, I was at work. This is something that I am doing. The circumstances that brought you to Haran had nothing to do with you! Nothing you did moved it forward. Without your own father even knowing it, the dream of Canaan was planted. I AM DOING THIS. **I got you there without any effort of your own toward this thing you now claim as your dream and mission.** *You were walking out my vision in that 400+ mile journey from Ur to Haran, and you didn't even know it. Because I AM DOING THIS!*

Wow! **Can you hear that?** Can you see the journey you are on with all its circles, back-tracks, brokenness, incomplete victories—as something that was set in motion even before your birth? Hear the word: "Your eyes have seen my unformed substance; And in Your book were all written the days that were ordained *for me*, when as yet there was not one of them." (Ps. 139:16)

THE CUTTING COVENANT

What the Father does next resounds with a declarative echo across all that will remain of time and space. I'm sitting here in disarray in my soul from a long season of anxious waiting—simply *looking at it* and *longing to believe it. Absorb it.* **Fully comprehend and live it.** He makes a covenant that now, because of Jesus, stands anchored in infinite perpetuity.

In response to Abram's honest question, "O Lord God, how may I know that I will possess it?" God uses the cultural norm—the understandable—to make something about his infinite character intimately known. He invites Abram to engage in a *cutting covenant*. If you're reading verses eighteen through twenty-one, and you are not familiar with the customs of the times, you're likely to find the whole exchange rather mystical, odd, and even brutally gross. (even though i've known of this part of the abram account for quite some time, i still am blown away when i stop to think that they actually did this!) Abram is asked to bring a heifer three years old, a female goat three years old, a ram three years old, a turtle dove, and a young pigeon. He cuts these each in two and waits. Again, if you are not up on your ancient Middle Eastern culture, you're probably lost.

Many scholars agree that what we are witnessing in this encounter is a very common (yet highly binding) covenant that would be made between two men in these days. John Davis provides a brief glimpse of the slang of the day, noting that the perspective guarantors would agree to "cut a covenant" together.[20]

According to what I have gathered from a number of sources, this is how it typically worked: Each party would provide an assortment of their personal livestock. These would each be "cut" in two and placed on either side of a ditch. The effect would be that the blood from the slain animals would then fill the ditch. What happens next is somewhat gruesome and a bit *over the top*. In order to make the covenant binding, each man in turn would walk barefoot through the blood-filled ditch, and upon reaching the other side, would say something to the effect that: "If I fail to live up to my end of the agreement, you can do this to me." (As you might guess, this was not a covenant to be entered into lightly!) It was used for major agreements where consequences for *failure to perform* meant permanent loss or death.

Perhaps this might help to explain the *terror and great darkness that fell upon him* in verse twelve.

If the scholars are right, and this is a covenantal practice that Abram immediately recognizes (in verse nine), you will also remember that this is a two-way covenant. He has just asked the Lord to give him a reliable commitment. Abram wants to trust the Lord, but it's been ten plus years since the original promise had been given. His request is not far from what we all really want when we are waiting on a promise. We want a sure-fire guarantee! However, given the nature of the covenantal practice God is offering here, it is completely reasonable to believe Abram is expecting an action on His part: a piece to bring to the agreement. God is preparing to give him what he wants, but with a catch: *with something Abram must do*. To that end, you might begin to guess why Abram is terrified. This covenantal ritual demands that Abram walk through the blood, look at his God and say: *If I fail, you can do this to me!*

---

[20]John J. Davis. *Paradise to Prison* (Grand Rapids, MI: Baker Book House, 1975), 187.

Refreshing your memory here, Abram has *already* failed to obey on numerous occasions. He quit on the promise in Egypt. He took Lot on the journey. He's entering into this with a Covenant Partner that is infinitely perfect, and—I suspect—he is well aware that *he* is not. This is an agreement that any sane person would be wise to reconsider! I think he knows in his heart that if any part of this is going to rest on his performance, then he's in really big trouble. After all, if he could have done it (made a baby and become a landowner) by now, *he would have!* These thoughts and fears are what may cause a double-take in response to what God does next. **After having prepared the covenantal ritual upon the ground, Abram waits for God to show up.**

I need to pause and ask if you have come to the place where you are so desperate to experience the promise, to get a clarifying word, that you would doggedly *wait* for something this risky? If not, you might want to go ahead and accept the likely fact that He may *make* you at some point.

As darkness comes, the Lord brings Abram into a deep sleep and a sense of His presence. It's here that the realization of what is about to happen hits Abram full-on. Verse twelve uses the word for terror and darkness. Terror is not simply fear. Fear can give you the *willies*. It can make you look over your shoulder and peak around corners. It can even paralyze you. *Terror,* however, is the most extreme experience of fear. So much so, that it gets its own place in the dictionary. Terror involves panic (possibly with the inability to think)—an adrenal rush into despair. There is no personal control in terror.

In the mix of that, God now speaks His covenantal promise. He lays out for Abram—in stark detail—the opening centuries of His promise. God reveals to Abram that he will have descendants. They will live as slaves in a land that is not theirs for 400 years. In the fourth generation of this enslavement, they will come out to the land that has been promised to them. The borders will be from the river of Egypt to the river Euphrates. They will have dominion over all the peoples now currently in the land (Gen. 15:13-21).

In the midst of these words, God (in the form of a smoking oven and flaming torch), *walks the ditch*—and then—**it is over.** On to chapter sixteen!

Whoa! Wait a minute——*TIME OUT!* What do you mean: "It's over."
EXACTLY! That was it.

Abram doesn't walk the ditch.

Abram expected to walk through the blood and risk his life, but in a *glory of glories*—a *relief beyond relief*—God alone walks the ditch! **God has just made a one-sided, unconditional promised covenant with Abram.**

If we can condense it into one statement, what is it? **I AM DOING THIS!** It's as if He can't say it, express it, or demonstrate it enough. Hear the chapter in cliff-note form and paraphrased: *Abram, years before I revealed the dream to you in Haran, I set your father in motion without his even knowing it.* ***I'm making a covenant with you today that requires nothing but belief on your part.*** *I'm revealing to you the secret of living in covenant promise with Me. I'M DOING IT! You don't have to scheme, dress a certain way, walk a certain way, live in a certain kind of dwelling, engage in a bizarre ritual,* ***anything.*** *You simply need to know that I'm doing something.*

If you're curious that this might sound a bit "too easy" or "too good to be true," **I will suggest that the real-life picture of what this looks like is a life that waits, listens, and acts upon revelation.** We wait and listen for revelation (direction)—and act as directed. In the middle of this, there will be planning, and there will be execution. But know that if it is to have favor and genuine forward-movement, it must be in the flow of what *He* is doing.

In the wrestling match you're likely to have with that, remember that Jesus cares way more about who you are becoming than what you are doing for Him! This means that in anything He is calling you to do, to chase, to join —an ulterior development of your character is a part of the point as well. Hear it again: **God wants His kids to trust Him. Apart from the ultimate goal which our sanctification will achieve (love), perseverance and trust are at the top of the divine currency chart.** In the end, I believe that will mean an unshakable trust, belief, confidence, rest, peace, and assurance that whatever it is you're hot after, exhausted in chasing after or waiting for, it is something that HE IS DOING. And as such, **trust** is the only option that ultimately gives peace.

here is trust again and that He is trustworthy. the idea that we are trusting in something that He is doing also brings to mind again proverbs 3:5-6—that as we lean in to trust Him, we have to let go of the tendency to defer to our understanding of the matter. paraphrased: we need to stop attempting to figure everything out, and then—rest in Him! this image of the one-sided covenant between God and abram is intense—and intensely beautiful. reader, the call on our lives may be compared to abram's!—a promise that God will be faithful, and we need only to be still. can we let our hearts believe that this is His promise over us? exodus 14:14!: "the Lord will fight for you, and you have only to be silent."

MAKING IT HAPPEN

And so…Genesis chapter sixteen. Wow! Is it possible to simply jump into the next chapter following that? In the real living and walking of life: yes. When chapter sixteen opens, we have no real frame of reference for the time that has passed from the covenant in chapter fifteen. As we look over the next chapter of Abram's and Sarai's journey, please keep the theme of chapter fifteen at the forefront of your mind. (*God is doing this.*)

One of the greatest sources of disappointment in my own journey has been an embarrassing tendency to take lessons learned for granted. To feel a sense of *arrival*.

When you see the events unfold coming off of the terror of the cutting covenant, it's easy to be a bit frustrated with Abram. Please remember to read these pages in *time perspective*. Abram and Sarai are obsessed with realizing the promise. The start of chapter sixteen has us coming back to something we've already discussed in the story. (I didn't entitle this book *Going in Circles and Actually Getting Somewhere* without reason.) It looks as if Abram's and Sarai's expectation following the intense encounter of the covenant is *NOW—FINALLY!* But, again—time is passing, and still no baby bump in the belly for Sarai. If the title of Genesis fifteen is *I AM DOING THIS*, the title of chapter sixteen is *MAKING IT HAPPEN*.

The chapter begins, "Now Sarai, Abram's wife had borne him no children...." (Gen. 16:1) Fresh off of the covenant, the facts on the ground hit harder than ever. Not sure how much time has elapsed since the chapter fifteen encounter, but I'm guessing weeks or months. We know, at the least, that they have been living in Canaan for ten years. It's a long time to wait for something that feels as if it should be obtainable. It's an even longer wait when you were in your seventies—now eighties—and the biological buzzer went off many years before. Sarai knows it better than anyone; her life's worth is wrapped up in producing this child. I think if we'll take an honest and transparent look at Abram's and Sarai's thinking over the verses of chapter sixteen, we'll find so much with which to relate.

First among these is the immense pressure and temptation to see forward movement in the walking season. **Failure to wait well opens the mind and imagination to justifications for means that can meet the end.** I will suggest that this is the case for Sarai and Abram in this season. According to verses two through four, Sarai (believing a son is to be born to Abram), has likely deluded herself into believing a "way has been provided." Please see the subtlety of what was just written. It wasn't an outright: *God, since you're dragging your feet—God, since you've decided not to do this through me, we'll do it this way—God, if You won't give us a child, we will take it into our own hands!* It's likely, in their desperation, they quite possibly feel this *must* be the way. She does put the failure of her own body to deliver on the Lord, but in the emptiness of mystery—trying to *figure it out*—she says, "perhaps."

How many times have I—have you—been in the hard place—exhausted, panicked, desperately grasping for ideas? Ways to "make it happen?" MacGyver was not a hit show and now pop-culture icon for novelty's sake. Americans, in particular, hold improvisers and contrivists in high esteem. *Perhaps* is the great distraction of the waiting season! *Perhaps*—seemingly more times than not—is a way to *make something happen.*

She says, **perhaps** *this is not coming through me after all, Abram. Let me give you my maid, Hagar. She's young—young enough to birth this child for us.* Something really important needs to be mentioned here: What Sarai is suggesting is completely acceptable at this time. Please keep in mind, this is pre-law! Even then, bigomy seems little-addressed. John Davis points out that the standard practice of these cultures extended the following provision: If a wealthy female slave-owner was unable to bear children, she could "give" her slave girl to her husband to be wedded as a concubine.[21] However, any children born by this girl would be under Sarai's authority.

---

[21]John J. Davis. *Paradise to Prison* (Grand Rapids, MI: Baker Book House, 1975), 188-189.

Even Hagar would continue to be under Sarai's authority. In this sense, we can see the justification that Sarai and Abram are making. Legally, the child does belong to Sarai. It just didn't come from Sarai's body.

If you're living in Sarai's time, the journey from *here to there* is every bit as relatable as our *here to there's* today. It wasn't a great leap—and that's what makes it so dangerous! Too often we think of satan's schemes in terms of *sex, drugs, and rock-n-roll*—when the real dangers lie in justifications for provision, means to meet ends, the little decisions we make that alter our short-term course, which over time—uncorrected—lead to vastly different destinations than our Creator intends.

The motives aren't altogether bad. Abram and Sarai want to see the promise fulfilled. They aren't giving up on it as they did in Egypt. They're simply looking for a way that it can believably happen.

A very real and truthful statement needs to be made. If you've got a high-lighter pen handy, you'll need to underline this one. Maybe even write it down if you have a journal. **Anything that is made by you or made to happen by you must be held together and maintained by you and the second law of thermodynamics (that over time, things become disordered) makes that impossible**—Not hard. Impossible! Not Doable! Waste of time! Vanity!

16:9 VS. 4:3

While this statement is true, the underlying impetus for pursuing these options is what I like to call 4:3 formatting. I discovered this for the first time in 1994, the year of my marriage to the beautiful and lovely Stephanie. A friend had taken me to Orlando on a bachelor party-type trip. While there, we decided to go and see what we thought was to be a straight-up typical Tom Hanks comedy: *Forrest Gump*. The film surprised us with depth and meaning, and I was absolutely floored and inspired! I laughed; I cried; I raged; I mused. It was a work of fiction that grabbed the heart and life as history. I liked it so much that I made at least three trips to the theater to watch it. (If you only understood how tight I was then, you would marvel at my value upon it!) Roughly six months later, it had made its way to VHS. I waited for it to go on sale as "previously viewed" and took it home for good. And then—disappointment!! Never before had I noticed the screen before the movie which reads, "This motion picture has been formatted to fit your TV screen," but this time, I did.

I noticed that when Forrest and Bubba were scrubbing the floor over a discussion of shrimp, that half of their bodies were missing from the screen! I noticed that when they sat back-to-back in the rain-soaked jungle discussing their future *shrimp'n business* that only one of their faces could be seen at a time. I was incredulous. To this day, (I am an avid classic movie watcher —Cary Grant, Bing Crosby, John Wayne, Fred Astaire) if the movie exists in 16:9 (widescreen!)—that is how I buy it! I want to see EVERYTHING the director meant for me to see.

When we begin to search for answers in the waiting season, satan is very good at delivering scenarios of deliverance, completion, and solutions in 4:3 formats. Applied to life, the pictures that satan frames show only the pleasure, relief, and satisfactory angles of the options and means to achieve that those methods provide.

another crazy example of this:

It was the third Discipleship Retreat that I had offered for students of our youth ministry. The previous year, we had been in St. Pete, Florida. It was beautiful. This year was to be in Cherry Grove, SC near North Myrtle Beach, but I was having a hard time finding an affordable house that could hold more than twenty youth and chaperones. Perusing the website of local rental homes in the area for hours that turned into days, I thought I had finally found "the one." It was gorgeous! To the left and right were wind-blown beach grasses. It was a two-story house which said it slept twenty-eight. It was a second row home which meant the beach was a very short walk across the street. Even the pictures of the water were beautiful. Blue calmed seas under a sunset, washed with a purple sky. All for a weekly rental amount that was in my budget! Obviously, I jumped on it.

When we got there, however, my making-lemonade-reflex (out of some very real lemons) kicked into overdrive. For the sake of the kids and parents attending, it was a *must*. Even before parking the bus, we met our very close-at-hand neighbors (these houses somehow were cropped out of the online pictures and...*were rented by warring fraternities*). Upon our arrival, hundreds of drunken, out-of-control college students on summer break were gathered about each house—one, to our immediate left, and the other, across the street, to our immediate right. Much of the furniture had been removed to the yard, which now contained passed-out girls and guys.

We were met by the owner of our rented space for the week—a very nice but weathered senior lady who was more than happy to have our group (as opposed to the fraternity she had hosted only days before). The house smelled like it: cigarettes, alcohol, and vomit.

With our amazing chaperones cleaning and fumigating the place, it was soon livable. However, with the girls from the neighboring frat houses flashing our young men as they walked by the house, it was apparent new plans would have to be made as to "how" we were going to spend our time there. Some of the most vicious hand-to-hand fighting I have ever seen happened in the evenings between these two houses. So, indoor, blinds-drawn activities became a necessity at night.

In hindsight, I laugh at myself, because I should have known better. I grew up going to this beach and have been there at every season of the year. There are no houses with fields to the left and right. There is certainly not *blue water* in North Myrtle Beach. This is the Atlantic, for crying out loud! It's light brownish, sudsy, and choppy. Regardless, what we had come to see was not in the picture. **We saw what the photographer wanted us to see, and it was enough to get us there.**

And there's the rub. The things we *MAKE HAPPEN* come loaded with unintended consequences. These are things which the enemy so cunningly hides from view. These things are hidden in the 4:3 format. We see this in Sarai's and Abram's story so often, yet most vividly here.

Apparently, in the story, it doesn't take long. In perhaps even less than a few months, Hagar discovers that she is pregnant. And then—the unexpected. (What Sarai had done for Hagar was a genuine gift!) Even though Hagar was still under Sarai's authority, she had her position in life permanently changed. In the grand scheme of things, when Sarai and Abram died, she and her son would become the heir to a literal fortune (and to their under-standing) heirs to the promise of a future kingdom. Any fear about provision, protection, and security had just been settled for Hagar. I'm guessing that Sarai expected some gratitude from Hagar for it all. For whatever reason, verse four emphatically shows that she doesn't get it. Maybe Hagar resented being a servant to Sarai. Maybe Hagar simply got a big head. After all, she delivered. Everything Abram's been waiting for, Hagar has just provided in a way that Sarai never has nor apparently can. Maybe she thought Abram would *have her back* in this. He doesn't. Neither of these women saw what was about to happen to them. Neither did Abram.

An unlooked for strife has entered the home, and Abram is in the middle of it! It's a strife that will have perpetual consequences in connection to the promises of God for Abram's seed. In the short-term, Sarai wants Abram to simply kick her out; however, even in this culture, legalities are now involved. In light of this, Abram removes himself from these issues by allowing Sarai to act within her own rights. Because Hagar is still under Sarai's authority, while Sarai cannot "legally" end the marriage to Abram or make the child *not* Abram's, she can make Hagar's life miserable. So— (without Abram's protection over Hagar), Sarai does exactly that, and under the strain, Hagar flees from Abram and company.

She is found days and weeks later (on her way back toward Egypt) by angels who have a specific word of promise for her. (This is where the unintended consequences heap on.) Hagar's pregnancy is confirmed, and the promise she thought would be hers in Abram's house is similarly given to her as her own: the son, Ishmael, will also become a new people. However, this is where things get hard. Verse twelve says, "He will be a wild donkey of a man. His hand will be against everyone, and everyone's hand will be against him...." (Gen. 16:12)

If you're paying attention to world events as they unfold, this word continues to haunt Abram's and Sarai's seed to this day. Even now, the radical Muslim world, populated largely by the seed of Ishmael, continues to rail against the world and the world rails against it. When the Jewish people returned from the 400 year enslavement and back into the land of promise, they would contend with the seed of Ishmael. **When Abram and Sarai moved to *make it happen*, you can know with certainty that none of this had entered their minds.**

A quick aside, if you'll permit: Even though we travel together as a community in the body of Christ, our decisions and journey into the heart of God are still individual pursuits. No one can do it for you or really even completely *with* you. It must be yours. In the end, the account you give when all is done is for your singular decisions. Even when made in company or collusion with others, what is judged is *your part*. With that said, understand that **individual choices hardly ever affect only you.** They have ripples that bless (and sadly sometimes curse) far beyond your personal circumstances or intentions—sometimes far beyond the times in which you live. **Waiting on the Lord grants perspective.** It grants revelation in the 16:9 aspect ratio and spares us the unintended consequences often generated when we are panicked and simply trying to make things happen.

waiting on the Lord grants perspective.
the big picture.
wide-screen.
i want to resist the urge to control the situation and make things happen in my strength.
psalm 46:10 says, "cease striving...."

GETTING DOWN TO CHARACTER
(BEING AND BECOMING)

Coming back to Isaiah 40:31, "Yet those who *wait* on the Lord." (italics mine) Those who qavah/qaveh—wait with an expectant hope as if holding on to a many-stranded rope that will not break (qavah) knowing that the wait has an end (qaveh).. .. ..*will not faint*. Abram and Sarai have *fainted* (Is. 40:31); they have fallen. Yet again, chapter seventeen dramatically reveals that the fall is not fatal.

It begins: "Now when Abram was ninety-nine years old...." (We're picking up the story roughly thirteen years from the birth of Ishmael.) Abram and Sarai have been journeying on a promise, a dream, a vision—for *twenty-three years*. This chapter opens with a confirmation from God, once again, of His covenant with and promise to Abram. However, this time, there is something a little different in the message. Previously, Yahweh had given directional words such as: *go here* or *there* and had progressively revealed the plot of the promise. He had given clarification of the promise...*every word thus far had to do with the **promise**.* Yet, verse one of chapter seventeen is different.

God says to Abram, "Walk before Me, and be blameless." (Gen 17:1) *This is a shift in God's dealing with Abram.* I'm bringing this up, because in looking back on my own journey, I can see the same shift from an obsession with *doing* (accomplishing an assignment) to *becoming*. In our local church circle, I have referred to it as the adventure of *being and becoming: being and becoming what God has designed and ordained me to become and be.*

If you're wondering what the meaning behind the circles is for you, it is about the forming of *character.* It is about driving you deep into the heart and knowledge of God. The pattern seems to flow in the many students that I've had the privilege to disciple through the years. The early years of our becoming acquainted with God often seem to revolve around the adventure of *doing.* We hear the Great Commission (Matthew 28:18-20), and we're all about it. (I realize I'm writing to believers who similarly have come into a genuine relationship with the Living Creative Christ: *knowing* and being *known* by Christ.) The Holy Spirit grabbed their hearts, and they were in the game. The concern early on is usually wrapped up in the *how* of accomplishing the mission. Where does the provision come from to do it? How can it be done better, bigger, longer, more impressively, more fruitfully, more *everything*?! (all from the purest motives!) Yet, inevitably, we find—or at least we *should* find, if we've genuinely pressed in with honest hearts—that there is more. The *more* is **character**—character that longs for presence with the Beloved. Character that, as C.S Lewis writes in Chronicles of Narnia, drives us to *"go further up and further in"* [22] (from *The Last Battle).* We become chasers and revelers in the Divine Nature and presence of God.

To that end, I would like to make yet another statement which may, to some, seem a wet blanket on vision and dream pursuit. Here it is: The dream and vision God has given you to pursue (as it concerns you) may have far more to do with the development of your character than the *thing* you have been called to do. While we find and place all value on the pursuit, God places the weight of His concern on our becoming. My personal experience has been that the pursuit of mission has been overwhelmingly disappointing. Very few outcomes have matched the expectations I had for them at the outset. There have been the welcome exceptions, but on the whole, I look back on most of it with embarrassment. I communicated *big dreams* and reaped wind. Sound depressing? No—what I just said (about reaping wind) was not altogether accurate. In fact, it is grossly inaccurate. How? Why? Because, my PAPA has yet to waste any of it.

What I see these days (more and more) is a journey deeper (and deeper!) into the heart of God. It has been a wrestling one. It has been a revealing

---

[22] C. S. Lewis. *Chronicles of Narnia* (New York, NY: Harper Collins, 2001), 753.

one. Brace for it: I now see the failures and incompletions as divinely-given and/or allowed. Am I blaming God?! Yes! Absolutely. I'm *blaming God*. He is Sovereign...

He also knows far better than I do what is needed to develop Christ fully in me (Gal. 4:19). In my spirit these days, I often hear His voice asking, *"Do you trust Me?"* (((there it is again...))) My answer is: "Yes; I trust You to do whatever is necessary—walk me through whatever is necessary—disappoint whatever is necessary to walk me into completion." For those of you who are reading aghast, thinking, "Well—what about the mission?! What about the lost people?!!! Do you love anything other than yourself in this journey????" Relax. Yes. Of course. But friend, what you will find is: hearts that brave the journey to go *further in and further up* will learn to love a *pure divine love*. I would press that if we could have had an afternoon coffee (and heart-to-heart) with Abram all through the early days of the pursuit of the promise, what would have most likely seeped through would have been Abram's need and desire for significance. Perhaps the right words would have been spoken about care of his people and the glory of God, but—in the end, at the foundation of it all (like it usually is with us in our early kingdom years)—would have been: *where—in it all—do I fit?*

immaturity looks similar in young saints, and pride is universal, isn't it? perceived need for significance is from birth. maturity, i think, brings a redirected glory. as we unlearn significance in accomplishment and begin to value significance in Him (to bring Him acclaim), we are able to delight in being broken open (sand-papered)—so eternally grateful to be rescued from our pride. worth all the sand-papering and trial! (pride would leave us ashamed and remorseful, forlorn, and without hope from our selfishness—obsessed with our perceived need. praise Jesus He doesn't leave us where we are!)

George Otis, Jr., in his book *God's Trademarks,* has a thought that I regularly keep close at hand. He says, "Many people talk about promoting the Kingdom, but what they really hope is that the Holy Spirit will promote them."[23] ohhhh ouch. (and we'll definitely hear this one again.. .. ..) Can you take a moment to recognize the incredible subtlety of that statement? This

---

[23] George Otis Jr. *God's Trademarks* (Grand Rapids, MI: Chosen Books, 2000), 60.

is not the peacock that causes us to feel simply annoyed. This is not the schemer constantly angling to move himself forward—not the politician (both secular and congregational). This is far more subtle and epidemically rampant. It applies to good-hearted pastors, youth pastors, Sunday school teachers, door-greeters, worship band members, childcare workers, etc. *needing significance.* A secret held even from themselves—that if they serve the kingdom, if they give, if they *love*, if they act in obedience—even extreme obedience—that the Holy Spirit will move on their behalf in promotion of their character or cause. Can you see it? All of our serving, loving, acting—works as a means to an end rather than for the purity that exists in and of each action itself. Otis, however, reminds us that, **the Holy Spirit has an exclusive contract to promote Jesus and none other![24] And so...we walk the circles of refinement. The circles where character is freedom-formed.** *i love this expression. formed—created—cultivated in me—freeing me from myself to bring Him glory.*

This is the theme of chapter seventeen for Abram and Sarai. So much so, that God gives them both new names: Abram becomes *Abraham,* meaning the father of a multitude of nations (Gen. 17:5). Sarai is renamed *Sarah:* the mother of many nations (Gen. 17:15). Both appropriate. I would imagine if Abraham and Lot met in these days, that Lot would hardly know the man anymore, such was the change that the journey had worked upon him.

I have been in the *winepress* of this kind of journey now for more than seventeen years, and I can honestly say that I am not the same person. In fact, because this is a life-journey for me now, if you haven't spoken with me in the last six months, it's likely that you don't know me all that well anymore. That is the nature of the journey. We go in circles as a process and come back around, but never in the same place.

we want to ^come back around^ to the circles of flying, running, and walking.

for the reids, going in circles has meant: ministry assignment with vision, excitement, expectation, work, work, and more work, resolution. ministry

---

[24] George Otis Jr. *God's Trademarks* (Grand Rapids, MI: Chosen Books, 2000), 60.

assignment with vision, excitement, expectation, work (times a lot), resolution. ministry assignment with vision, excitement, expectation, lots of work, resolution. and...repeat.

each circle and the life processes God works in us through every assignment and in every bit of the work and vision and expectation (even and especially when resolution brings with it disappointment)...is a beautiful process of the Savior of our souls working in us to cultivate perseverance, peace, and zoe-life in the flying and running and walking— and in the waiting. and—He gets glory in who we are becoming in the process.

CIRCUMCISION

To mark the shift, God brings to Abraham yet another covenant. It was circumcision. Bizarre though it may seem, I believe it offers tremendous insight into the aims of the Lord upon Abraham's and Sarah's lives. If you're paying attention, it will have a huge one in your life as well, friend.

So, why circumcision??? I'm putting three question marks there because —wow! Of all the ways—of all the things God could use to "mark" His people in perpetuity, why this one? Let's take a moment to put the health science hat on.

In my perusing of sources, it quickly became clear that a good deal of debate on the matter exists. However, a few things aided me in "picking a side" (concerning whether to circumcise or not to circumcise). The first of these was the divine fact the God does nothing arbitrarily. He moves and acts with purpose. The second rested upon our definition of sin: *anything that hurts you emotionally, mentally, spiritually, physically, or someone else in the same way.* After long months of slow-walking through the law of Moses, I became aware that every commandment—every law—either provided for or protected the people, individually and corporately.

As I looked over the benefits, which are nearly all preventative, it was rather easy to see a practical purpose for circumcision among His people. Not wanting to get too graphic here, but assuming middle school eyes will not have gotten this far in a book of this nature, I'll share with you the basic findings of my search. Because it yielded nearly identical information from multiple sites, I picked one and am quoting from www.WebMD.com.

It lists the health benefits of circumcision:

- A decreased risk of urinary tract infections.

- A reduced risk of some sexually transmitted diseases in men.

- Protection against penile cancer and a reduced risk of cervical cancer in female sex partners.

- Prevention of balanitis (inflammation of the glans) and balanoposthitis (inflammation of the glans and foreskin).

- Prevention of phimosis (the inability to retract the foreskin) and paraphimosis (the inability to return the foreskin to its original location).

Circumcision also makes it easier to keep the end of the penis clean.[25]

You may be saying about now, "Do I really need this information? Can you do me a favor and please make your point another way?" Well...I would, except for the fact that God didn't. Again, the practical reasons that God would require this at the beginning of the Judaic race are obvious: God cares deeply about the health of his kids. All of the law of Moses points to it! Even in today's cultures, there remain vast numbers of people groups who suffer from inadequate hygiene practices. (This, in a world which has come far in understanding microscopic dangers that lurk in unwashed places.) The command to circumcise in this day is revolutionary. Knowing that the discoveries of the spread of bacteria will not come for thousands of years makes it even more of a divine confirmation.

However, a closer look reveals a theme among Judaic laws that would later be given. If the benefits of circumcision can be condensed into one concern, it would be cleanliness. There are at least thirty-four different passages in the Old Testament that deal with *washing* of some sort. There is even an entire section of the law which declares what food sources are *clean* and *unclean*. Remarkably, all of the unclean animals listed (pigs,

---

[25] WebMD Medical Reference Reviewed by **Dan Brennan, MD** on December 22, 2015 http://teens.webmd.com/boys/circumcision-faq#1.

shellfish, reptiles, etc.), are terrible food sources if you're concerned about your health. Again, cleanliness is the concern.

Yeah, I know: "get to the point!" Bearing in mind that the Old Testament stories are recorded for our benefit (Rom. 15:4), let me just come out and say it: the point is **PURITY.** God is addressing character (Gen. 17:1). He is addressing who and what Abraham and Sarah are to become—what their posterity is to become. They are to be marked by it, protected by it, provided for by it. Deuteronomy 10:16-18 would later reveal His character in this:

So circumcise your heart, and stiffen your neck no longer. For the Lord your God is the God of gods and the Lord of lords, the great, the mighty, and the awesome God who does not show partiality nor take a bribe. He executes justice for the orphan and the widow, and shows His love for the alien by giving him food and clothing.

While God could have chosen any washing ceremony He would later prescribe, none carry the intimacy of circumcision. All of the others are dependent upon discipline to remember and resource of water at hand to complete. This one alone marked the body as a permanent binding benefit and yes, reminder. God was not content to leave it to convenience, nor memory. Purity in the most intimate of places designed for the most intimate of acts was to be insured. This new nation—this new birth—would be free from the taint of foreign bacteria. It's what a good Father wants for his kids: freedom from that which sickens, hurts, diseases.

Those who decide to journey with Jesus will, in New Testament days, endure what Paul calls the circumcision of the heart. Rom. 2:28-29: "For he is not a Jew who is one outwardly, nor is circumcision that which is outward in the flesh. But he is a Jew who is one inwardly; and circumcision is that which is of the heart, by the Spirit, not by the letter; and his praise is not from men, but from God." Later, Paul would write by the inspiration of the Spirit: "and in Him you were also circumcised with a circumcision made without hands, in the removal of the body of the flesh by the circumcision of Christ." (Col. 2:11)

What's the connection? "Blessed are the *pure* in heart, for they shall see God." (Matt. 5:8) It matters. "For out of the heart come evil thoughts, murders, adulteries, fornications, thefts, false witness, slanders. These are the things which defile the man; but to eat with unwashed hands does not defile the man." (Matthew 15:19-20) **God is after purity. The longer you**

walk the seasons of flying, running, and walking with intentionality, the greater the transformation there will be *upon all that is you,* and the closer you will be to the heart of God. Abraham, now over twenty years into the journey, is beginning to catch a glimpse of what God is actually after: hearts and lives that can be made to walk with Him once again.

Chapter seventeen finishes out in classic *circles* fashion. God is again stretching Abraham to the breaking point. It's another word of promise. Twenty plus years of promise *undelivered* have left Abraham doubtful (to say the least). Watch him in verse seventeen: "Then Abraham fell on his face and laughed, and said in his heart, 'Will a child be born to a man one hundred years old? And will Sarah, who is ninety years old, bear a child?'" Did you catch that it was *in his heart* that this was said?

I think many of us, like Abraham, are not dumb enough (or at least have enough fear) to keep some things *unspoken,* yet—Abraham is dealing with the All-Knower! Nevertheless, he reveals his heart by asking God to short-cut the process and simply allocate the promise through Ishmael. However, like so many of us on the journey, Abraham is still missing the 16:9 of what God is doing. Ishmael is pre-circumcision. He is conceived and born of human (and unclean) intervention.

God is birthing a people defined by purity. He is cultivating a Divine personality within Abraham and Sarah. Yet again, grace comes to the honest heart of Abraham by way of *more revelation*—this time with specifics on timing! God reveals that his son will be born to him at *this season next year* (Gen. 17:21). Not only does he get timing; he gets a NAME. Abraham's response? **Immediate obedience.** Everybody—Abraham included—is circumcised, and thereby, purified. He is entering a new season.

ABRAHAM RUNS!

Chapter eighteen opens with Abraham sitting in his tent door at Mamre enjoying the shade during the hot part of the day. All indications are that this happens on the heels of the covenant in chapter seventeen. It has at least been long enough to heal, but certainly not much longer. If his strength has been renewed, as I expect, he's likely mulling over and over in his head the recent word of the Lord. (It's what I do.) Upon those things for which I'm waiting (in my case, a seventeen-year wait so far), the Lord comes in season to remind me of the vision and often to shed a little more light on it. What follows is a head full of possibilities.

The Lord comes to Abraham yet again, and *three men* are standing in the distance with divine words for him and for Sarah. My understanding is that these surprise visitors are angels. Abraham seems to reverence them as such, and they display the power of the angelic in the next chapter. Whatever the case, Abraham intuitively knows from whence they come and does something very out of character for a man in his position: *He runs.*

Again, an understanding of the culture is helpful here. In his culture, men of Abraham's stature don't *run* unless it is for sport or battle. They don't fetch; they have servants to do that for them. One reason for this is related to the dress of the time. There is simply no way to run gracefully in a full-length man-gown. To move with any speed at all requires Abraham to hock the whole thing up and engage in the *waddle run,* which is very awkward and certainly undignified. Furthermore, Abraham is the master of his domain. If he wanted a word with the strangers, he would simply command a servant to run with the invitation to come to the tent.

Have you ever been so excited for news, so on the edge to hear what the Lord has to say that your dignity flies out the window? I get that way watching Carolina Panthers games at times, because I am an avid fan. In celebration or frustration, I am in rare form. I try to imagine the look on the servants' faces when Abraham began to run—on Ishmael's face— on Sarah's and Hagar's faces. *Are we seeing what we think we're seeing???* Abraham is beside himself.

He offers them bread and water to refresh themselves, and then runs back and has a full-on meal prepared with a hand-picked calf on the menu. If that is not enough, he leaves everybody scratching their heads as he, the master of the house, stands in the place of a servant while the guests recline and eat—at HIS table! I'm guessing that Abraham has a serious *timing expectation.* If Sarah was to birth a son at that season the following year, then he should be getting news very soon that Sarah is pregnant. Flying and running seasons can be like this. Revelation seems to flow, and things seem to come together. They are exciting times.

However—and this is good to remember—your season doesn't always match up to those of your companions and/or community. Abraham is full of belief, yet Sarah is still where Abraham was in chapter seventeen. You'll remember that Abraham laughed when God reiterated the promise in Genesis 17:17. Now, it's Sarah's turn. The angel-men ask for Sarah (who is now standing at the tent door, probably wondering why her husband is standing while these men eat his best calf), and she overhears their proclamation that she will birth a son at that time next year. Sarah's response is somewhat like Abraham's. (She laughs but doesn't fall on her face.) The Lord's reply is somewhat telling as He asks a question meant to both chastise and challenge their hearts: "Why did Sarah laugh, saying, 'Shall I indeed bear a child, when I am so old?' Is anything too difficult for the Lord?" (Gen. 18:13-14)

METHOD IN THE MADNESS

Perhaps, here is the method in the madness of the circle process. At the fall, we lost far more than innocence. We became knowledgeable of the loss of divine relationship. With that knowledge and loss came the perception of *ability*.

We became men and women who were forced to depend upon what we could learn and do to survive. We weren't designed to live that way, yet there we were.

The second law of thermodynamics has ever since been the enemy of all we do, and we have become dependent beings, attempting to live independently, and—failing miserably. In this place, all unredeemed men and women remain today.

*We are all born to this pattern of life-living. The processes of flying, running, and walking (and of James 1:2-4) are largely about recognizing our God-sized **dependence factor**.*

In my journeying, I see the revolutions of my experience consistently culminating in circumstances that are beyond my help or control.

The dreams I receive in the flying seasons grow far beyond my strength and abilities as the walking seasons near, and I'm left utterly helpless by human means. God could have given Isaac to Abraham and Sarah twenty years prior, and it still would have been an amazing story that established the line of Jesus! Yet, He didn't. The character of His people was far too important for that timeline scenario. He obviously wanted to leave zero doubt about Who exactly was MAKING THIS HAPPEN and who wasn't. At ages ninety-nine and ninety, God—*the Life-breather and Sustainer*—was the only way it could happen.

I love what happens next. Sarah knows she's *stepped in it* and says, "Uhhh...I wasn't laughing...." (Gen. 18:15) Too late. The Lord replies, "Oh —but you did laugh." It's small, but we need to catch it.

In this process, you can't hide your thoughts and motive from Him. They are being confronted all along the way in His divine grace. As we said at the beginning, if you'll come to this process with a brutally honest heart (with yourself), you will begin to *see* and *experience* Him in ways and depths beyond anything you've ever known.

needing to pray now as i read and reread: Jesus, thank You for confronting my thoughts and heart in every circle. david prayed, "don't take Your Holy Spirit from me" (psalm 51:11). i plead this in the process. Your Spirit convicts. convict and reveal, Redeemer.

RETEST

My memory is a bit fuzzy at the moment, so I can't remember if it was my junior or senior year of high school; I do, however, have a very clear memory of the occasion and event. It was the Monday following a Friday exam-day in US History, toward the beginning of class. Mr. Burke was sitting at his desk, waiting for us to find our seats and settle down a bit. (Also working as an assistant basketball coach, many of us had a relationship with Burke outside of the classroom. He was, to say the least, a fun teacher.)

On that morning, he was in the process of feigning disappointment. Looking sternly at the class, he gave a grim assessment of our performance on the previous Friday's test. It wasn't good. He remarked in stunned disbelief that he could not begin to understand how a subject covered that well could be failed so miserably by *everyone* in the class.

As Burke was going into all of this, my friend, Matthew, happened to be sitting on the corner of his desk. Matthew is one of the most gifted and brilliant people I know. (He was good enough to serve as a board member of our youth ministry nonprofit in our earlier days. Today, Matt coaches a local college basketball team. I love this guy.) But, like all of us (especially me), he could have his *moments.*

So toward the end of Burke's "you don't look very intelligent right now" speech, our dumbfounded teacher made the following happy announcement: "...and I know you won't believe this (and you're so incredibly lucky it's true), but I have somehow *misplaced* your tests." *Note that the tests were sitting poised on the corner of his desk in plain sight.* "I can't find them anywhere, so...you'll have to take it again."

Now, as he was saying *misplaced*, Mr. Burke's arms swept the tests into the trash can beside his desk. You could hear the collective sigh of relief ripple in a glad whisper throughout the classroom.

Matt, however was perplexed. He quickly shot his hand up. (May I remind you that he is sitting on the opposite corner of Burke's desk?) "Mr. Burke, they were on the corner of your desk." Burke quickly interjected, "No, Matthew, they were *lost. I can't find them..."*

*"But, you just knocked them into the trash can," replied a thoroughly confused Matt.

"I don't think you understand, Matthew. Those tests are lost and can't be found," responded Burke. "But...."

Mr. Burke, looking Matthew squarely in the eye with incredulity but a completely deadpan face, "Matthew, the tests have been LOST, however, I'm sure that if I look hard enough, I can find *yours."* It was then that Matthew looked at the giggling, astounded, *horrified for some,* and frustrated faces of his classmates and—*got it.*

Mr. Burke had graciously decided that what was needed was a second chance and a *retest.*

When I come to chapter twenty of Genesis, it helps me to see through the lens of a *retest.* In some ways, the opening of the chapter reveals real growth in Abraham. You'll notice, we've jumped from Genesis 18:16 to pick up the story here. The reason is that a sort of *aside* is appropriate to tell of God's dealing with Sodom and the surrounding valley cities: This is the second time Abraham has received news that Lot was in danger. On the first occasion, Abraham is off to the rescue. On this occasion, he takes on the role of intercessor. God honors Abraham's heart and extends a rescue to Lot via his most recent *visitors.* It's not the only thing Abraham will have to face for a second time.

For reasons unknown (at least none that are revealed and without existing evidence to clarify them), Abraham departs from Mamre and once again makes his way down into the Negev. Some have postulated that perhaps his livestock had depleted the pasture lands, or maybe there was political unrest in the region.[26] We don't really know. Given the fear that both he and Sarah exhibit, I am more likely to believe his move to the region of Gerar in the Negev has some sort of underlying necessity. Regardless, we find Abraham and Sarah in a very familiar circumstance. (In fact, if you ever make it on to Jeopardy and pick the category of Bible Patriarchs receiving the following prompt: *She was my wife, but I told everybody she was my sister so————————— wouldn't kill me,* you would have a 50% chance of getting it right!)

Abraham circling back around...

So alike is this account to Abraham's and Sarah's experience twenty-five years earlier with Pharaoh, that you feel like you're reading the same narrative twice. The only seeming difference is the name Abimelech and location in the Negev, rather than Egypt.

Maybe it's so familiar that I'm getting ahead of myself. If you haven't read it recently, verse two of chapter twenty records: "Abraham said of Sarah his wife, 'She is my sister.' So Abimelech king of Gerar sent and took Sarah."

Somewhat like Pharaoh, Abimelech is a king—not of a regional power, but of a city state/region of Philistine nationality. Abraham, for good reason, fears this pagan culture and, by extension, the possible reaction of Abimelech regarding his decision to put down permanent roots in his realm. If we know anything about Philistine culture, it does not fear God and engages in cult practices of the worst kinds. (They would be a problem to Abraham's seed for generations to come.)

Again, even in her 90's, Abraham is worried that Sarah is going to attract attention, and his concern proves to be founded. (Just an observation from *captain obvious* here, but Sarah must be the most genetically freakish age-defying woman of all time! She's past child-bearing age but still attractive enough that royalty pursues her based on the word that spreads *about*

---

[26] John J. Davis. *Paradise to Prison* (Grand Rapids, MI: Baker Book House, 1975), 209.

128

her??? What's it like to be Abraham at ninety-nine and still have this problem/blessing???)

Whatever the case, nearly everything we said about Abraham in chapter twelve can be repeated here in chapter twenty. But I think, when we look at it as a *journey* (or rather a work in progress that receives the Master's nuances as it continues), we can glean some rather significant observations. It's the same—but it's not. Some new principles are at play that we need to take in. Again, we are *going in circles and getting somewhere*. In the midst of this chapter of Abraham's and Sarah's story, we can make note that when you go in circles, you are very likely to come back around a second and maybe even a third time to relive seasons of your past. *Retest.*

retests, like the welcomed second chance in scott's history class, are sometimes joyous and relieving. yet, other times, grueling and painful. we are figuring this out.

This has been very true of my own story. I shared with you earlier of the misadventure of our sponsored concert that would preclude the beginning of the end of our community youth ministry—and with that event—the abject failure that we felt leading to disillusionment and depression.

It would sadly repeat itself eight years later.

>>WE INTERRUPT ABRAHAM CIRCLING WITH A REID RETEST<<

By this time, I had served for several years in youth ministry at two different churches near our home. The summer of 2007, we had taken students on our second tour of children's homes. Following our experiences in those settings and because of important influences in our lives and our ministry at the time, we had a vision for something a little more *adventurous* in 2008. The dream was to visit the inner cities of East St. Louis, Toronto, and then, St. Petersburg, FL. To kick this adventure off and to raise awareness and funding, we had invited the *Charlie Hall Band* to join us for an early winter retreat at Fort Caswell. It didn't take long in our planning to see that we had bitten off more than we could chew. A downsizing was in order. (Ft. Caswell is a Baptist youth camp on the coast of North Carolina which sleeps nearly 1200 students.) We weren't even close to getting the registrations needed to pull it off, so we downscaled considerably and decided to make it local.

With ticks and flashbacks still in my system from the failure associated with the event eight years earlier, I avoided the Finch Auditorium like the plague! I pored over every small to mid-sized venue in the Triad of North Carolina. (Hint: There are a ton of them!) To my dismay, one-by-one, the doors shut on each. Every city venue as well as every high school and middle school auditorium closed to us. In the end, I had no choice but to contact T. Austin Finch Auditorium. (Keep in mind that the issue was not the facility. It's a very nicely kept professional performing arts theatre.) I was simply terrified of reliving our event in December of '99.

In my praying, it became very clear that I couldn't escape it and once the reservation had been made (looking back in hindsight), nearly everything about the process leading up to *Come As You Are* was an eerie re-do of eight years prior.

we were coming full-circle—with trepidation, but also, hopefulness.

Learning my lesson (or so I thought), we decided that ticket sales in Thomasville, NC were not the way to go. After all, this wasn't a concert as much as it was an "awareness-raiser." However, the same effort to promote was every bit as intense as before. There are 1000+ churches in the Triad of North Carolina. We mailed and directly called ALL OF THEM. As the date of the event approached, I began to get an all-too-familiar feeling. Not enough people were going to come.

You'll remember that eight years before, just prior to the event, Steph's mother had suffered the car accident that would eventually claim her life. Fast forwarding to four days until launch, this time around I received a devastating phone call that a very precious member of our extended family had passed unexpectedly from a heart attack. (Many strong extended families have *that* person who breathes life and vitality into family gatherings. Dale was that person. In fact, Dale was the poster-child for that person. He placed a mark on our family when he married in and left a gaping hole when he was taken from it.)

Once again, on the cusp of one of the most important events of my life, my immediate and extended family was thrown into crisis. Once again, I found myself pleading with the Lord for rescue. My hope and faith wheeled like

a feather on the wind. Up, down, over here, over there, on the ground, etc.
—you get the picture.

As we had experienced previously, we were financially leveraged to the hilt for this event. The costs associated with producing something of this nature are quite extensive, not the least of which is the agreed upon and contract-sealed commitment of artist honorarium.

The evening of *Come As You Are* had arrived. Fifteen minutes to start—and I was set back eight years. Staring from the side curtains to look upon hundreds of empty seats, a darkness began to invade my spirit. I was in trouble.

The night was programmed for meaningful impact. A dear friend opened our evening with worship while my mentor and friend who had made the trip down from Indiana gave a talk that only he could deliver.

It was during these moments that my greatest fear was confirmed: the donations taken at the doors were woefully inadequate to meet the expenses of the evening. However— unlike before—there was no one with a savings account to come to our rescue.

The rest of the evening was spent in the knowledge that the entire evening for me was going to end in the most disappointing and awkward conversation of my life. I was mortified and horrified. Perhaps to suspend my misery, Charlie and the band, recognizing that we had much to break down, offered for us to *settle up* in the morning before I took them to the airport.

This was a financial and dream-stealing disaster that couldn't be hidden from our team. My countenance through the evening and the sheer number of empty seats gave a rather obvious clue. At two a.m. in my living room that night (with our disappointed team slunk into our living room couches), I gave the run-down and sent them home. So distraught that I didn't even bother to get in my bed, at three o'clock in the morning, I put on the most obscure mind-numbing musical I could find: Robin Williams in *Popeye* and watched ALL OF IT. After the credits, I simply stared at the ceiling, too depressed and panicked of spirit to even cry. (I *wanted* to cry for the sheer relief it might bring, but the tears simply wouldn't come.)

At 7:30, in the hotel lobby just separated from his bandmates in the breakfast area, I broke the news to Charlie. After paying the Finch Auditorium, I was now handing over to him EVERYTHING we had, which was way less than half of the contracted amount. Nobody enjoys disappointing someone they like. (Most of us are horrified at the thought of letting someone down whom we admire and respect. This is even worse when we factor in the honest heart that admits we desperately want to earn their admiration and respect as well.)

After seeing off an obviously disappointed yet graceful Charlie, I headed home to prepare to attend a funeral and to wonder if the dust of destruction would ever settle. After a few weeks, I was still wondering if I had grown at all. I simply couldn't believe that HE had *done it to me again*. I was humiliated, furious, livid, hurt, wounded, confused, disillusioned—everything I was before—but now intensified. (Largely, because I felt I *deserved better*. After all, I had endured the same test eight years before. If anything, this was to be the redemption tour. ›instead, it was the roughest sort of character sandpaper to date.‹ Obviously, there was more to learn. And nine years later, I'm laughing a bit at myself. *It was so true.*)

I'm sharing this with you not so that you can know my story (or even feel the things we felt necessarily). *It is to give you a heads up that the processes of the Lord upon your life will very likely have you walking out very similar seasons of your past.* In particular, these may come in the familiar forms of past failures or trials that have previously marked you. Don't be surprised if you find yourself walking out eerily similar circumstances in your lifetime. Why? Because at the core of our doing and dreaming lies the divine initiative to make something of us. *Our* doing is encapsulated in *His* doing. He will accomplish what He purposes to do in us, and for that, retests are often needed.

If you're wondering—yes, we eventually paid Charlie in full. It took a solid year to do it. And in 2011, we had yet another opportunity to host him for a concert (but not until after another incredibly embarrassing flop in 2010 with a nationally recognized speaker—story for another time.) This time, Charlie's contract was paid in full, in advance. The previous experience enjoyed a bit of redemption, but not before a few more rotations in the circles had been traversed. we definitely want to praise Jesus for the beautiful redeeming grace in allowing us to host charlie's band again—and to praise Him for refining us in the process.

HOPE FATIGUE

Still on chapter twenty (*back to genesis!*), I wanted to be sure that we catch another tidbit before moving on. It has to do with emotional endurance. When Abraham decides to make the trek into Egypt in chapter twelve, he is perhaps more than a year into the journey. Again—we don't know—but given the miles covered and the numbers of people traveling, we can infer that Abraham has had enough time since the dream and directive given in Haran to become challenged in the journey. Yet, Abraham's decision to move down into the Negev in chapter twenty is coming on the heels of his visit from the angels in chapter eighteen. The promise has not only been reiterated; it has been confirmed with a name and divinely-given time expectation. On the surface, this shouldn't be a point of self-doubt for Abraham and Sarah but is in reality. It begs the question, *why?*

I would like to suggest fragile emotions and—*hope fatigue*. While current behavioral science would accept the idea of emotional fatigue—*also, maybe adrenal fatigue*—I'm not sure anyone is talking about *hope fatigue* these days. It might not be the correct phrase—but it's the best I can do at present. I would say that this is very closely related with the ideas we discussed earlier in reference to enlargement and impregnation that happens while dreams and *calls* gestate. Twenty-five years into the journey, Abraham has been *played before* (coming off these encounters). *Finally, it's here now—turned into:* **not yet—not even close—disappointment.**

I find the longer I am forced to wait for something, the more emotionally fragile I can tend to become. But you say, *Wait a second. I thought the whole purpose for this process was to create endurance!* It is. Yet, because it is directed by a Divine Infinite, it operates at a scope that has no regard for our immediates. It sees a final product. He is *producing* endurance. He's growing something larger than your soul—inside of your soul. But for endurance to be created, a breaking point has to be reached. (The fact that I am emotionally raw only indicates that I still may have a ways to go.) *It is not yet time for the delivery and birth.* As I have mentioned thus far, I am in a seventeen-year wilderness journey. The last year has had me remarking until I can hardly stand it in my own ears, "I'm so tired in the waiting—holding hope is exhausting me." **There is a divine energy, a zoe life that is needed to hold hope.** If you haven't yet realized it, go ahead and know that you will reach a place where your emotion may snap rather than bend and your hope holds at best through a very heavy chest.

worth repeating: "there is a divine energy, a zoe life that is needed to hold hope." it's why we named our third child, our daughter, hope. bethlehem hope...

I think this is where we find Abraham at this point in the story. It's the only thing that I can think of that would explain his surrender of the promise yet once again. Let's make no mistake here. This is exactly what this is; Abraham has no further excuse. The Lord has been crystal clear. Isaac is to come through Sarah. Abraham has just given her away to another man and at ages ninety-nine and ninety, it's for good. His hope has failed. The emotional strength needed to hold it has snapped. As I sit here writing this, I am thinking to myself, "How many times have I simply wanted to throw it all away, but I couldn't?" Some reading may have tried to do exactly that. You walked out on the promise. You quit on the dream. You quit on the calling.

But yet again, like Papa Eagle, the Father swoops down to rescue Abraham, Sarah, the promise—and Isaac—who is still yet to be born. Abimelech, like Pharaoh, gets the Divine *heads up* to find that his house is stricken and his wives are no longer able to bear children and that—he's a dead man walking. Like before, Abraham is not only permitted to depart—*with Sarah* —but once again—he journeys on, loaded with gifts. **The fall is not fatal. The promise is safe.**

A FINAL NOTE FOR GENESIS 20

While all of chapter twenty does look like abject failure for Abraham, there is a bright spot that can be caught regarding development in Abraham's character as well as in his relationship with God. While revealing to Abimelech Sarah's true position, He refers to Abraham as a *prophet* (Gen. 20:7) and informs Abimelech that if he desires to be healed and have children, not only will he have to give Sarah back, but he will have to humble himself and ask Abraham to pray for his healing and the healing of his wives. In verse seventeen, Abraham does exactly that, and Abimelech and family are healed.

Looking at this passage, I am warned in spirit to be careful making guesses as to why Abraham is commissioned to pray for Abimelech after nearly getting him killed. So I do offer the following as a possibility: an admired friend once said to me and another friend over breakfast that **if God is**

doing one thing, you can be sure that He is doing a thousand other things somehow connected to it. Perhaps that is the case here. Maybe God is granting a divinely-given respect and fear of Abraham to Abimelech and his people.

The Philistines are as thoroughly pagan as it gets. Respect for life is not one of their strong points. I wonder if God is elevating Abraham in their sight to ensure his security as well as the security of his company during their stay. Yet, He calls him a prophet, and in verse seventeen, Abraham seems to naturally act like one. His flow and communication with God that seamlessly transitions into a prayer for Abimelech indeed results in his healing. The *what if* here for me is the distinct possibility that the Father also wants to remind Abraham of his special relationship to Him. Despite his (Abraham's) personal failure, the Father had not lost his way, was *still doing this*—was still going to use him. Yes. In the midst of a place in the story in which it looks as if Abraham has gotten nowhere, we find that in truth: he is *nowhere near* where he started. (there is hope for jack and jill, scottie.)

FINALLY ISAAC!

If the story of Abraham were a work of fiction, I'm pretty sure most writers would have ended it after verse eight of chapter twenty-one. Verse one begins, "Then the Lord took note of Sarah as He had said, and the Lord did for Sarah as He had promised." In regards to the seasons we're speaking of, you can be sure that they're flying high. If I can read up to these verses of the story, blocking out what comes next, it is a triumphal climax for Abraham and Sarah. **For twenty-five plus years, they carried what became an impossible dream. They carried it to the brink. Twice, they nearly threw it over the brink. In the end, they can only confess: HE IS FAITHFUL.** I see Sarah's deliriously happy heart, and I want to laugh and cry with her (v. 6). I wonder how tightly they held that child.

What joy, elation, gratitude, reverent thanks, holy-*other* emotions were in their hearts as they held baby Isaac in those days? In quiet moments, when Abraham had time to think, did he vindicate His God as he mused upon the journey and affirm to himself that it was all worth it? What might the relief of birthing an expectation SO LARGE have felt like? Did God fill the cavernous space left by the waiting with joy unspeakable? Confidence unshakable? Trust deeper than the oceans? I'm watching Abraham in my mind's eye perform the circumcision upon his son with incredulity!: *Is this really happening? Am I really getting to do this....?!!!*

I'm living these days in the heartache of hope that longs to see that kind of delivery upon my dreams and desires. To see the ever-enlarging chasms of my soul filled by anxious waiting to climax in a glorious birth and then filled with the fruits of joy, gratitude, and the *other* of the Holy Spirit. If I could confess one fear, and it really is ONE fear—for when I think about every other fear I may have, they rest upon this *one*. It is a fear that I shall be as Moses and not get to walk over into the land of promise on this side of life-living.

I want so badly—I long so intensely—to see God throw open the doors of His favor and abundance upon me and the initiatives to which He has called me. My dream is a dream of fruit-bearing. I want to be a thing doing what it was made to do and doing it well with the favor and provision of the Almighty flowing all over it, declaring to all who would see, a God who is ALL I ever wanted and ALL I ever needed and the ALL anyone ever needs. **I want so much more than the *theology* of Him. I want the *Him* of Him and the *everything* of Him, the *experience* of Him, the *nature* of Him, the *essence* of Him, the *flow* of Him, the *completeness* of Him, the *foundation* of Him, the *love* of Him, the *care* of Him, the *thought and understanding* of Him, Him, Him, Him, Him!**

VICTORY, MAINTENANCE, & CELEBRATING

I'm laughing at myself now. Having bared my soul to you, what comes next in the very same chapter of GLORY is a warning and a heads up to us all. As long as our birthday suits are still on (as long as we are still living/breathing), we are still on the journey, and God is not finished with us yet. *Our greatest moment of victory is only a platform to prepare for the next place.* Please don't misunderstand. I'm not suggesting every "next" place will be as hard as the birth of Isaac, but—we haven't arrived.

Steph and I had a dream and vision for the house we are currently living in. We essentially bought land and this antiquated uninsulated termite heap came with it. But it was *our* antiquated uninsulated termite heap, and we loved it. Our dream was to renovate and restore it. That was a major dream of ours, and—*we did it.* and it was a dream realized. a vision hoped for and waited for and worked for. God was faithful to answer our prayers and to *provide*. *Yet now, thirteen years later, it requires much maintenance.* We have even added rooms since then. (We keep my silver Ford Ranger with 400K plus miles on it simply because there is always something more to do on the house and a need to run to the hardware store for something that doesn't fit in the back of the Honda.)

Life-living in the Spirit of Christ is no different than the maintenance needs of an old home. Circle-walking doesn't stop until our birthday suits *fall off.* What Abraham does do—and what we should do as the seasons come and go—is celebrate the victories. On this occasion (the birth and weaning of Isaac), it is a huge celebration—and rightfully so (v. 8)! *Celebrate the victories when they come.* It makes the heart of Jesus happy.

16:9 VS. 4:3 REVISITED

Having settled into the victory of parenting Isaac, a fourteen year-old issue rears its head yet again: Hagar and Ishmael. The true 16:9 of human manipulation is just now coming into focus. The strife that seemed to have settled has re-entered the Abraham home. Ishmael is caught picking on the *promised one.* I don't know if Hagar shared the Lord's promise over Ishmael with Abraham, but if she did, this incident really shouldn't have come as a surprise. I am a father of four. I look at this and say to myself, "Yeah, and—welcome to parenting!" I'm guessing the issue here is the nature of the mocking. Perhaps Isaac is being a bit of a *Joseph,* unwisely remarking of his inheritance of *the promise.* Then again, maybe not.

It's hard to imagine—after all of the celebrating—that Isaac is held in a higher favor. The idea that boys will be boys (Ishmael being perhaps a *wild donkey of a youth*), is enough to beware of the potential explosiveness that could exist between the two as they grew. Regardless, at Sarah's demand, God requires Abraham to say goodbye to a son. Verse eleven makes clear that this is no small thing for Abraham.

I think I haven't adequately considered what this meant for him. For fourteen years, Ishmael has been the ONLY, and then—eldest son of Abraham. We forget that Abraham has pled with God to pass the promise through Ishmael. The love that Abraham has for *his son* can only be recognized as just that: a father's love. But God is doing something, and Abraham will have to trust. (It is a lot more trust than the story reveals.) If he was to part with Hagar and Ishmael, there had to be a better and more provisional way to do it. Surely, he could have found a place in a neighboring city-state to settle them. Surely, some kind of *severance package* could have been granted: enough to make a new start—but nothing. In essence, Abraham now knows that everything he has is designated to the promise. Hagar and Ishmael have no part in this plan. He will have to trust the Lord completely for their sustainment and provision.

I wonder in my spirit what kind of hope Abraham had for them when he sent them out with *some bread and water* (v.14). The Lord had just promised him a future for them, but to Abraham's mind, I have to wonder if he considered: *but when, and through what, and how long will they have to wait for it?* It wasn't for him to know. For Abraham, it was the painful letting go of self-inflicted, self-obtained responsibilities, to protect the victory and promise he had finally realized.

We should go ahead and expect a continued pruning to protect the fruit the Lord births in our lives. (This is especially true when we consider those things we have self-generated—in our striving—to make the promise happen along the way.) It is not unusual for the 16:9 view to take years to develop. Jesus reveals this principle in the parable of the tares and wheat. There's really no way to tell them apart at the beginning. They can only be found once the wheat has started to grow. The tares have to come out later (Matthew 13:24-30). in this pruning, there is a similarity, and He will be careful to protect the health of what He's already done in us. The circle process is really good at bringing these things back around to us at the perfect time. I believe if we can trust the Lord for anything, we can trust that He will not be satisfied until He has accomplished *all* of His purpose in and through us. To that end, the details matter. 16:9 is always the way to go.

GETTING TO THE SOMEWHERE

I'm a little hesitant to even start this section of the chapter. It's too important. It needs to be shared—yet, I feel inadequate in communicating this truth that is still working itself out in my walk. I can say it, but the *truth of it* is not yet fully realized in my illuminated motive and heart. It has to do with the object of my affection. I opened my heart and desire to you only moments before, and if you look closely, you will discern it: I am often caught—as the depth of my heart is revealed—with a love for the *promise* that burns greater than my love for the *Promiser.* I have no defense, as my daily anxieties and sleepless nights testify against me.

Times beyond count now, the Holy Spirit has gifted me disappointed hope to prove it to me. The longer I have walked these seasons, the harder and more acute the test has become. Yet, I believe this kind of heart and motive examination is the door to a destination for all that we hoped for when we set out with Him. It is not *pass/fail*; the test is a *revealer.* Yet, the Lord already knows our hearts. It's about knowing them ourselves. It's not an academic assessment but, rather (as just stated), a *revealer* test. Like a litmus test, it only lets you know where you are—or what you have—or what you don't have.

and sometimes—He allows us the humbling work of the examination? not harsh, like humiliation, but a gentle nudge and hand mirror placed before us to pick up when we're ready? (i know what comes next in the abraham and isaac story, and i know where you're going with this, jack—i feel vulnerable in the examination already.) i mentioned earlier that i have always been excellent at cramming for and then, acing the test. this is an altogether different kind of measure. no A through F scale; no plusses or minuses or curves. just a mirror to reveal. no cramming necessary or no. 2 pencil...

If God wanted Abraham to see how far he had come, and to get the full-on view with understanding of what the entire journey had been about, this test was perfectly placed and timed. So much so, that I would almost describe it as a test so refined, so incalculable in its timing, so diamond hard—without any loophole—that only an Infinite Other could come up with it. It is the perfect test, because it gets to the foundation of what the Father demands. If we can wrap our heads around it, it gets us to the *destination*—the somewhere.

LOVING GOD MORE THAN THE PROMISE

Genesis 22:1 reads, "Now it came about after these things, that God tested Abraham." Immediately, another *time-out* is in order. I don't know about you, but I sort of thought the entire journey for Abraham up until now had been *a test.* For crying out loud! They had the baby! They had a son for whom they had waited more than twenty-five years! Ishmael had departed. The timing of it all had taken them into the twilight years of their lives. What more could God possibly want? If you're consumed with dream and vision, it'll be really hard to imagine *what else. And*—if you're consumed with dream and vision—the climax of the story is over—complete. *Yet, the Father is after something entirely different.* All along, He has cared way more about *who Abraham was becoming* than *what he was doing.* After all, we've established that even in all that Abraham was *doing,* the cutting covenant made clear that God was really *doing it.* The real story in the story is: *what is God doing in Abraham?*

Genesis 22:1-19 gives an unambiguous, unequivocal, pronounced final answer. I hope that you catch it. If in all your *circle going,* you long for a destination—that is, a final destination—this passage will reveal it to you. Yes, I know it's in the Old Testament. ancient, but foundational —> —>—> *God has not changed, nor has His desire to see you reunited in fullness back to Him.* This test is the litmus for everything the cross of Jesus makes available to you. **It is the end destination of all of our circling.** Let's walk it out.

God says to Abraham, "Take now your son, your only son, whom you love, Isaac, and go to the land of Moriah, and offer him there as a burnt offering on one of the mountains of which I will tell you." (Gen. 22:2) anticipation that this was coming only increased its meaning and gravity. the story isn't over quite—and the test is our heart-exam too.

Just last night, as we were relaxing for the evening, my eight-year-old son sat cuddled in my lap while my elder sons led us in worship with their guitars and my daughter tinkered with a craft beside Steph on the couch next to me. Resting together as a family, I observed Aiden's small frame still fitting perfectly into my arms. He was drawing a coffee table with a man seated at it. The innocent focus of his *little boy eye*s captured my affection. The rise and fall of his lungs, the grace of his little hands, the sounds of breath, the resting of his head from time-to-time into the side of my cheek—all stealing my heart. I could hold him in those moments forever. I delight in his questions when they come. I am his champion-*can do everything*-fix-it-all dad, and he is my buddy! Anything that harms him draws my immediate ire. I see him in the morning with his bedhead and think to myself, "Man, I missed you in the night." I love Aiden Journey Reid, as I do my other three. I read Genesis 22:2, and my heart stops. I don't know how to hold it. I don't know how to approach it. I certainly can't conceive it. But there it is. *Abraham, in verse three, setting out in the morning on a journey of the impossible.*

As just mentioned, this is a test of refined precision. There is no out. Even the travel is part of the test. From his current location, the trek to Moriah was a fifty-five mile journey. According to verse four, it took at least three days to get within sight of it. Some have challenged the distance, noting that it should have only taken three days *total* to get there. If you're a dad, you'll understand the delay. What were those nights at the campsite like? Did Abraham stare at his son asleep through the night? Did he listen intently to Isaac's voice, desperately trying to trap the sounds of his son deep in his memory and subconscious as they walked the path? I would suspect so.

Was Abraham listening intently, searching for a sign—any sign along the way that would release him from this? I wonder. The time taken in the journey seems to suggest something of the sort. As previously mentioned, this is an unforgiving test. God could have commanded the sacrifice of Isaac right then and there. But he didn't. Abraham gets a long road upon which to contemplate his loyalty. He has time for justifications to sneak in, time for excuses and alternate plans to develop—and time to savor his son before losing him FOREVER.

Yet, this is not the Abraham that set out from Haran. This is not the Abraham that quit on the promise in Egypt and yet again, in the land of Abimelech. Abraham has journeyed with God and has been witness to His faithfulness and now—he's walking beside Him for the entire fifty-five mile-long journey. The expanded soul (emotion, will, and intellect) of Abraham has traveled an amazing distance and arrived at a place the Father delights in. Abraham has belief, trust, and confidence in the Father. Let's say it again: the Father wants His kids to trust Him. So much so, that you can be sure He will grant the opportunity over and over again to keep trusting. You catch it in verse five as they approach the mountain of sacrifice. Abraham says to the two young men who had made the journey with him and with Isaac, "Stay here with the donkey, and I and the lad will go over there; and we will worship and return to you."

One of two things is happening here: (1) Abraham has no conceivable way to explain to these two young men what he's about to do. They've been traveling with Abraham all their lives. They probably attended the weaning party and probably watched Ishmael leave. Isaac is everything to Abraham and Sarah, and they know it. Abraham may fear that they will try to stop him, so he's just letting them think, "Oh, it's just Abraham off to another '*God*' meeting. Wonder where we'll be off to next..." OR (2) (and I think verse eight bears this out) Abraham's faith in the word of the

Lord—in the promise of God Almighty—is not wavering. Nobody knows better than Abraham that the promise flows through Isaac. It's either Isaac —or a broken promise. Perhaps he's remembering the *cutting covenant* years before. It's Isaac—or God slays himself, lies in the ditch, and Abraham has the right to trample the Divine blood underfoot and down into the mud. Whatever is running through his mind, he is able to say with a straight face: *We're going to worship with a sacrifice, and **WE** will be back when we're done.*

If it's a ruse to keep everybody calm, then he continues it while he and Isaac, alone, head up the mountain. Yet, Isaac can't help but notice the obvious. They've got wood. They've got fire. They're approaching the site of the offering—they have a *place.* Yet, something incredibly conspicuous is missing: the lamb for the sacrifice. *Dad...are you forgetting something? Uhh. Dad... where's the lamb?...* Abraham's reply is beautiful: "God will provide for Himself the lamb for the burnt offering, my son" (v.8). Again, if God is going to keep the promise, He had to provide.

My mother-in-law said often to Steph and me, "God is seldom early, but He is never late." *comforting AND uncomfortable all in the same thought.* I chafe at that statement every time it comes to mind. My personal experience these past seventeen years has been that God is rarely early; He is never late—but He is almost always, always, very, very way too last minute for my comfort! Indeed, I'm pastoring a church in the middle of a building renovation and move. Nearly everything I have touched for the past two months has been met with delay, obstacle, deadline-pushing-back frustration. It's been a lot of me waiting with baited breath and hopeful expectation: *Is He going to show.?...Is this getting done today—sometime—at all???*

By verse nine, *last minute* has arrived. Abraham (with emotion—clinging to the promise), has to be in a surreal world. Could he possibly be building an altar upon which he will be asked to sacrifice the promise—his only son? Was it a dream he was desperately trying to wake up from?

Did he tie Isaac up to keep him from struggling? Had Isaac's fight-or-flight instincts kicked in? We don't know. We only know that with the last seconds of Isaac's life passing—the knife raised ready to descend into the precious body of his son—God finally shows up: "Abraham, Abraham! Do not stretch our your hand against the lad, and do nothing to him, for now I know that you fear God, since you have not withheld your son, your only son, from Me."

And there it is. You have arrived at your destination. Can I place it into our context for you? Here it is. Here is the test: **Do you love God more than the promise?**

Abraham, in all of your journeying with Me through all of these years, have I been the means by which to achieve and gain the promise, or somewhere along the way, did I become the end through which all of the means served to bring you here? It was the final test in Abraham's journey of the dream.

If you're still reading this, I must assume you are serious and have been seriously involved in your pursuit of God for some time. You are a person with *skin in the game.* You may have had a few go-rounds in the circles. Regardless of where you are in the Isaiah chapter forty process (flying, running, walking), you are a person that is wrestling with holding and keeping vision. Perhaps you've fainted a few times along the way. Whatever your current condition, if you haven't discovered this truth yet, you will. The purity of your love, loyalty, devotion, and adoration toward Him is the destination. You will have to be confronted by the journey and the test which anchors your love and affection to Him above the promise.

MOST SATISFIED IN HIM

Hannah Hurnard's *Hinds' Feet on High Places,* I think, speaks my heart better than I am able to these days. *Much Afraid,* after having come into the service of the *Chief Shepherd,* has now journeyed far in pursuit of the promise given her. The *Chief Shepherd* has promised her freedom from her *fearing* relatives. He has promised her that her distorted face and bent crippled ankles will be healed and made able to leap with Him in the high places. The two companions He had given her, *Sorrow* and *Suffering,* have led her through many unexpected detours along the way. They have gone down into the desert of Egypt, walked the *Shores of Loneliness,* been confronted at the *Old Sea Wall,* mounted the *Precipice of Injury,* endured the forest of *Danger and Tribulation,* and walked through the *Shrouded Mist.* After each adventure, *Much Afraid* has felt the time for the delivery of the promise was then eminent. Yet there was one more detour, one more test she would have to endure: *The Valley of Loss.*

Only moments before in the story, the *Chief Shepherd* had asked *Much Afraid* if she trusted Him as much as she loved Him. Did she love Him so much that if He wished, He could *deceive* her about the promise? At this turn in her journey, her heart would be tested. With the high places (which held the healing streams that could restore health to her face and legs) in view, the path veered yet once again—down into a valley. It was a valley far lower than the *Valley of Humiliation* from whence her journey had begun so long ago. To go into that valley would be to lose every bit of the altitude gained through all of her toils and adventures.

She panics in her soul. Up until now, at every turn, she had opportunities to turn back. Her *fearing* relatives had dogged her the entire way, both tempting and intimidating her to do so. Up until now, she had not relented nor seriously considered it—but this seemed too much. To leave now, however, would mean *to leave the Chief Shepherd altogether.* **It was no longer the promise that she couldn't live without! It was the Chief Shepherd Himself:**

"Shepherd," she shrieked, "Shepherd! Shepherd! Help me! Where are you? Don't leave me!" The next instant, she was clinging to Him, trembling from head to foot, and sobbing over and over again, "You may do anything, Shepherd. You may ask anything -- only don't let me turn back. O My Lord, don't let me leave You. Entreat me not to leave thee nor to return from following after thee...If you can deceive me, my Lord, about the promise and the hinds' feet and the new name or anything else, you may, indeed you may; only don't let me leave you. Don't let anything turn me back...."[27]

The heart of *Much Afraid* had been changed in the journey. (and her name was changed—she was now **Grace and Glory!**) The *flying, running, and walking* of life-living with the Shepherd had shifted the foundational object of her affection *without her knowing it*—until now. Looking back on it, she mused:

The awful glimpse down into the abyss of an existence without him had so staggered and appalled her heart that she felt she could never be quite the same again. However, it had opened her eyes to the fact that right down in the depths of her own heart she really had but one passionate desire, not for the things which the Shepherd had promised, but for Himself. All she wanted was to be allowed to follow him forever.

---

[27]Hannah Hurnand. *Hinds Feet on High Places* (Uhrichsvill, OH: Barbour, 1987), 149.

Other desires might clamor strongly and fiercely nearer the surface of her nature, but she knew now that down in the core of her own being she was so shaped that nothing could fit, fill, or satisfy her heart but he Himself.[28] (italics mine)

More and more, I believe this is becoming true in my life. My longing for the fruition of the promise and dream *clamor fiercely* on the surface of my soul, yet deep in the interiors of my spirit, I have become like Peter in his response to Jesus' questioning, "Will you leave me also?"

>>"Where can I go? You have the words of life...." (Jn. 6:67)<<

I have **nowhere** else to go. In point of fact, I do not. My life verse, "To live is Christ, to die is gain..." (Ph. 1:21) *There is nothing else!*—has increasingly become true in me. Don't misunderstand, I want to see my dream of life fulfilled more than ever, yet if I must choose—in my heart of hearts—what I most need, most want, am most satisfied with—is *Him.*

Even so, even now, my circles are continuing to walk me through that test and through the divesting of all that would lead me to confuse the means with the end. But oh, the reward of soul rest and peace I believe I'll experience when the processes of God have solidified this work in me! "The Lord has promised good to me. His word my hope secures. *He will my shield and portion be* as long as life endures"[29] (from *Amazing Grace* —verse four, bold italics mine.)

Then Abraham raised his eyes and looked, and behold, behind him a ram caught in the thicket by his horns; and Abraham went and took the ram and offered him up for a burnt offering in the place of His son. Abraham called the name of that place, The Lord Will Provide. (Gen.22:13-14)

Yes! Right there in the place where the temple of God would eventually sit, in the region were the ultimate Alpha and Omega of *provision* would be crucified, buried, and resurrected, the Lord *PROVIDED.*

---

[28] Hannah Hurnand. *Hinds Feet on High Places* (Uhrichsvill, OH: Barbour, 1987), 152.

[29] John Newton. *Amazing Grace. Best Loved Songs And Hymns.* Ruth W. Shelton, ed. (Kendallville, IN: Ellis J. Crum, 1961), 228.

It's what the life of Abraham displays. It's what the Exodus journey through the forty-year wilderness declares. It's what Jesus, in His many parables and life stories, proclaims. It's what the cross and resurrection shout out: *I am a Father who loves you, and I will provide!*

Abraham has walked a more than twenty-five year journey with God who has prospered him in a land inhabited by violent peoples. He has given him a son that will become a nation in miraculous biology-defying fashion. And when the object of His affection is made clear to him, THE picture, THE archetype of provision is lavished at the perfect time.

HE CAN BE TRUSTED

Can I express to you what this process of *flying, running, walking,* and *"James 1:2-4ing"* will do? Your Father will put in you a dream and vision that you will not be able to achieve independently of Him, and you will come to know that HE IS THE ONE DOING IT. In the pursuit of said dream and vision, the objects of your affection will be sifted until it is *Jesus* that you will want more than anything. In the mix of that, you will be confronted with NEED. **Nearly all of the sin that you will commit will be directly related to your attempts to meet need independently of God.** Walking in 4:3 vision, you will over and over again manipulate and justify means to meet the end, and our Father will allow life circumstances that test the objects of your faith.

If you don't believe we have a misperception of provision, listen to Craig Hill's revelation: "The New Testament actually contains 215 verses pertaining to faith, 218 verses pertaining to salvation, and 2,084 verses dealing with the stewardship of and accountability for money and finance. Sixteen of Jesus' thirty-eight parables deal with money."[30] If we also factor in those things we do related to need of significance, security (often financial), love, companionship, etc.—we find that most of our lives are lived as black holes of NEED. So much of Abraham's journey (and so much of our journey), is the Lord demonstrating that He will provide—so relax and enjoy Him. Love Him. Engage with Him.

---

[30]Craig Hill. *Living On the Third River* (Littleton, CO: Family Foundation International, 2002), 5.

Ann Spangler's *The Names of God Bible,* makes a remarkable catch on Abraham's calling on the name of Yahweh Yireh. She notes that Yireh is a derivative of the Hebrew word *raah* which means *to see.* Here, it is translated as *provide.* Hence she writes, "Since God sees the past, present, and future, He is able to anticipate and provide for what is needed."[31] He is a God who *sees.*

Can you remember the opening pages of this book—of the beginnings of understanding the process of the Lord? God says to those who are tired, to those exiles in a world of need: "Why do you say, O Jacob, and assert, O Israel, 'My way is hidden from the Lord, And the justice due me escapes the notice of my God'? Do you not know? Have you not heard?" (Is. 40:27) He says, **I *see* you.**

All of our striving is birthed in the lie that *He has lost our way.* So we strive, manipulate, lie, cheat, justify, connive, exploit, cajole—and when these fail—we are tempted to quit in despair. (All the while, failing to *see* that **He *sees*.**) Spangler observes that even our English word, *provision,* is laden with this truth. It comes from the Latin, meaning *to see ahead.*[32] This is the comfort that is given to us. He loves us. He see us. *He sees ahead for us.* He has already *provided* in that time and space. He can be trusted. He didn't guess or forecast your future. He ordained it. He wrote it. It is not a shaky bridge that will require great courage to cross. It will only require courage if you doubt it. If you are confident that it is more like the Hoover Dam, you can walk across in peace. What's more—and what's *most*: you can fly, run, and walk it all out with HIM.

"He loves us. He sees us. He sees ahead for us. He has already provided in that time and space. He can be trusted...."

If you're curious, Abraham would go on to live another sixty+ years. He would bury Sarah not long after the test at Mt. Moriah. He would remarry and have many more children. The remainder of his life would be marked by blessing and fruit. In the end, his epitaph would read: "These are all the years of Abraham's life that he lived, one hundred and seventy-

---

[31]Ann Spangler. *The Names of God Bible* (Grand Rapids, MI: Revell, 2011), 38.

[32] Ibid, 38.

five years. Abraham breathed his last and died in a ripe old age, an old man and satisfied *with life*; and he was gathered to his people." (Gen. 25:7-8)

PART THREE:
HE MEANS TO MAKE MUCH OF OUR CIRCLES

the day is awakening as the sun comes up on this friday morning, and i sit with my computer once again—to finish this last day of edits. i just read the epilogue for the fourth or fifth time now—my heart heaved and fell again—and my cheeks are wet. (ah ah ah—don't skip ahead. but, then again, it really wouldn't hurt anything.) scott reid is vulnerable in these pages. the journey has been uphill. and unexpectedly HARD. and we're still in it.

we think we heard in prayer in florida—when he did the bulk of the writing—that he was coming out of the wilderness. this remains to be seen, but we are hopeful. we are living loving the Promiser.

237 pages here and almost 88,000 words of writing about how God uses our circles like character sandpaper. how He means to make much of our journey—our flying, running, walking—and every bit of the waiting. He means to speak through our false expectations, our shifting plans—like sand sometimes. He means to redeem.

He means to make much of our wilderness journeys. He means to make much of Himself in these days and in our circles.

CHAPTER 8

this chapter also intentionally LONG (because usually these journeys are)

WILDERNESS JOURNEYS

When I started on this book, it was originally intended to be written in two parts. As part one became much longer than intended, it became evident that it would need to be book one and a sequel. (with each book sectioned into parts. not saying anything about being on the long-winded side of things, jack.) I have debated in my mind for nearly a year where this chapter on *Wilderness Journeys* should go. It is a trial that has large significance to both the macro- and micro-processes of God in life-living. In the end, I have decided to address it in both. It's that important.

Many who will set their face towards the Son in life pursuit will most likely walk into a season of wilderness. Unless your birthday suit falls off at a young age, I am nearly certain at some point, you will experience the desert of delayed hope and dream. We are going to look at this, because it's very important to understand that a season of walking and the place of wilderness are not necessarily the same thing. They may have or share some familiar characteristics, but a wilderness journey will typically transcend the flying, running, and walking seasons and can possibly consume years of life. As I have mentioned a few times already, I am in a personal seventeen-year wilderness journey.

The hopes and dreams birthed in me as a young man in my twenties remain unfulfilled. Unlike so many, I have yet to put them down. I have yet to really quit. (from chapter seven—late in jack's account of abraham's circling>>>) I have pursued Jesus from then until now longing *so intensely to see God throw open the doors of His favor and abundance upon me and those initiatives to which He has called me. My dream is a dream of fruit-bearing. I want to be a thing doing what it was made to do and to do it well with the favor and provision of the Almighty flowing all over it, declaring to all who would see: a God who is ALL I ever wanted and ALL I ever needed and the ALL anyone ever needs.* I am not there yet. I have not experienced that yet. However, in the pursuit of it, my strength for the journey has been renewed over and over again.

We're going to look closely at this principle and see a good Father at work who is determined to see Christ fully formed in us (Gal. 4:19).

THE JOURNEY DEFINED

If you were reading Watchman Nee, he would call it an extended season of the *breaking of the soul*. In A.W. Tozer's writing, it would be referred to as *the crucified life*. C.S. Lewis may simply call it good old-fashioned discipline and tell you to *count the cost*. Regardless (and whatever it is called), the aims are the same. Its recognition by the Spirit-filled *mystics* (as Tozer would identity them), testifies to the universality of the principle. Of all of the tools in the Father's tool belt for the shaping of His kids, none is more invasively thorough than the wilderness journey. Book two will deal with this truth in greater depth. But for now, be reminded that whatever this desert journey becomes for you, HE IS DOING IT. and He can be trusted.

and really important note!: What empowers this journey is the indwelling Spirit of Christ, as so beautifully written by Andrew Murray: "The Holy Spirit is the Inmost Self of the Father and the Son. My spirit is my inmost self. The Holy Spirit renews that inmost Self, and then dwells in it. And so He becomes to me what He was to Jesus, the very life of my personality..."[33] I hope you caught the fullness of that.

Murray continues as he explains the workings of the Holy Spirit:

The distinction is of the deepest importance. In the new spirit given to me, I have a work of God in me; in God's Spirit given, I have God Himself, a Living Person, to dwell with me. What a difference between having a home built by a rich friend, given me to live in, while I remain poor and feeble, or having the rich friend himself come to live with me, and fulfill my every want![34]

If your soul is to be broken—your life to be crucified—your days, months, years to be filled with discipline, the Holy Spirit in the midst of it all will be the prime Mover, Stabilizer, Comforter, Demolisher, Healer, Builder,

---

[33]Andrew Murray. *The Spirit of Christ* (Fort Washington, PA: Christian Literature Crusade, 1963), 18-19.

[34] Ibid, 18.

Secret-sharer, Friend, Prophetic Voice—the Quiet, Loud, Firm, Direction—and *Mystery* in it all.

In a word, as to the nature of the journey, it is an extended season of *discipline*. Hear clearly the writer of Hebrews:

For consider Him who has endured such hostility by sinners against Himself, so that you will not grow weary and lose heart. You have not yet resisted to the point of shedding blood in your striving against sin; and you have forgotten the exhortation which is addressed to you as sons,"My son, do not regard lightly the discipline of the Lord, Nor faint when you are reproved by Him; For those whom the Lord loves He disciplines, And He scourges every son whom He receives." It is for discipline that you endure; God deals with you as with sons; what son is there whom *his* father does not discipline? But if you are without discipline, of which all have become partakers, then you are illegitimate children and not sons. Further-more, we had earthly fathers to discipline us, and we respected them; shall we not much rather be subject to the Father of spirits, and live? For they disciplined us for a short time as seemed best to them, but He *disciplines us* for *our* good, so that we may share His holiness. All discipline for the moment seems not to be joyful, but sorrowful; yet to those who have been trained by it, afterwards it yields the peaceful fruit of righteousness (Heb. 12:3-11).

Of the Greek dialect used to carry the idea, this passage uses three different words. The writer uses *paideia* in verse five, telling his readers to remember and regard as significant His parental relationship over and for us. Whatever you think of the *hard* of life circumstances that He grants to come your way, the love of a perfect parent urging you forward goes with it. *Paideuo* is used in verse seven, again carrying the idea of one who chastises, who educates, and who even punishes as a good parent must. It is a testimony of our daughter or sonship. Lastly, *paideutes* is used, reminding us that we've all had parents who have sought to *teach and correct us* (and while they have done what they could), it does not compare with a Father who will engage us in discipline that will *yield the peaceful fruit of righteousness* (v.11).

The grind of this extended journey will be one that disciplines (i.e. educates, instructs, wears out, tests, chastises, punishes—all of the above!) To that end, I believe that Watchman Nee nails the nature of the wilderness journey: "The Holy Spirit has not ceased working. He makes sure one event after another and one difficulty after another come to us. These disciplinary workings of the Holy Spirit have but one purpose—to break our outward man so that our inward man may come through."[35]

Yet herein lies the challenge of such an extended period of time in the *winepress* of life. (It is called such, as there is no wine until the grapes are thoroughly trampled, crushed, bruised; until the fullness of the flavor in the grape is released.) We don't like such seasons. Let's be brutally honest here. We don't even tolerate such moments! Nee comments on the fact:

Yet here is our difficulty—We fret over trifles, we murmur at small losses, and we complain about insignificant things. The Lord is ever finding and preparing a way in order to use us. Yet when His hand slightly touches us, we begin to feel unhappy—even to the extent of quarreling with God and having a negative attitude. Since the time when we were saved, we have been touched by the Lord many times in various ways—all with the purpose of breaking our outward man. Whether we are conscious of it or not, the aim of the Lord is to break this stubborn vessel called our outward man.[36]

So much of what this desert journey *is* initially, is wrapped up in coming to grips with this truth. My guilt in cursing the discipline of my Father in my daily life-living is embarrassingly mountainous. **Even now, sitting here, I am shamed in my own eyes at the raging that has passed in my thoughts in the quiet hours of the day. I am a man under the trial of fire, and the God of Abraham, Isaac, Jacob, and Moses is burning away day-by-day, month-by-month, year-by-year, my resistance to His invading light which sears the self of the false me away.** To that end, we must "recognize **WHOSE** hand is dealing with us. It is not a human hand. Nor is it our family's hand. It's not the brother's and sister's hand in the church. But **it is God's very own hand that is dealing with us. We need to learn how to kneel down, kiss the hand, and love the hand that deals with us....**" (bold mine)[37]

In this journey we will find, as C.S. Lewis writes: "The Christian way is different: harder, and easier. Christ says 'Give me All. I don't want so much of your time and so much of your money and so much of your work; I

---

[35]Watchman Nee. *The Release Of The Spirit* (New York: Christian Fellowship Publishers, 2000), 15.

[36] Ibid, 15.

[37] Ibid, 19.

want You. I have not come to torment your natural self, but to kill it.'"[38]

In its place, as Lewis notes, a new life will be given to you. A life that is His and therefore eternal and indestructible. A soul that can feel what He feels, think what He thinks, and acts in step with Him (in reference to James 1:21).

What will this mean for you? It will mean disappointed hopes and delayed dreams. It will most likely mean the *long way around* to the things you want most. Why? *Because Jesus cares way more about who you are becoming than what you are doing for Him.* Who you are now is a person with far more of the world in your thinking than you can sparsely imagine. (You may no longer engage in sins of your past. You may attend church. You may even pastor one. Yet, under the intense light of extended hard circumstances, your heart motives will be laid bare.) The *why* of what you do and what you think will be given every opportunity to rear its ugly head, so that you can repent and be free of it all.

Does all of this make you a bit nervous? The late Dr. Charles H. Stevens studied long the wilderness journey of the Jewish people. He writes, "CRISES DO NOT PRODUCE HEROES, nor do emergencies make cowards; However, extraordinary circumstances often serve to reveal strengths or weaknesses that have long been dormant."[39]

What he says next is profound:

The storm that felled the mighty oak only brought to light the hidden decay that had been eating at its heart for years. The outburst of a glaring weakness or evil tendency in an unguarded moment only serves to bring to attention that which is but the climax of a protracted course of thought and purpose. We are not what we are because of what we do; we do what we do because of what we are.[40]

---

[38]C. S. Lewis. *Mere Christianity* (SanFrancisco, CA: Harper, 1952), 196.

[39] Charles H. Stevens. *The Wilderness Journey* (Chicago, IL: Moody Press, 1971), 171.

[40] Ibid, 171.

Because the cloud of witnesses speaks rather loudly concerning these truths, these pages seem to be filling up with quotations of their shared insights. Here, Nee echoes Stevens' sentiment:

At the beginning of the Christian life, we are concerned with our doing and not with our being; we are distressed more by what we have done than by what we are. We think that if only we could rectify certain things we could be good Christians; therefore, we set out to change our actions. We try to please the Lord, but we find that something within us does not want to please Him. And the more we try to rectify matters externally, the more we realize how deep-seated the problem really is.[41]

If you're listening closely, what you are hearing is that this is a work that takes time. It's why so many have come to recognize it as a *wilderness journey*. It is wilderness because it feels solitary. It will feel like a *fruitless place* while your character is being challenged and built. At times, you will wear your patience on your chest, and it will crush upon your heart and lungs, laboring your breath. In truth, there will be fruit—yet, in your heart —you will know there is more. If you're like me, you will ache for it. You will find as I have, however, that there is no shortcut. There is only quitting (which is easier said than done), or there is moving on. However, if we make the journey we will find that, according to Stevens:

God has a way of turning "disappointments" into "His appointments." It is everlastingly true that our losses, our loneliness, our sorrows, our disappointments, and our sicknesses turn out to be within the loving providence of God. These are the means used by God to enrich the lives of His own children and bring them closer to Himself... There is no part of life from which He withholds Himself."[42]

Welcome to the heart of God in the least likely of places: in the desert, waterless, bare-necessities wandering.

---

[41]Watchman Nee. *Secrets to Spiritual Power* (New Kensington, PA: Whitaker House, 1999), 21.

[42] Charles H. Stevens. *The Wilderness Journey* (Chicago, IL: Moody Press, 1971), 80.

GOOD MEDICINE

George Otis, Jr., in his book *God's Trademarks,* writes of *good medicine* for his people. It speaks much to the aims of the Spirit in the heart and motive of man. One of these *medicines* is **wandering.** He says, "...we can hardly appreciate that He would lead us in circles. But wandering is not so much about detour as it is about delay. Sometimes God slows our pace that He might divest us of a flawed mentality or worldview."[43]

The image of *medicine* in terms of the circumstances that seem to come in these journeys couldn't have been better chosen. While most children's medicines come flavored in grape, orange, and cherry—adult medicines do not. In fact, most *grown up* medicine is disgusting and even downright painful or inconvenient.

A few years back, I had somehow contracted a strep virus in my uvula (the flap of skin that hangs down in the back of your mouth). Through the night, it had swollen to the size of a rather large grape! I remember driving to the urgent care the next day with my head angled down just enough to keep my uvula out of my air passage and still see the road!

After the nurses and physician assistant nearly panicked, they took a few x-rays and sent me to the pharmacy located across the street for a rather serious antibiotic. Opening it right there on the spot, I was dumb-founded when I saw that it was the largest *horse pill* I had ever seen. Looking up at the pharmacologist—pointing at the back of my mouth—(speaking with my uvula *sitting on my tongue*), I mumbled out, "You've got to be kidding me." She looked a bit horrified and shrugged her shoulders. My reply was, "Do you have smoovies?" In the end, I ground it to powder right there in the CVS, mixed it with my smoothie and was exponentially better by seven o'clock that night. It was good medicine. It was the right medicine at the time. But, it was no fun to take. at the time, the prescribed medicine was what was needed to fix the emergent problem. i was away on a trip when jack's THROAT ALMOST CLOSED OFF, and i'm really glad that i didn't ever see him struggling to keep his air passageway unobstructed like that! (and definitely glad that he took the medicine.)

---

[43] Otis Jr., George. *God's Trademarks* (Grand Rapids, MI: Chosen Books, 2000), 81.

I am reminded of a line that stood out to me from the obscure sequel to *Aladdin*. The line was so distinct in my memory that even after one viewing, I still recall it. Jafar had promised that he would not kill Aladdin. His evil sidekick was reminding him of that fact when Jafar quipped, "I'm not going to kill him, but you would be surprised what he could live through."[44]

When speaking of journeys of this nature, I believe that what we most fear are challenges that we may have to go through and what our Father may deem *good medicine* in our lives. C.S. Lewis writes:

> When I was a child I often had a toothache, and I knew that if I went to my mother she would give me something which would deaden the pain for that night and let me get to sleep. But I did not go to my mother—at least, not till the pain became very bad...I did not doubt she would give me the aspirin; but I know she would also do something else. I knew she would take me to the dentist next morning. I could not get what I wanted out of her without getting something more, which I did not want. I wanted immediate relief from the pain: but I could not get it without having my teeth set permanently right. And I knew those dentists: I knew they started fiddling about with all sorts of other teeth which had not yet begun to ache. They would not let sleeping dogs lie, if you gave them an inch they took an ell.[45]

i picked up <u>Mere Christianity</u> to check this reference, and kept reading. i am so thankful for thinkers who write their thoughts, like lewis. he writes, "Our Lord is like the dentists. If you give Him an inch, He will take an ell." i'm not sure what an "ell" is, but i assume it's an awful lot. "He will cure it all right..." lewis continues (speaking of some particular sin one may go to the Lord with for a cure):

"but He will not stop there...'Make no mistake,' He says, 'if you let me, I will make you perfect. The moment you put yourself in My hands, that is what you are in for. Nothing less, or other, than that. You have free will, and if you choose, you can push Me away. But if you do not push Me away, understand that I am going to see this job through. Whatever

---

[44] *Return of Jafar.* Directed by Toby Shelton, Tad Stones & Alan Zaslove, Walt Disney Pictures, 1994.

[45]C.S. Lewis. *Mere Christianity* (SanFrancisco, CA: Harper, 1952), 201-202.

suffering it may cost you in your earthly life...whatever it costs Me, I will never rest, nor let you rest, until you are literally perfect—until my Father can say without reservation that He is well pleased with you, as He said He was well pleased with me. This I can do and will do. But I will not do anything less."[46]

He means to make much of us. He won't relent in discipline if necessary. He loves us too much to leave us broken.

WALKED INTO FAILURE

We need to ask a hard question over these next few pages. If wilderness wanderings are one of the strange *medicines* prescribed by a loving Father that seeks your ultimate good (and understanding that wilderness has to do with delay and divestment which is experienced by and through life experiences): **is it possible that the Father would call you out to an assignment and intentionally walk you into failure?** Perhaps you may need to hear it another way: Is it possible that the Father would call you to an assignment where your failure has been providentially foreseen by Him, and allow you to walk it out anyway—even command you to do so, without your knowledge at the outset that failure will be the outcome? For some, your faith may be too fragile, your emotion too raw to even consider the question. But you will have to. If you don't, you will most likely come up with manipulative defense mechanisms to cope with the circumstances that James 1:2 and John 16:33 promise will come your way. The *discipline* of the Lord will be coming your way, and you will be *despising it* (Prov. 3:11; Heb. 12:6). (And you may stay in the wilderness far longer than needed.)

These are the kinds of circumstances that cause us to ask, *Would God do that?* To begin an answer, let's look at Peter's walk on the water.

According to Matthew chapter 14, it had already been a really long day. It began with Jesus receiving word that John the Baptist had been martyred by Herod. What had started as a morning of seclusion (perhaps to mourn and pray) was quickly interrupted by a sea of need.

---

[46] C. S. Lewis. *Mere Christianity* (San Francisco, CA: Harper,1952), 202.

The fame and compassion of Jesus was spreading quickly. Imagine a world with near 100% mortality rates for modern day *over the counter* issues of pre-twentieth century medical advances. A chance at life, a chance at walking, a chance at seeing, a chance at living *without pain* would certainly draw a crowd. Let's not forget that the disciples are privy to all of it. Hour after hour—they ushered; they watched; they conversed—as their Master *won* against death, infirmity, and disease *without fail*. In not one instance was there a disappointing moment. Jesus delivered *every single time*.

It may be tempting to ascribe some sort of negative motive to the disciples when they suggested to Jesus that it was getting late and folks would need to make the journey back to find a bite to eat. I'm not sure it's necessary. Most likely, they were pointing out the obvious. It was desolate, and it *was* getting late. Sure, they may have been hungry and tired, looking for a break, but why not? They needed rest too. But Jesus wasn't finished *accomplishing, winning, delivering the hurting!* The long day was just getting started. (And by long, I don't mean bad. I mean *long*—extended, sensory-overloaded.)

So, Jesus decided to feed everybody with five loaves of bread and two fish. While it was Jesus who did all of the *touching* until now, the disciples got to personally pass a miracle by *hand* to thousands. (Have you ever begun a given task with uneasy timidity—only to grow in confidence and speed— as hand, foot, eye, and mind seemingly mastered it?) I would like to have had a camera on the face of each disciple—edited with a time elapse—to watch shifts of facial expression throughout the serving.

and following this crazy miracle.. .. ..The story reads in verse twenty-two that "immediately He made the disciples get into the boat." I'm not sure if that means they *ate and ran* or took theirs *to go*. Whatever it was, it was literally on the heels of a momentous day—a really full day of success upon success upon success. And now, where were they off to? Well—more success; right?

According to the story, it looks innocent enough. Jesus was sending the exhausted disciples on ahead while he dismissed everybody, maybe catching up on that quiet time that was interrupted earlier in the morning. What could go wrong?

well.. .. ..
Everything for the next few hours.

160

By the fourth watch of the night (sometime between three a.m. and six a.m.), the disciples were still fighting a nasty headwind and the waves that go with it. (I've done some mean things in my time—like practical jokes that went gloriously well—but if this had been a practical joke, it would have topped them all. Happily, it was no joke.) If we assume they entered the boats as light was fading, we can estimate that they had been laboring to cross for eight plus hours...much of it, with Jesus watching from the shore. Those poor men! Already exhausted, they thought they were moving across for a night of uninterrupted sleep.

I've always thought it's super hard to have something go so wrong after so much has gone so right. These days, when I read this passage, I don't spend a lot of time pondering what the disciples may have been thinking. I get frustrated, tired, scared, and angry enough that I feel I kind of know much of that already. What captures my imagination is: what was Jesus doing and thinking for the eight or so hours on the shore. Did he laugh? we know that He was genuinely concerned for them in the struggle, but we also know that, in His sovereignty, He was excited about what He was getting ready to teach them through a crazy display of His power! Assuming he knew the individual thought of each as they struggled, was he disappointed, pleased, angered, grieved??? Certainly, He wasn't surprised. He may have been a man, but He was also God, and I have to assume nothing was transpiring that He hadn't already seen. Yet, there He was, watching the men He loved so dearly in a desperate fight to do *something He had told them to do*. It wasn't their idea to go across. It was His. They didn't know the sudden change of wind that would come *when* it did or the *way* it did, *but He did.* You would think with that foreknowledge engaged, He would have held them up until the folks had left and then made the trip with them. He is the One, after all, who would say to the sea, "Peace, be still." (Mk. 4:39) But, not here. He watched hour after hour as they fought, struggled, and failed to move forward.

I love all of the messages that get preached around this passage—most of them from the negative aspects of the ravages of doubt and disbelief. After all, it is the take away that Jesus gives in verse thirty-one. And it is much of what we've been getting at so far...*that the Father wants to be believed*, right? Right—but I think there is more.

In those early morning hours, Jesus approached the boat by foot. Again, in and of itself, a lesson in belief to be sure. Who does that? *Jesus.* Some really relatable responses come from the boat, one of which has somebody

161

shouting and gripping the closest neighbor in horror saying, "It's a ghost!" (v. 26). And then the *wow*! It's *Jesus*. What happens next is legendary. It will be preached, exhorted, exposited—millions of times this week! The catch phrase, "You gotta get out of the boat!" will be uttered on every continent today. Coaches with no knowledge of the scriptures will tell their teams to *keeps their eyes off of the waves*. But for all of that, a nuance of heart motive is revealed in these verses that can begin to answer the question, "Would God do that?" It has already been introduced in the disciples beginning the journey across the lake. But here, with Jesus' command for Peter to *come out of the boat,* something very significant can be gleaned that wrestles with *faith and belief* in a highly counterintuitive way.

WIND, WAVES, &...FAILURE

In the mix of all the success they had that day—and now the unexpected struggle—Jesus stood on the water in full view of the dumbfounded men. *Winning again.* He had covered the same amount of ground (well, water, jack.) in thirty minutes that they had in more than *eight* hours. Oh...and he did it on foot! What can't Jesus do?! *What can't we do with Jesus!?,* seems to be the question on Peter's mind. The flow of the conversation becomes very important. Don't miss it: "Peter said to Him, 'Lord, if it is You, command me to come to You on the water.' And He said, 'Come!' And Peter got out of the boat, and walked on the water and came toward Jesus" (Matt. 14:28-29). Did you catch it? When this story is paraphrased, it is often paraphrased (in our heads): *Hey Jesus, can I come??? Hey Jesus, please, oh please, let me come out of the boat.* But, this is not what happens.

I want to make a leap here, because I believe a bit of the nature of a Christ-believing man is on display in Peter. It's really, really subtle, yet needs to be caught. My opinion is that Peter is being clever. Not in a malicious way, yet rather, in a *base-covering* sort of way. He's not stupid. He can't—in and of himself—walk on water. Period—Fact. But, Jesus can. (Peter also can't multiply food. Yet, earlier in the day, as he passed it from hand to hand, the food did multiply. He didn't make it happen, but Jesus did, and Jesus was the One who had told him to pass the basket.) So Peter *wisely* says, *Command me to come to you on the water* (v. 28). So? What are you saying, Scott? Precisely this: Peter's thought—our thought—is that if Jesus initiates the call, the assignment, and gives the command to act, then that which I do under His command will *SUCCEED*.

But. It doesn't.

Peter does walk for a moment or two, but then...waves, wind, and...failure. And his faith is questioned.

My theology—and my understanding of what Jesus knows and doesn't know—greatly affects my processing of this true tale. Before Peter ever took the first step upon the water, Jesus knew the outcome. He knew every emotion. He knew what every wave would look like through Peter's eyes. He saw his panic as Peter sank to his neck in a sea that was bigger than his faith. And yet—He *commanded* him to come. You could say, *Yeah, but Peter was being manipulative.* Oh...for sure. But—he was speaking to *God.* And God is, in truth, manipulated by no man nor demon, however persuasive. An *un-manipulated* God gave the command. For Peter to back down at that moment would have been disobedience to His Master's call. He had to step out onto the water.

Foreknowledge accounted for, Jesus called Peter into failure. *Foreknowledge accounted for*—Jesus sent the disciples into a night of frustration. HE DID THAT. Did Peter doubt? Yes. Did the disciples doubt? Yes. How were their failures made into teachable moments on the water that can instruct and build our faith today? Failure. Failure *by design.*

Would God intentionally walk you into failure? Yes. But as with Peter —*always* with great purpose. Watchman Nee writes:

All that comes to us is ordered by God. To us as Christians, **nothing** is accidental. We should ask God to open our eyes to see that it is He who is striking us by all things and in all areas of our life. One day, when we are enabled by His grace to accept the ordering of God in our environment, our spirit will be released and ready to function.[47]

THIS IS PERSONAL FOR THE REIDS

For seventeen years, I have lived this truth, one failure after another. I've written of the failure of our concert events and the TV show. **These were only a few episodes in a lengthy saga.** In 2009, Steph and I attempted to plant a church; it never got out of its fledgling early days before God

---

[47]Watchman Nee. *The Release Of The Spirit* (New York: Christian Fellowship Publishers, 2000), 41.

had us make a left turn. By 2011, I was back on staff at a local church serving as a youth and college pastor again, reflecting on the disappointed hopes of an evangelistic mission stifled as we were redirected once again.

Around that time, ever bent on seeing a full-scale citywide transformation, our nonprofit ministry hosted a community evening of worship at the local middle school auditorium. *this night was one for the books that left us seriously scratching our heads...!!* Finding out that we would go over time *by half an hour,* the principal made a special trip to the school to shut us down! Our guest speaker (a well-known communicator whom we had flown in from out of state), was fifteen minutes into his talk, when, under threat of police intervention, I had to *interrupt him and ask everyone to leave.* The next morning, he informed Steph and I that we had made it in to the top two *weirdest* things that had ever happened to him. Coming from a man raised by Iranian refugee parents, that's quite a distinction!

I've shepherded three youth groups beyond comparable numbers to general congregation size only to watch each dissipate for various reasons. Please be aware that none of these were whimsically entered into. Steph and I are intercessors. I hardly purchase a candy bar without it becoming a spiritual encounter. *To Live Is Christ To Die is Gain...there is nothing else* (Ph. 1:21) has been my life's pursuit. Every step, as far as we knew at each turn, has been by a perceived *divine come.* (I'm not suggesting they all were *divine comes.* In the early days of the journey, I now feel that some may not have been—but at the least—we had said as Peter, *"Command us,* and we'll go.")

I HAVE FAILED. **But! I fully believe that I have failed with great purpose!**

C.S. Lewis writes:

When a man turns to Christ and seems to be getting on pretty well (in the sense that some of his bad habits are now corrected) he often feels that it would now be natural if things went fairly smoothly. When troubles come along—illnesses, money troubles, new kinds of temptation—he is disappointed. These things, he feels, might have been necessary to rouse him and make him repent in his bad old days; but why now? Because God is forcing him on, or up, to a higher level; putting him into situations where he will have to be very much braver, or more patient, or more loving, than he ever dreamed of being before. It seems to us all unnecessary; but that is because we have not yet had the slightest notion of the tremendous things He means to make of us.[48]

I have chosen to fully embrace the statement above.

me too! ^^^

I have traveled these circles for my entire adult life. The last several years have been with spiritual eyes wide open, gleaning the lessons, wrestling with the implications, all the while, watching *the me of me* transform before my eyes. I am not where I started. The journey has done its work; there is no longer any regret.

This is not to say that I *enjoy* it. I have *joy*, but I haven't celebrated the *hard*. I've celebrated the many rescues as they have appeared after the hard times have come and gone—after Jesus has pulled me back up out of the water. After Jesus has said to the wind and waves, "Peace, be still." (Mk. 4:39)

yet, we still ache with each disappointment. catch the tozer quote in the next paragraph, though. don't miss it.

I hope so much that in the reading of these thoughts, you are not discouraged. These things are hard. It is the purpose for which they come, however, that grants a capacity for joy. If these words are only serving to focus you on the *hard*, they are missing their mark. The aim of it all is to introduce you to the glory of *the One* who is moving you into Himself. A.W. Tozer understands this danger quite well and encourages his readers:

Those who persevere will find that instead of breaking into the clear bright sunshine, just ahead of them are more discouragements, doubts and deceptions... Those who have been so discouraged—those who have bumped their foreheads on the ceiling or scraped their chins on the sidewalk—and have gone down in some kind of defeat are the very ones who are getting nearer to God....those who have found things going against them—those who in their longing and yearning for the crucified life, those who wait for Jesus Christ to lead them and instead wonder if He is discouraging them—they probably don't realize that they are very close to the kingdom of God.[49]

---

[48]C.S. Lewis. *Mere Christianity* (San Francisco, CA: Harper, 1952), 204-205.

[49] A.W. Tozer. *The Crucified Life* (Ventura, CA: Regal, 2011), 137-138.

that is ALL we want, Jesus. to be close to Your kingdom.

DELAY & DIVESTMENT

I want to go back a moment to something shared from George Otis, Jr. He wrote,"...we can hardly appreciate that He would lead us in circles. But wandering is not so much about detour as it is about delay. Sometimes God slows our pace that He might divest us of a flawed mentality or worldview."[50]

We can get hung up on the failures and drown in a sea of self-pity if we are not careful. If indeed, it is a divinely-appointed *wilderness journey* you have found yourself in, these failures might be better-framed as delay. **Delay is frustrating, but not final.** As my dear friend, Mike, used to fondly say, "We like to put periods where God puts a comma." So much of Abraham's story is filled with: *and then.*

You are in a flowing story. Time passes and you float upon its current. It's the divine wind spoken of in Genesis, and all things drift at its speed. I believe Otis is right. It's not about *detour,* it's about delay, BUT...delay for a purpose. The purpose? Divestment. Divestment of what? Of everything that hinders you from being fruitful and enjoying Him. It's why the Father disciplines us as children in this way (Heb. 12:4-11). The Israelites who came out with Moses came out as slaves. Some came out worshiping the Egyptian gods. Nearly all were immersed in pagan culture. The forty years in the desert consumed those things that would keep them from inhabiting the promise and inhabiting it well.

And yes; God would do that. Delay is a powerful enlarger of capacity. It strains hope and endurance like nothing else can. It tests them. Like hydraulic lines, the pressure of delay fills the arteries of life, stressing hard at the joints. Where they are weak, they will burst. They will leak. The weak places will be revealed—not broken to be tossed away, but illuminated to be repaired, strengthened—even made new if need be.

---

[50]George Otis, Jr. *God's Trademarks* (Grand Rapids, MI: Chosen Books, 2000), 81.

START PAYING ATTENTION

So, if you're in a wilderness journey, what do you do? *Start paying attention.* While I maintain that all of life's circumstances in all seasons are full of the voice of the Holy Spirit, perhaps none are as *jam-packed* and *loaded*—as the wilderness. If delay and failure provide anything, they provide **lots** of opportunity for meditation! This is a protracted time in which God is doing something very real, very constructive, and highly sensitive in your being. HE'S TRYING TO TELL YOU SOMETHING!!!! Look for it. In it, you will find *character sandpaper* (yeah, I totally just made that up—but definitely made its way on to the front cover and consequently throughout the book to this point!), as well as awkwardly effective emotional mirrors, even heads-up for what the journey ahead might hold.

thank You for everything that has been character sandpaper in our journey, Jesus.

DISNEY SANDPAPER

In August of 2014, Steph and I took our first extended (by extended, I mean more than three days)—*no kids*—vacation and anniversary trip to Venice, FL. One of the eight days, we had planned to do something I had dreamt of doing with Stephanie from our dating days in the early 1990's. I wanted to spend a day in the Magic Kingdom with my high school sweetheart and now life-love and partner of then, twenty years! I was so incredibly stoked.

My mother had a number of one-day park-hoppers leftover from previous trips, and never was I more careful and intentional about anything than I was at making sure the tickets could be redeemed! I was also careful about obtaining reservations for our anniversary dinner. Belle's Castle was booked, so I settled on a place that had become my favorite down through the years —the restaurant in *Mexico,* located in Epcot.

The morning of the *Disney day* dawned bright and clear. It was an incredibly pleasant drive over to Orlando. Just as they had promised over the phone, the old paper tickets were quickly transferred to the new plastic cards, and we were off across the *Seven Seas Lagoon* to the land where *dreams come true. i am literally laughing at this build-up, jack. so cute.*

Before continuing, I need to catch you up on life-happenings for us leading into these days. In the Fall of 2013, we had begun a second attempt at planting a church, thinking maybe this was God's timing. Already, there had been much promise and then disappointment. The first location that we looked at to host our young team was in the hands of questionable owners, so it ended up needing to be scrapped. Then, a local church had verbally agreed to allow us to lease their auditorium, but two weeks before we were to launch, they took on an interim pastor who informed us that they were leery of *being seen as supporting a church plant. yeah....* When I stepped into the park that August morning, our church had most recently put a proposal in the hands of a children's home in our city to inquire about the use of an old chapel on their campus. Speed bumps and delays felt as if they were becoming a way of life for our young church, and my eyes were wide open, as I was looking hard to see what the Father might be doing in it all.

back to orlando and the magic kingdom.. .. ..

While August is not the busiest season for the Disney parks, it is still fairly crowded at this time of year. Our first priority was to make our way to a *fast pass* kiosk and see what was available. It wasn't altogether helpful. The first passes were not available until seven p.m. that evening! (I've been three times since and have received fast passes starting at nine a.m.) Our first and only round of passes were for seven, nine, and ten *p.m.* With a crowded park, I was starting to get the feeling that there was going to be a lot of waiting. However, in spite of that, I was with my best friend in the whole wide world, and for that reason alone, it was going to be an amazing day.

Our first ride was *Pirates of the Caribbean* (a favorite from childhood days). The listed wait time was thirty minutes, but about fifteen in, an announcement came through the speaker that the ride had temporarily stopped and would resume shortly. (*Forty-five minutes later*, we were still in the roped-off line outside of the building, and an *hour and a half after that*, we were finally on the ride—when less than five minutes into the ride itself, *it stopped with technical difficulties!*) At approximately 11:30 a.m., we were finally out of *Pirates of the Caribbean*, having nearly all of our morning "looted" in the Pirate's ride.

After lunch, we made our way across the park to *Tomorrowland*—and to let our meal settle a bit before engaging a fast ride—(*if you've been there, you may recall that space mountain is in that section of the park*)—we decided to relax a bit on the *People Mover* (a rather pleasant and restful extensive tour of the surrounding attractions). Approximately seventy-five yards from the finish, the cart stopped, and for thirty minutes, we sat motionless in the *People Mover* cart as occasional messages came through the speaker systems encouraging us about our *temporary delay*. Finally, a park employee made his way to our cart and manually opened the doors, escorting us to the disembarking point. (For that one, we received an additional fast pass to be used later that evening.) It was two o'clock, and we had yet to do anything that hadn't broken or delayed.

With our reservation for Mexico anticipated at Epcot at five p.m., we decided to catch one more ride in Tomorrowland before heading that way. We opted for the *Carousel of Progress* as the doors had just opened to it. The carousel is a rotating theater observing numerous changing scenes from one man's kitchen through the decades. Nearing the completion of the last rotation, out of the corner of my eye, I noticed a very young Hispanic boy walking up and leaning against the stage. At this, the show was stopped. The attendant in the corner requested through the intercom that everyone be seated for the ride to continue. The young boy appeared to have gotten the message, taking a few steps back from the platform as the scene started again—from the beginning. Hardly had we gotten halfway through, when the young boy was once again at the stage front. It stopped again. The announcement came again. The boy moved again. The scene started from the beginning...again. Nearly at the completion of the LAST scene, he was back. By this time, I had come to the conclusion that neither the boy nor his mother, brothers nor sisters spoke English. Apparently, the third stop and raising of the lights did the trick. The third start from the top was yet again attempted and this time—success!

It was 3:30ish and time to make our way to Epcot. If you can believe it, we actually rode the monorail all the way over without one delay. Having gotten there with an hour to spare, we made the decision to ride *Spaceship Earth*. Despite the rain that was beginning to fall, we were a bit refreshed as there was no line, and we were able to walk straight on.

Less than two minutes in, however, we experienced the first of three breakdowns—on the same ride. Thirty minutes later, we were getting off the ride with just enough time to make a leisurely walk over to Mexico for our much-anticipated dinner.

After removing our rain ponchos, we made our way to the reservations desk and gave them our name. She asked us to have a seat, and she would be with us in a moment. As the moments of our reservation came and went, I inquired about the delay. To my dismay and displeasure, they had us down for six p.m. instead of five. In the end, it turned out that not only did they misplace the reservation, they had recorded the wrong phone number, the wrong reservation number, and held the five p.m. reservation under the wrong name. After a wait of an hour, they finally recognized their error and gave us a seat. I've got to say however, that Steph and I were so into being with each other, that none of it seemed to matter (though we were noticing a trend!)

As seven o'clock and our first *fast passes* were quickly approaching, we made our way back to the Magic Kingdom and over to *Thunder Mountain*. Ironically, it was under a *thunder*storm delay. So, we endured the line for *Splash Mountain*. (It only broke down with us on it *twice!*) It was at this point that I considered the idea of placing a warning sign on our backs for anyone wanting to enjoy a ride without mishap: DO NOT RIDE WITH US. SUBJECT TO MULTIPLE BREAKDOWNS AND DELAYS IF WE ARE ON IT! I had wanted to ride *Peter Pan*, but one look at the line in lieu of our success rate with wait times that day, we decided against and opted to give the *People Mover* another chance (as there was no line and our second fast pass for *Splash Mountain* was coming up). Halfway through, it stopped again. After a really good laugh and conversation revolving around the theme the Lord had seemed to place on our lives that day, it resumed and completed its journey.

Back at *Splash Mountain,* we enjoyed the ability to walk straight onto the log. (One of the few times that day we had done anything without waiting —but it wasn't to last.) Again, the ride was stalled for technical difficulties. With our last fast pass to *Space Mountain* coming up in the next half hour, we elected to have a seat on the ground near Belle's Castle and take in the fireworks. It was truly one of the more pleasant parts of the entire day. Sitting with my beloved as she took picture after picture with my phone— it's three years later as I write, and they are still there! Finally, waiting in the fast pass line of *Space Mountain*, we endured one more delay as *Space Mountain broke down with us in line*. Incidentally, it was the last ride of our long-anticipated anniversary Disney day.

From nine a.m. to ten p.m. during a moderately busy day, we had endured *eighteen separate delays riding nine rides.*

We arrived back to our Honda Civic in the Magic Kingdom parking lot at approximately 11:30 p.m. and began the nearly two hour drive back to Venice Beach. During the drive, as Steph went in and out of sleep, my mind was eager to hear from the Spirit regarding the events of the day. Again, in the wilderness journey, *He is speaking.* In nearly every circumstance, He may be heard. The image that was developing in my mind was one that seemed to be foretelling our immediate future. It wasn't a picture I wanted to see, and I did much over the next two years to ignore it. In light of what the remainder of 2014 held—on through the present—I look back to that epic time now as one of the most significant prophetic days of the entire journey. That one day has been a microcosm of the last two and half years.

My heart and hope was for this trip to be a page-turning to a new season. It was. *(but not how we'd imagined.)* With hope high—the new delays coming were harder to stomach. We weren't home a few weeks before learning that the children's home would not be able to host us. They would only make the chapel auditorium available (even though other adjacent rooms would have been adequate for nursery and children's areas)—they would not make them available for rent. Again, weeks before a launch, we hit another wall.

A few weeks later, a local elementary school opened their doors to us. (An elder's wife worked at the school and had a good relationship with the principal who happened to be a preacher's kid herself.) Like so many church plants, we were setting up and tearing down on a weekly basis in the school's gym/auditorium. It felt like blessing, though, because while we did have to set up, it was minimal as most of our lighting and sound could stay in place on the platform during the week. However, coming into May (with the current principal departing), it came to our attention through the city office that our presence there was in violation of city policy. We would have to start looking again. With much grace, the superintendent's office permitted us to remain through the summer.

At that time, we came across another building in downtown Thomasville on Salem Street. It seemed perfect! 12,000 square feet in the downtown of the city we feel called to saturate with the Gospel. We had an unexpected connection with the owner who attended the church I had recently served. The plan was to lease the space for the first year with the option to purchase or continue the lease at a much higher rate the next year. Yet, while the building's exterior was solid, its internals were not. A previous tenant had filled the space with classroom and office walls, and—nothing was to code. The *fire walls* weren't real fire walls. Electrical junction boxes were sitting hot and open above the ceiling tiles. A/C ducts were improperly run through "fire walls." The ceiling leaked in multiple places, and the smell of mildew was oppressive in the summer heat. (The realtor expressed to us that the air simply needed to move and carpet replaced—and all would be fine. We did both; it wasn't.)

In the end, we tore out 30,000 pounds of drywall and dropped 12,000 square feet of ceiling tiles. What we found was a light concrete deck that was covered in mold. The upfit on this space would exceed $250,000. That's if we volunteered all of the labor excluding the cost of the remediation company. The owner was in the difficult place of having to ask far more than the property was worth. The total amount needed for our very small church plant to make this place happen would have exceeded half a million dollars. After much work, lots of praying and pleading in the Spirit, we came to a familiar place. We had to put it down. In the meantime, we had moved our Sunday morning worship gatherings to our barn. This was in the fall of 2015.

Without a doubt, the barn is one of my most favorite places on the planet. It's my dreaming place, writing place, resting place, project place, family party place, neighborhood party place. It's a 1000 square-foot blessing to the Reid family. Built to replace the original barn which had been there previously for nearly one hundred years, it now provides our family of six some leg room from our really old, 1400 square-foot farmhouse. In the barn, we can seat roughly seventy-five people. The space is insulated and heated with an old woodstove which sits in the corner. In the summer of 2016, we had five *expectant* ladies with us. With the help of my dad and some connections of our treasurer, we put central air in to keep them happy! At this writing, we're still there.

As much as we love it, it was not intended to host a church on a weekly basis. For two years, Steph and I have hosted our small church family. Because it's *our home* it has been hard not to do more than typical pastors do. It's *our yard and field*. So, we mow it on Saturdays to be ready for everyone to park. It's *our barn*, so we make the coffee and put out the refreshments. It's *our place*, so we put away the chairs, sweep, and clean when everyone leaves. It has turned into quite a job to keep things up and ready week in and week out. While we count it an honor to serve people we love with all of our hearts ((*so worth it all, and we would do it all over again!!!*)), we would be lying if we told you we're not worn thin.

As we were letting go of Salem Street and the frustration I felt in my spirit about it all, the Lord came near to me. What I heard in those moments stand now as another of those *place markers* of life-living that demarcate real direction change. What I had specifically heard in my spirit was that I had taken this church plant as far as I could. I was not gifted to take it any farther —Ouch! I was so raw and worn from the waiting and disappointment that it really wasn't that much of a surprise. The next thought that came was a question: *If you could do what you wanted to do, what would it be?* The answer came fast. It's always been my bucket-list career: Write/ Travel/ Speak/Teach. That's it. If there is anything in my life that seems to breathe life into me, it's those things. I am happiest when engaging in those endeavors. The opportunity, however, has never presented itself, so I've engaged them on the edges within the ministries I've been placed.

What became clear in those moments was that this book, which had begun eleven years ago, was to now become a priority. At present, Steph and I are still attempting to discern our role with our young church. We wrestled for months about next steps: if we were to resign, would we bring on co-laborers and possibly become a singly-focused *teaching pastor???* Even now, we don't have the answers to those questions. What it did do was move us to take a two-month sabbatical to hear what the Spirit had to say and to finish the manuscript of this book.

In the midst of this, December of 2016 brought unexpected blessing. (You'll remember that our original plan was to plant this church on East Main Street in Thomasville, NC.) In early December, my dad, walking memory lane in the old *Hudson Belk*, found himself in a conversation with the current owner of the property on East Main. It is now an Antique Emporium housing a cafe and coffeehouse. For *whatever reason,* she opened up to him about her battles with the city inspections department. For *whatever reason,* my dad felt I needed to get to know her. So, about ten days from Christmas morning, I stopped in, walked toward the back of the building, and there was Ms. Ruth carrying a pot of soup down to the coffeehouse. I gave her my name, and she immediately asked if we could sit down and talk. Taken aback, I agreed.

It was a remarkable conversation. She thought I was there to commiserate about city inspections. I thought I was there for—well—I didn't know why I was there. I didn't have a problem with city inspectors. I happen to like the city inspectors. I was there because my dad said I should meet this sweet lady. However, after listening to her, it sounded like a potential partnership could be forged. She needed help with inspectors, and we needed a place in Thomasville to gather.

A few days later, I had another meeting with Ruth to discuss the possibilities. It ended with her needing to speak with her son. While on a holiday trip, Ruth gave us a call and asked if we could sit down when I got back. We did. What she and her son offered dropped our jaws. She asked if we could take over the coffeehouse and use the small space behind it for our worship gatherings. The rent was incredibly agreeable, with options for future purchase that we could have scarcely imagined a month before when we put Salem Street down. We signed the lease which became effective in February of 2017. Everything was finally coming together. We could see it, taste it, and smell it. Then, the work began.

While it was high stress for Stephanie, her part was getting done, and the coffeehouse somehow came together literally the day before our departure.

It was not so for me. If I touched it, it delayed. Having invited a dear friend to join us as executive and worship pastor, he and his family were not able to arrive until a week before our departure for the sabbatical—no fault of their own. (Our hope had been to have at least a month together with them prior to our time away.) The permit to finish out the worship space never arrived. While I did what I could (stripped floors, painted walls, rigged production equipment, etc.), I could not achieve my primary goal which was to have our church family in their new worship space before Steph and I would leave them for two months. Everything I had imagined, hoped, and prayed concerning how we would walk into this sabbatical was in abject ruins. *this is recent as of the time of this writing—very fresh on our minds, and we are processing.*

I'm sitting in Venice Beach, FL right now writing this and would you like to know what the first two weeks of this sabbatical have been? ***Scott, do you love ME more than the promise?*** Through A.W. Tozer, He has spoken to me:

174

With words all carefully laid out and knowing just where to put your finger on this or just where to put your finger on that, you are too smart for God to bless you. You know too much. You can identify everything, but the dear heavenly Father knows you do not really know much at all. He lets things happen to you until you recognize that you do not know what is happening. Your friends do not know what is going on either. And when you go to somebody you feel you can trust, that person will not be able to help you either. That is actually good news.[51]

From there, He says daily: *Scott, be quiet and simply be. Put the promise down. I love you.*

as of this writing, we are still very much in a waiting place.

Scott, are you honestly suggesting that God is responsible for the journey you just described??? Yes. And He has told me as much in my spirit. He has something great to *make of me* (and me. and our church family.) ...and I doubt much—as long as I'm willing to walk it out—that He won't continue.

Yes—God does that!—Embrace it.

INDIVIDUALS WHO JOURNEYED IN THE WILDERNESS

If you're still wondering and possibly struggling with the thought that God would intentionally walk His kids through things like this, perhaps it would help to have an overview of the biblical witness from those who have been blessed and favored through it. What are we looking for? *Wilderness journeys* are not single season challenges—not even tragic single-season trials. Wilderness journeys will most likely encompass years, and those who walk them will experience the processes of God *(flying, running, walking)* even as they walk in pursuit of their hope. We are looking for individuals (even corporate groups) that have been met with extended delay to achieve the primary dreams and visions for their lives.

ABRAHAM (A REVIEW)

We've looked at Abraham's story already in great and lengthy detail, so we'll just hit the highlights here. At seventy-six years of age, Abram received the promise, the dream, the vision. (He seems a bit old to be receiving a

---

[51]A.W. Tozer. *The Crucified Life* (Ventura, CA: Regal, 2011), 108.

dream of this kind. Yet, God delights in doing things that leave His indelible mark.) By the time Abram and Sarai reached the area between Bethel and Ai, he was already starting to wonder, *Hey...where is the baby?* It was after calling on the name of the Lord in this place that he encountered his first major test: famine.

He had just gotten started in the circles, and already, he attempted to quit —handing Sarai over to Pharaoh. In Canaan, Abram—now separated from Lot—was finally walking in full obedience and the Lord came to him again, not only renewing the promise, but clarifying it. This was met with Abram's second major trial in lieu of the nagging one that never went away (the unfulfilled promise): Lot was taken. Abram had to do the one thing that he had carefully avoided while traversing the land: make enemies. Abram was forced to fight to deliver Lot and those with him.

It was after this episode that the Father had His most intimate encounter to date with Abram—*cutting the covenant*—that declared so much of what we have to learn on this journey. HE WAS DOING THIS. Chapter sixteen (being ten years into the journey), describes Abram and Sarai taking matters into their own hands by completely legitimate means. Abram, now eighty-six years old, had just unwittingly made the remainder of wilderness far more difficult—and thirteen years later, Abraham was still waiting on the promise.

At ninety-nine, God clarified the promise and more, this time giving details about timing. He sealed it with a covenant that was wholly unlike the previous one. The first one was about what God would do; this one was about the character and health of the new people. ((circumcision)) Fresh off this covenant, Abraham and Sarah were *re-tested* and failed miserably. Abraham quit on the promise again, giving Sarah to Abimelech to protect his skin. Yet, God delivered them from harm—*delivered the promise*— **again**.

By chapter twenty-one, with Sarah at ninety years old, and Abraham at one hundred years old, God finally "came through": Isaac was born! Hear this. See this. Do the math on your fingers if you have to, and consider the distance. Consider the life and trials lived in between. Isaac was a dream *twenty-five years in the making*. Knowing what was coming up for Abraham at Mt. Moriah, it was those twenty-five years of wilderness-shaping that empowered him to make the impossible journey of sacrifice—a walk of divine sacrificial love—unsurpassed until the hill of Calvary.

JOSEPH (A SURVEY)

When I read Joseph's story, my inclination is to weep with him. Aside from Job, no story seems so wholly *unfair.* I find myself sitting in prison with Joseph, thinking of the lost years in my father's house and the *might-have-beens.* Perhaps it's an ability the Spirit grants me to read these stories as if I do not know their endings. (If you can read as though the ending is yet to be, these life-walks become **so intensely viral to the emotion**. I want to ask you to make the attempt.) We're going to take our time with Joseph, and in the mix of that, it is hoped that you can see and feel the tensions of a divine wilderness experience.

For me, the entire journey begins with the words: *Joseph, when seventeen years of age*...(Gen. 37:1). Spoiler alert, he will be *in his forties* before any kind of conclusion dawns. We're talking about another story with very little resolution over a twenty-three year period.

Some background might be helpful. jack will be tracking from genesis 37-50, if it is helpful to have a bible close for reference.

No doubt, you're familiar with Joseph's coat of many colors. You're familiar with the fact that Joseph was the youngest of several brothers and that he was the favorite. You may be familiar with the reasons his brothers would have been jealous of the unique gift and preference his father had given him.

What I had often missed in the story was an intimate look and feel for the tensions that would have been present in this burgeoning family. Central to this whole story is *the promise* given to Abraham, Isaac, and now Jacob. It might benefit you to read through Jacob's story and to gain an appreciation for the consuming passion that *he* had for the promise. (He connived and deceived to obtain it from his father. He cheated and manipulated through his entire young adult life. He wrestled with God to *see* the *blessing.*) The promise is everything to this family.

If there's one thing we've learned from these periods and cultures, *oral tradition* is as unquestioned writ. For all of their young lives—at meals, walks in the fields, trekking to the next place to set up camp—they have heard Abraham's story, Isaac's story, and their father's stories about *the promise:* a promise that until now, had passed to the oldest. Yeah, I know,

Jacob was the younger twin. Yet, he knew that it was *supposed* to go to the older; he'd manipulated his way into the promise. (Genesis thirty-eight makes it clear that Judah was the son to inherit the mantel of Abraham and Isaac, even though Reuben was the oldest. It is in this greater tension that this story is recorded.)

It opens with Joseph pasturing his father's flock with his brothers, and immediately, we see it. We don't know what his brothers were doing, but whatever it was, Joseph saw to it that their father knew. I've been reading a bit in various commentaries and resources to glean what I can. For the most part, concerning Joseph's character at this time, commentators generally fall into two camps. Camp one sees Joseph as a spoiled *snot*. He's not a bad kid, but maybe the kid you want to punch in the face because he's good, and he knows it. The other camp sees Joseph as an honest full-on God-seeker, only looking out for his Father's best interests. He's not out to rub anything in anyone's face. He's a *boy scout*.

Having spent more than twenty years of my life pastoring youth and college students, and now raising teenagers of my own, I would like to toss my hat into the ring. I'm going to suggest that what we see in Joseph is *both*. The whole of Joseph's life does scream *BOY SCOUT!* A clearer eye might fairly label it: *integrity*. However, integrity can be wielded with great immaturity. It can be wielded with an over-developed sense of justice. Perhaps you've met the busybody who finds it his/her duty to police the behaviors in every social circle in which he/she finds him/herself. In youth, this is often a developmental stage. The world is black and white, and the black should be challenged while the white should be spoken. This stage of life can leave a youth with false confidence knowing one-eighth of what they actually think they know. (I'm taking the time to flesh this out because it has much bearing on understanding what happens next.)

At age seventeen, Joseph has a dream. Again, let me suggest that Joseph is not a *spoiled snot* so much as he is a young soul of *high integrity*, acting out in naive immaturity. (Otherwise, Joseph would not be a safe person in whom to posit this dream.) It's not just any dream; this is a vision—a vision that has ramifications for the survival of *THE PROMISE*. The Messiah is going to be preserved based on how this dream is accomplished! Keeping in mind all that is about to go down, it would take an individual of iron will and stone-faced integrity to walk it out. Yet, because of immaturity, it will require a wilderness journey of hardship to shape it into the Father's purpose.

JOSEPH'S DREAM

This is the basic run-down of the dream: Joseph and his brothers are in the field tying together stalks of wheat, when all of a sudden, these bound-together stalks take on personalities of their own. Joseph's bundle stands up, stiff and erect. His brother's bundles then seem to face it and bend in the middle as if bowing to Joseph's bundle (Gen. 37:6-7). You don't have to be a *rocket surgeon or brain scientist* to catch the implications of this one. (pretty simple—all types of surgery and science unnecessary.. .. ..)

Here's where the immaturity comes in. Because this family is all about *the promise* and dream of moving it forward, Joseph assumes much in sharing this vision so quickly. He correctly interprets the dream—that it does, indeed, relate to the family. He also rightly discerns its origin. It is from the God of Abraham, Isaac, and his father Jacob. To Joseph's mind, his brother's *liking or not liking it* is completely beside the point. God has decreed it. It must be spoken. Oh...but wait—there's more. He has another dream.

In this one, he sees the sun, moon, and eleven stars, all of which bow down to him. I'm laughing a bit now trying to imagine the naive, astonished face of Joseph relating this dream to the livid, teeth grinding, jaw clinching, *can you believe this* _____?-faced brothers.

If you were paying attention above, you'll catch that this occasion is far more than sibling rivalry boiling to the surface. What Joseph is relating in this dream is life-altering. If it is, indeed, from the Lord, it changes everything for these brothers—especially for the eldest, or so he would think. What it seems that Joseph has just told his brothers and father is that *THE PROMISE* is going to flow through him. Even Jacob seems taken aback. (After all, if this is true, the dream should have come though *him*. He is the head of this family until his birthday suit falls off, and according to family tradition thus far—it is *he* who will be the one to physically lay hands on and pass forth the anointing, blessing and *promise*.)

Naturally, Jacob pushes back. Nothing about this dream seems in order as Jacob—and his other sons, Joseph's brothers—would have understood it. (There is a reason for this that will remix the way you view this story.) In our typical telling, the brothers are all jerks, and Jacob is left privately scratching his chin, pondering it as a possibility (Gen. 37:11). However, it may just be that their anger is somewhat justified. Their actions are not; their resentment is not—but, maybe, just maybe, they all know something in their subconscious thought that Joseph doesn't know. We'll have to address the narrative out of order, but I think it'll help us catch a major *impetus* for wilderness journeys.

Almost inexplicably, right when we're getting hooked into Joseph's story, there is an abrupt turning into a portion of *Judah's* story. It takes up all of chapter thirty-eight before jumping right back into Joseph's story in chapter thirty-nine. (Francine Rivers turns it into an entire novel!)

I have to credit this catch to a gentleman who befriended me at a Panera Bread one random morning. He drew my attention to the subject matter of the chapter. The cliff-note version follows a parallel track of Judah and Tamar.

Judah leaves his father's house, takes a wife and has three sons. The eldest marries Tamar, but is taken by the Lord. (He apparently was *a snot.*) So Judah gives Tamar to his second son who refuses to impregnate her, which is a serious indignity to place on Tamar, and a direct disobedience to his father. The Lord kills him. Then Judah sends Tamar back to live with her parents until his youngest son is of age. (The truth, however, is that Judah is now paranoid about giving another son to Tamar. Judah is about to fail the family line and his part in *the promise.*)

However, Tamar, getting news of Judah's whereabouts, goes ahead of him, dresses as a prostitute and is solicited by Judah and becomes pregnant with Judah's fourth and fifth sons, Perez and Zerah—and then—back to Joseph's story. Yeah, I know—what is that all about?

You have to go to the opening chapter of Matthew for the *"aha!"* Right there, in the first sixteen verses of Matthew chapter one, we see that *Jesus,* the ultimate fulfillment of the Abrahamic promise (Gen. 12:3), comes of the line of *Judah* through Perez!

SO??? So let's go back to Joseph's dream. It seems obvious that Joseph's interpretation of the dream was that the *promise* was coming through him!

180

It is safe to assume that he understood it that way and related it that way. Yet, right here at the beginning of Joseph's wilderness journey, we, the readers, are given a spoiler alert. This dream—this vision—did not make Joseph the *carrier* of the promise. It was making him the *protector* and *shelter* of the promise.

Of all the things the wilderness journey does, clarification of the dream and vision is often a major part. We've already mentioned this, but let's hear it again: *There is a major difference between hearing the Lord and understanding Him.* Did Joseph wrongly assess in the dream that his father and brothers would be subject to his authority? No. He was right—they would, and they were. (It was everything in his current context and imagination that he attached to it that was wrong.) He *heard* the Lord correctly. But it is obvious that he did not understand Him.

To Joseph—and to us, if we haven't read ahead—there is nothing there to even remotely suggest that Joseph would be in charge of all Egypt some day! So Joseph does what nearly all do. We hear the word of the Lord inside of our current circumstance and *comprehend it* in that light. Chapter thirty-eight is about clarifying what Joseph's journey is and is *not* about. Chapters thirty-nine through forty-five are about divestment and preparation for those things he first sees at the age of seventeen. As we continue on, let's keep in mind that Joseph is not privy to the information in chapter thirty-eight. In fact, when we pick the story back up, his mind is likely running wild with possibilities. Joseph hasn't a clue that his entire world is about to be ripped from him.

JOSEPH'S WILDERNESS BEGINS

Right there, at seventeen years old (with a glorious future ahead of him), *his brothers take it all away.* He is thrown into an abandoned dried up well —and if not for Judah, their plan was to leave him there to die. I would like a window into the mind of Joseph in that hour while his brothers ate their lunch. Was it all a joke? Was it a warning??? Did they really mean to leave him to die? Any questions to that end were quickly confirmed when he was sold to the Midianite traders.

How do you reconcile a turn that violent in your journey? How many miles had he walked tied or chained before the dream began to haunt him? For the justice-inclined, integrity-gripped, *promise*-bound Joseph, everything in his world is shaken to absolute dust. There are those things which come to us that shake our circumstance and reorient our thinking and world, and there are those things that come that seem to kill it altogether. The latter is Joseph's introduction to a wilderness journey.

I think the beginning of chapter thirty-nine possibly reveals some reasons for Jacob's partiality to Joseph. The primary reason given is that he is a child of his old age and comes from his true love, Rachel. Another reason might be that Joseph (even at this young age), is gifted administratively. Given his iron integrity, *he is worth his weight in gold.* I'm guessing the Midianite traders picked up on it on the trek to Egypt. This kid was not the usual house servant. This one was worth something. Joseph's landing place bears this out. Of *all* places, Joseph finds himself serving the man in charge of guarding the most powerful leader in the world—Pharaoh.

We should catch something in Joseph's story that can seem counterintuitive to a spiritual desert journey. Genesis 39:2-6 makes it clear that in this season of Joseph's life, God was *with him, favored him, blessed him*—and by verse four, Joseph is running the house of Potiphar. And not only is he running it—it is flourishing under his gift and skill. Again, a wilderness journey is an extended delay in the call and dream you have for your life. All of the seasons of flying, running, and walking can be experienced in it.

In these days, I want to get inside the head of Joseph. Yes, he was a slave—but he was in a sweet spot. He had his master's favor and trust. We can estimate that Joseph served in Potiphar's house for at least seven to ten years. As those years passed and Joseph's anointing and favor continued to grow, I have to wonder if a hope of release for good service was in the forefront of his unspoken thought. If the dream given at seventeen had yet to die in him, I have to think a light at the end of the tunnel had to be conceptualized in his hope. The injury of his brothers and all that had been taken from him would continue to be a bitter pill...but God was *with him.* Surely, the end was on the horizon.

But—Joseph serves a God *That Would Do THAT To Him.* Enter Potiphar's wife...

We don't know her name. We only know that she had a thing for Joseph. We know that she would be yet another devastating tool for divestment in Joseph's journey. Again, if you were questioning Joseph's character back in Canaan, get it settled in your mind now. Joseph was a high integrity individual. While some may be taken into the wilderness to address moral behaviors, the examples given in the scriptures are not so. They are taken to address matters far more intimate—matters of the soul. The emotion, intellect, and will are on the operating table. *or sandpapered on the Carpenter's workbench.. .. ..*

Potiphar's wife threw herself at Joseph on multiple occasions, only to be rebuffed. Joseph was looking at his circumstance in 16:9. On the periphery of his screen was a chance to make the journey back home. But his purity of purpose would cost him. This accusation may have stung in a more poignant way than his brothers' betrayal. (His brothers were simply jealous. Their actions toward him vindicated his righteousness. He was wronged— unjustly so. Yet, his character—his integrity—was not impugned.) This false charge, however, assaulted Joseph in every way that hurt most.

In view of those whom he had spent the last seven to ten years serving faithfully—honestly—fruitfully, he now found himself an accused and convicted rapist—an unfaithful slave who had been given everything, and in his insolence and greed sought to wantonly take more. Some scholars suggest that Joseph taking Potiphar's wife may have been seen as an attempt to take Potiphar's position. I'm unsure of the truth of this, but of one thing we can be certain, to be wrongfully and publicly accused is the mother of all insults and injury to a high integrity person. No doubt Joseph would have pled his case, presented his long faithful, fruitful service to his master. But no one listened. On the edge of a potential *out,* he's repressed further *in*—all the way into Pharaoh's prison.

PROCESSING AND RECRIMINATING

"recriminating" —> 1. to bring a counter charge against an accuser. 2. to accuse in return.[52] *i think jack is using it more along the lines of self-accusation or—not exactly accusation—but calling to mind/intense processing of personal life happenings.*

How's your *life-living* memory? Mine seems to be near photographic. I can't remember numbers or lists given me on the fly. I have to write that stuff down, or my bride ends up with half her list delivered upon my return

---

[52] "recriminate". *Dictionary.com Unabridged.* Random House, Inc. 6 Feb. 2018. <Dictionary.com http://www.dictionary.com/browse/recriminate>.

from Trader Joe's. But, life memories—seasonal life circumstances—play at 4K HD in my mind and emotion. I can you tell you the floor pattern and carpet colors and draw the floor plan of the single-wide trailer I spent my first four years of life in while my dad built our house. I can walk you, hour by hour, through my movements on the day of my wedding —even the day before my wedding (twenty-three years ago).

Maybe yours isn't as vivid as mine, but I would bet if there are any circumstances in your memory that stand out more than others, they would be moments of deep disappointment, injustice, failures, and hurt. These have a way of burning themselves into our memories like nothing else. When I am down emotionally, it takes little-to-no effort for these memories to emerge. It's a rather Herculean effort to conger a good memory. Good memories generally need mental permission to flash, while bad ones often come uninvited. I'm willing to suggest that this is true of Joseph as well.

For seven to ten years, how often had he replayed the dream and the looks on his brothers' faces when he shared it with them? How often had he contemplated his last words to his dad before walking out of the tent opening to that fateful encounter with his brothers? How often did he see in his mind's eye the looks on his brothers' faces as the Midianite traders bound him and led him off? What imaginations or incriminations danced there? We'll never know. Later on in the story, you'll see that his emotion remained strongly engaged on the matter. But here—now—in the prison, what agony of spirit must Joseph have endured, having the dream taken from him once again? (Only this time—seemingly forever.)

He was not in a common prison. He was in Pharaoh's prison. As Potiphar was the chief of the bodyguard for Pharaoh, it would be inconceivable to think that Joseph is unfamiliar with this prison or its officials. No happy endings come from this place. But...again: "the Lord was with Joseph and extended kindness to him, and gave him favor in the sight of the chief jailer." (Gen. 39:21)

Kindness! Are you kidding me?!!! *Kindness* would have been for the Lord to give the Midianite traders a heads up on what was really going on, and beaten the _____ out of Joseph's brothers and spared Joseph this entire excrement sandwich in the first place! *Kindness* would have been for Potiphar to listen to Joseph's story and gain Pharaoh's permission to pay Jacob's sons a little visit to set matters straight. You know—he could have. When playing out the circumstances with no real knowledge of the *greater thing* the Father is doing, it can feel like that. Sorry to be so *raw* with it, but white-washing eloquent 4:3 screened (how we *should feel*) doesn't get us any closer to the place these kinds of circles take us. **A brutally honest and transparent heart gets somewhere, because it is laid bare to the One who is healing it.** So try to *feel* with Joseph. Better yet, let your honest heart-reaction surface. If you find things there that are not pretty, express thanks that it is revealed and engage in repentance. It's what these circles are about. If you're looking at this story with blinders to its outcome, this is more of a *mercy crumb* than a kindness. Yet the truth of the matter is, something huge is coming down the pipe for Joseph. This is—in point of fact—*amazing KINDNESS!*

As God had done with Joseph in Potiphar's house, He does yet again in Pharaoh's prison (Gen. 39:22). It is not long before Joseph is *running the prison.* Did I mention that Joseph is high integrity? How many convicted *master-betraying rapists* end up running the prison? Again, I have to wonder at Joseph's thoughts in this season; in particular, those days before his encounters with the baker and cupbearer. Was he simply making the best of a miserable situation? It looks as if it was a pattern with Joseph. Regardless, he was living the title of this book. Joseph was going in circles and getting somewhere. But—where? At this place in the story, the only view is a dead end.

A NEW HOPE

Sorry—no Jedi here. Just another glimmer of hope that the dream of going home to *the promise* might not be as dead as Joseph thought. We're not sure how long Joseph was in the prison before interpreting the dreams of the baker and cupbearer. Most would assume at least a year prior, yet it is quite possible that it could have been up to three years. In that place, we see the heart of Joseph still able to grab on to any possibility. It comes in the form of interpreting the dreams of his new companions.

I don't want to do any injustice to the portrait of Joseph's overall character. We catch a glimpse of his indomitable spirit in verse seven. In that dead-end place, Joseph playfully engages these two dejected men: "Why are your faces so sad today?"

Joseph is not a walking black hole of depression. The hurt is there, to be sure. You'll see it come out later. Yet, in the day-to-day, he has the strength of heart and character to *live*. For sure, in that place, it could be worse. One has to wonder, how many men had he witnessed being carried lifeless from prison? How many left and didn't come back—or go anywhere else???

Joseph had been given the *kindness* to receive a somewhat secure position, even there. But now a chance—*a new hope*—is dangled in front of his eyes. The opportunity lay with the dreams of these two men. The baker would be hung. The cupbearer, however, would be restored to his position. It was an important position. Author John Davis notes that these positions were far from menial. Both the baker and cupbearer had responsibilities not only to Pharaoh, but to his tomb as well. These individuals looked after the mountain of food and drink that flowed as offerings into this all important facet of Pharaoh's ending.[53] (Some have even suggested that the chief cupbearer would personally ingest any beverage given to Pharaoh as a check against attempted assassination via poison.) Whatever the case, the cupbearer would be in close proximity to Pharaoh. Joseph seizes the chance, asking the cupbearer to *put in the good word* for him once he was restored to his position. He says, "Only keep me in mind when it goes well with you, and please do me a kindness by mentioning me to Pharaoh and get me out of this house." (Gen. 40:15) Can you hear Joseph's inflection? "Get me out of this house!" *Get me out of here. Release me from a life of injustice.*

Better yet, can you imagine Joseph's anxious anticipation as the cupbearer was led from the prison? Did he find a quiet place to laugh, cry, weep, pray, and plead??? I would have. I wonder if his hands trembled at his task that day as his unfocused mind triggered at every move of the chief jailer. Did he sleep that night? Any movement might be word coming that he was to be released. How many days and nights did he live this way before hope turned to questioning—questioning turned to pleading in his spirit—pleading turned to hurt—hurt turned to bitterness—bitterness turned to resignation. I don't say despair. Despair seems somehow removed from Joseph's character. But concerning *the promise,* was there a point in the two years that followed the forgetful betrayal of the cupbearer that he began to be resigned to the thought that for him, there was no *promise?* The dream had been just that—*a dream?*

---

[53] John J. Davis. *Paradise to Prison* (Grand Rapids, MI: Baker Book House, 1975), 273.

How many times have you opened your email and checked your text today hoping for a communication that will change things? Heal the relationship, get the follow-up interview—get the first interview?? How often have you anxiously flipped the mail from the box through your fingers hoping to receive relief from financial strain? Day after day after day with no response —no rescue—nothing.

Joseph is in a very familiar spot. Betrayed. Left. Neglected. It's a circle he's walked before. It's another retest. However, without his even knowing it, he is actually getting somewhere unbelievably significant.

OUT OF PRISON

For two more years, Joseph would be left in the prison he did not deserve. Forgotten. His *chance* having been squandered. But then (there it is again), *Pharaoh* had a dream—a dream so vivid that he immediately summoned magicians and wise men from his kingdom to interpret (v. 8)—but to no avail. This dream did not emanate from the spiritual darkness through which his magicians and wise men worked. This was a God-dream, and they could not help him. And then—finally—the cupbearer *remembered* Joseph (Gen.41:9) and recounted the remarkable accuracy with which Joseph had foretold the very events in which the Pharaoh himself had participated.

This is what *God-timing* looks like. *At this point in the story*, Pharaoh was going to have a dream—and he was going to demand an interpretation. Yet, before he was going to be willing to listen to a slave who was accused of attempted rape by his chief bodyguard's wife—before giving Joseph the time of day—he was going to need a track record and voucher from another of his chief court officials.

In the middle of our desert wanderings, it seems as if the world is stilled. Yet, God is at work from a thousand different places for a thousand different purposes—achieving a thousand different ends—all clamoring in an explosive—*silence*. Joseph couldn't see any of it coming. But there it is— all of its parts moving with divine precision, accomplishing the movements He has set for them.

Verse fourteen says that Joseph was *hurriedly* brought from the prison. Those days immediately following the release of the cupbearer, *this* was what he was waiting for—*expecting*. Two years later, what was his thought when they came to get him? *What have I done now—did I kill the chief jailer's pet cat???* **A few moments for a clean shave and some clean clothes would see Joseph walking into an entirely new season of life.** The Joseph that now approached the throne was not the young man who eagerly shared his dream with his brothers. This is a wizened, humbled, servant-minded Joseph that stood before Pharaoh.

When his interpretation was demanded, Joseph in no way placed himself within the doorway of understanding. He wanted it understood that while his mouth would be moving, it would be *God's words* flowing (Gen. 41:16). He was directing Pharaoh's complete attention to the Dream-giver. Joseph had now become the ultimate servant. He'd had a lot of time to get really good at it. George Otis, Jr. writes:

Are we willing to open the door in such a way that our shadow is not cast across the Master? Where we stand in relation to Christ is no small question. It can determine (at least temporarily) whether and in what measure a spiritual pilgrim is able to look on the object of his or her search. If we choose to stand behind the door (like courtiers or butlers), then all will be well; but if we position ourselves in the doorway (like royalty or celebrities), His visage will be hidden. In the end Christ's profound humility has left Him vulnerable to our movements and priorities. He has left amateurs to stage manage the appearance of a King.[54]

this idea is wrecking me right now—wrecking my need for significance, my need to receive encouragement about how well i am carrying out the tasks God has given me at any given time. it is confronting my battles with insecurity over the years also (which is ultimately self-focus), especially recent years—and well, recent days if i am transparent. can **insecurity** (not just boldness, arrogance, celebrity.. .. ..) actually block the doorway? if i LIVE to hold the door for Jesus to be seen, can all of this dissipate?

humble joseph opened the door wide for the visage of the Dream-giver to be center.

i pray divestment of self will work this in me as well.

---

[54]George Otis, Jr. *God's Trademarks* (Grand Rapids, MI: Chosen Books, 2000), 61.

"i am crucified with Christ, and i no longer live" (galatians 2:20).

At thirty years old, Joseph's high integrity—matched now by his thirteen-year humiliation—prepared him for his initial steps out of his wilderness journey. So much so, that we should hear Pharaoh's recognition of him: "Can we find a man like this, in whom is a **divine** spirit?" I hope that is what is recognized in me as I traverse this journey—the divine Spirit of Christ *being formed in me* (Gal. 4:19).

MANASSEH & EPHRAIM

But, he was not there yet. Even after accurately interpreting Pharaoh's dream of plenty and famine—once again—being placed in the position of managing another master's responsibilities, *the promise* is still a world away. Even so, this is an amazingly sweet time for Joseph. Again, I have to wonder how these days began to reframe his journey from Canaan, to Potiphar, to prison, to—manager of a world superpower? Hear this again: the cycle of flying, running, and walking can and should be experienced in a wilderness journey. This is a flying season for Joseph—even an oasis of healing in many ways. When you don't take the time to place yourself in Joseph's story (deeply pondering the years involved), the favor he appears to receive in Potiphar's house and the prison almost seem to promote a *care-free, easy-come-easy-go* Joseph.

The naming of his children painted a different picture, however. The people of this culture did not whimsically pick their children's names. Namesakes often represented the journey of the parent. Having managed the affairs of Egypt through the seven years of plenty, Joseph was given a wife by Pharaoh. That alone was likely a faraway fantasy for nearly all of his young adult life. And before the seven years of famine arrived, *Joseph became the proud papa of two boys.*

The first he named Manasseh: *bittersweet.* It meant, "God has made me forget all my trouble and all my father's household" (v. 51). If you were thinking that Joseph was the *donkey at the bottom of the well merrily shaking the dirt from his back as his owners attempted to bury* (or *rescue?*) him, (you've heard the illustration and catch phrase—"shake it off and step up."—up, up, and out of the well)—no, if you hold this image—you are missing Joseph. The journey had been full of hurt. He was sold by his blood relatives. He was *robbed* of *the promise*; his character was falsely impugned and life placed in mortal danger. Then, he was left to rot by a friend he had comforted. He was never *ok with it.*

But now, in view of all of the pain and suffering, God gifted him a joy that he thought he may never have again. The hurts and all that was stolen were too deep—but—God did something that eased the pain he felt about his journey—even the enmity he felt toward his brothers. His second son continued the healing: Ephraim—"God has made me fruitful in the land of my affliction" (v. 52). Somehow, in this wilderness of the soul—in his utter loneliness (when he thought his name may die with him in a foreign land), God instead *furthered* his name. The name of Joseph would live. It was a gift beyond his hope in the days of his imprisonment.

FULLY REALIZING HIS DREAM

What more could there be? It's the *well-off*—to *abject poverty*—to *prison* —to *riches and ruler-of-a-super-power* story! But, there would still be more to go for Joseph to fully realize the dream he had shared with his brothers all those years ago. Before they showed up on the scene in chapter forty-two, Joseph seemed content, even happy in his work. The arrival of these traitorous, hard-hearted, self-serving, jealous, _____ (!) illuminate something altogether different welling up from deep inside.

We pick the story up in Genesis forty-two with Joseph personally handling the grain sales. It's one of the many moments in the scriptures where I would have loved to have posted a candid camera in the room. For Jacob to send his sons down into Egypt reveals the desperation of their plight. I would remind you of how Abraham traveled (the load and the people). Multiply that possibly by quite a bit, and you can see how significant a transaction this would need to be. This was not a few destitute men needing some food. This was a large scale transaction that needed Joseph's approval. This falls under the umbrella of *foreign trade. that's hyberbole but likely close to reality, jack. too funny.*

It's highly likely that Jacob's sons were well aware of Zaphenath-paneah's (Joseph's given name by Pharoah) place of authority. So they were very careful to act appropriately. Upon entering Zaphenath-paneah's presence, they bowed to him. (v.6) —— Let me write that again —— **they bowed to him!** Joseph was now at least thirty-eight years old. The dream he received at seventeen finally saw its fulfillment—twenty-one years later!!! And even

190

though verse nine acknowledges that the dream came back to his mind, I'm not sure he fully caught the significance of it in the moment. It all happened in the most unexpected of ways.

Verse seven says he spoke *harshly* with them. My personal thought here is that Joseph was caught in a flash of anger. What flashed in his emotions in those moments is beyond my ability to relate. The last time he saw them, they had ripped his coat from him, probably roughed him up a bit, and forced him into an abandoned well. He had pleaded with them for his life. He likely overhead their negotiations with the Midianite traders to sell him. Who knows what threats his brothers and the slave traders plied to silence him for the journey from all he had ever known. His life had ended on that day.

And on *this* day, they had come unexpectedly through his door, bowed at his feet, asking him for help. I believe what we are reading in these verses (seven through seventeen) is Joseph wrestling with his anger and hurt. If we could have heard his internal debate, it would have been a raging storm, brewing between vengeance and the many things he could do with it. His initial reaction was to imprison all but one of them. He gave them the option to send one brother back to retrieve Benjamin. Joseph wanted the whole sibling gang together, even though Benjamin had nothing to do with it. Perhaps he wanted Benjamin as a witness to the evil his brothers had committed. We don't know. Whatever the motive, the brothers apparently needed time to consider. In truth, *Joseph himself needed time to think.*

The men were held in prison for a further three days. Keeping in mind that Joseph had yet to reveal his identity to these terrified men, it all had to seem so surreal to them. What had they walked into? Three days later, Joseph had had time to soften and returned telling them he feared their God as well. Under the ruse that he suspected them to be spies, he gave them his terms (along with grain to return with), but if they wanted to ever see Simeon again, they would have to come back with Benjamin thereby proving their honesty.

The conversation that his brothers now had in their native tongue seemed to change everything in Joseph's heart. What must it have been like to overhear his brothers' confessions and remorse? What did Reuben's rebuke of his brothers mean to Joseph in those moments? Verse twenty-four says that he *turned and wept.* What had begun in anger was softening to hurt.

I believe much of what follows in chapters forty-two to forty-four is a *mash up* of much of what is roiling in Joseph's emotions and fears. Joseph desired to test his brothers. Would they do to Simeon what they had done to him? Would they abandon a brother to rot in a foreign prison? Before he could open his heart to them, he needed to see if they had changed. Again, whatever the motive, Joseph endured an emotional roller coaster in these days—until it all came to a head in the opening verses of chapter forty-five.

By now, the entire sibling family was back in Joseph's presence, trying to explain their way out of the latest trap that he had set for them as a test. According to Joseph's design, Benjamin's life was now endangered. Judah stepped forward and did what to Joseph would be the unthinkable. This man that had come up with the idea of selling him off as a slave was now offering his life in place of the youngest brother. I imagine that Joseph could see the whole of his life pass before his eyes. Oh my! How everything had changed. Joseph broke.

practically a third of the genesis account is joseph's story. this feels real, and it's evident why God inspired it all to take up such a chunk of the patriarchs' stories. we find ourselves in the hurt and betrayal, remembering offenses committed against us and wondering if we can put them down the way joseph did—all the while feeling with him the hurt—and then later, the healing.

my avid movie-watcher recounts the passion of another individual—though fictional—vividly portraying the passion of his life passing before his eyes and the hurt of years coming to the surface...

There comes a moment in *Forrest Gump* toward the end of the movie when Forrest (who has been sitting all the day long, telling his tale at the bus stop) is finally reunited with the other lead character, Jenny. Jenny is showing him her scrapbook of clippings from Forrest's running adventures when *little Forrest* is dropped off by the babysitter.

Forrest's eyes grow wide in wonder, exclaiming, "Jenny—you've got a son. What's his name?"

Jenny replies slowly, "It's Forrest. I named him after his daddy."

The always-innocent, naive Forrest responds, "You mean, he's got a daddy named Forrest too?"

"No. *You're his daddy, Forrest.*"

And then—you see it. Panic fills Forrest's eyes as he backs away toward the wall. Jenny fears, but even she misunderstands Forrest's reaction.

He says, "Is he smart—or dumb like me?"

Jenny—with understanding realization—replies, "He's smart Forrest, real smart."[55]

Forrest's hand goes to his mouth and great expressions of relief shine out through his tears.

All those years—every insult, every condescending look; he had heard them all. They had hurt—they had hurt him *deeply.* Nothing could be more tragic to Forrest than to pass that hurt onto something so entirely precious. In that moment, *the hurt of all his life comes out for all to see.*
the hurt of allllll of his life comes out.

It's hard for me not to feel the moment with Joseph. Serving as the happy warrior, the unjustly injured, forced-servant, making the best of it all—*he finally breaks.* Joseph, through tears and emotion bulging at the seams to erupt beyond all control, shouts for the room to be emptied of all save his brothers—*and the flood spills over.*

"He wept so loudly that the Egyptians heard it, and the household of Pharaoh heard it" (Gen. 45:2). It was a cry and release that defied all dignity —all of it bottled for so long. He was never really, really ok. The longing never subsided—*the journey always needing to make sense somehow.* It had been sitting on his chest for over twenty-two years. It had been held in the soul as it grew and grew and grew and then...*birth!*

Joseph revealed himself to his brothers—and something else happened as well. Somewhere in those days since he had first laid eyes on his brothers

---

[55] *Forrest Gump.* Directed by Robert Zemeckis, Steve Starkey and Rick Carter. Paramount Pictures, 1994.

(perhaps even in that moment), the dream he had received at seventeen was clarified and fulfilled. The injury that would have gnawed his sleep for twenty-two years—*What about the dream?—What about the promise?*—was brought to his mind in 16:9. He said to his brothers some twenty-two years after telling them his dream: "Now do not be grieved or angry with yourselves, because you sold me here, for God sent me before you to preserve life...God sent me before you to preserve for you a remnant in the earth, and to keep you alive by a great deliverance. Now, therefore, it was not you who sent me here, but God...." (Gen. 45:5-8)

Joseph had gone around, and around, and around—*and had gotten somewhere.* The man that imagined himself *lord* over his brothers at seventeen was now their servant. As seen in Jacob's blessing upon Judah, Joseph was not the *carrier* of *the promise* but rather, a partaker and *servant* of the promise. The authority he now had was but to serve. The wilderness journey had again accomplished its intended design.

YES. GOD WOULD DO THAT.

Would God do that? Would he give a young man full of life and vigor, who loves and honors Him, a dream—then have him kidnapped and sold into slavery, nurture his hope, only to leave him in a prison—a convicted, supposedly disloyal rapist—build his hope again, only to let him stew another two years in an unjustified prison, bring him face-to-face with the men who "did that to him," so he could repay them with kindness unspeakable... .....*Yes!.....to make something great of him.* **Yes, He would do that.**

The list of those whom the Lord has chosen to *take into Egypt* and into a *wilderness journey* is long and distinguished: Abraham, Jacob, Joseph, Moses, Job, David, Hosea—to name a few. Paul, shortly after his conversion and initial forays into Gospel-sharing, disappeared from the scene for awhile (Gal. 1:14-18). Even Jesus, the Firstfruit of our kind, walked His divinely-appointed wilderness (Matt. 4:1-11).

All who have received it have been blessed in it and through it. All who have traversed its trials have come out enlarged, wizened, softened, enlightened, filled, increased in the fruit of the Spirit—coming to a place totally *other* than that which they had departed. Those who knew them before they journeyed out do not recognize them if ever they see them again. Indeed, it may be possible that not all His servants are asked to walk this wilderness, but for those who do and come out on the other side—*they are wholly and beautifully changed.*

SHORTCUTS & WANTING OUT

Nearly a year ago (at the time of this writing), Steph and I, with our two youngest, were in St. Pete Beach, Florida. We were touring children's homes with a young couple seeking to enter the domestic mission field full-time. Our hotel was booked for Venice Beach. The plan was to visit some familiar spots in Pass-a-grille, then take the I-275 skybridge shortcut over to Bradenton. That turnpike turns an hour and a half drive that runs through Tampa then down to Sarasota via I-75 into a thirty-five minute scenic wonder as you cross over the gorgeous blue waters of the bay. We would be there in time for a beautiful sunset and swim with the kiddos. One problem. As we neared the entrance ramp, a Florida Highway Patrol officer blocked the way. Somewhere along the skybridge, a kerosene tanker had caught fire and exploded! Both sides of the skybridge were completely shut down. ALL traffic was being diverted through Tampa. The thirty-five minute shortcut had just been turned into a *seven hour* detour and delay!

didn't i end up reading you an entire book that night in tampa, scott?

If there is one thing that is certain in divinely-appointed wilderness journeys, there are no real shortcuts. Attempted shortcuts are almost certain to turn into even longer delays. We look for these when we fail to discern the season we're in and are ignorant (or perhaps forgetful) of the Spirit's discipline over our lives. We even become indignant at God for allowing the trial, failing to see any real purpose in it. Listen to C.S. Lewis once again:

When a man turns to Christ and seems to be getting on pretty well (in the sense that some of his bad habits are now corrected) he often feels that it would now be natural if things went fairly smoothly. When troubles come along—illnesses, money troubles, new kinds of temptations—he is disappointed. These things, he feels, might have been necessary to rouse him and make him repent in his bad old days; but why now? Because God is forcing him on, or up, to a higher level: putting him into situations where he will have to be very much braver, or more patient, or more loving, than he ever dreamed of being before. It seems to us all unnecessary: but that is because we have not yet had the slightest notion of the tremendous thing He means to make of us.[56]

---

[56] C. S. Lewis. *Mere Christianity* (San Francisco, CA: Harper, 1952), 204-205.

When we come to that place, questioning the very reason for the season, at best we begin to look for shortcuts—at worst, *we look for a way out.*

I mentioned *Much Afraid* in her journey to the high places earlier and the many detours along the way. Earlier in her journey, having come through the detour of the desert, she was now walking hand-in-hand with her given companions, *Sorrow* and *Suffering,* along the *Shores of Loneliness.* It had been a cruel time, as her enemies dogged her footsteps—*Resentment, Self-Pity, Bitterness,* and *Pride*—all shouting contemptuous thoughts from behind every rock and tree. *The promise was a ruse—you'll be left here to die—the more you give, the more He'll ask for—it will never end*—and on it went. But as the story pointed out, already *Much Afraid* was a much different person than the defenseless girl who had once lived in the *Valley of Humiliation.* She was resisting them now.

On one day in particular, while her companions rested, she walked on ahead alone and found herself cornered by her enemies. Even though her cry for the *Chief Shepherd* was met with immediate rescue, she wondered why her adversaries had nearly taken her again. The *Shepherd's* response now hangs on my office wall on canvas with a little flower painted upon it. He says to *Much Afraid:*

"I think," said the Shepherd gently, "that lately the way seemed a little easier and the sun shone, and you came to a place where you could rest. You forgot for a while that you were my little handmaiden Acceptance-with-Joy and were beginning to tell yourself it really was time I led you back to the mountains and up to the High Places. **When you wear the weed of impatience in your heart instead of the flower Acceptance-with-Joy, you will always find your enemies get an advantage over you.**"[57]

This was a flower *Much Afraid* had found in the desert of Egypt, poking up from the sand from behind a tent where just enough sunlight passed to give it life and where a small drip from a tank kept it watered. She had marveled at this plant growing in the harshest of places, and it had a name —*Acceptance-with-Joy. Much Afraid,* inspired by its lovely courage to live with joy in such a place, appropriated the name as her own.[58] For those

---

[57]Hannah Hurnand. *Hinds Feet on High Places* (Uhrichsvill, OH: Barbour, 1987), 88.

[58]Ibid, 78.

196

of us in the long-waiting environments of the wilderness journey, this is the heart that must be maintained—if not nourished or outright created in us—through the trial: *Acceptance-with-Joy.*

Impatience and weariness in the waiting will open the doors to enemies—enemies named Anxiety, Doubt, Fear, Resentment, Delusion, Despair. When these have opportunity to assail through the door of the impatient heart, the temptation to find a shortcut or quit the pursuit is all but inevitable. The outcome from these endeavors will result in *fainting* (Is.40:31) and disillusionment. Hurnard is inspired in naming such impatience a weed.

A weed is pernicious because of its root system. It has a way of tangling deep into the foundation of neighboring root systems. Removing it can sometimes mean taking everything else with it. It's the very thing the enemy delights in "nurturing" in the interiors of your life, and negative thought upon negative thought give it a detestable mangling life. **When it comes to the wilderness experience, the long way is the short way.**

^^^quotable.

Watchman Nee excoriates our tendency to reject the journey as it comes to us. He writes:

> The Holy Spirit has not ceased working. He makes sure one event after another and one difficulty after another come to us... Yet here is our difficulty—we fret over trifles, we murmur at small losses, and we complain about insignificant things. The Lord is ever finding and preparing a way in order to use us. Yet when His hand slightly touches us, we begin to feel unhappy—even to the extent of quarreling with God and having a negative attitude.[59]

remembering nee's thought from earlier. so worth reading again.

These are the attitudes that lead to attempted shortcuts. They are also the very attitudes the Lord means to prune as He seeks to make much of us. Continuing Nee's thought:

> Let us remember that the one reason for all misunderstandings, all fretfulness, all disappointments, is that we secretly love ourselves. Hence, we plan a way whereby

---

[59]Watchman Nee. *The Release Of The Spirit* (New York: Christian Fellowship Publishers, 2000), 15.

we can rescue ourselves. Many times problems arise due to our seeking a way of escape—an escape from the working of the cross...Many go up to the cross rather reluctantly, still thinking of drinking vinegar mingled with gall to alleviate their pain. All who say—*"The cup which **the Father has given me, shall I not drink it?"***—will not drink the cup of vinegar mingled with gall. [60]

Perhaps, it would help to see what *self-rescue* achieves in the desert wanderings. No doubt, my own story has tasted far more of these calamities than I have the heart to share in this space. I would imagine this is true for many of us. After all, there are very few real masochists. If we had known that the shortcuts were not really shortcuts, we never would have attempted them. But like Abram and Sarai bringing Hagar into the picture, we find ways to justify the *umph* we're providing to God's plan for us. Like Abram and Sarai these *umphs* often come in the form of presumption gathered from things *we would like to be hearing in our spirits*. Book two will address this in a very detailed manner, but suffice it to say for now, the pressure of the wilderness journey can produce really well-intentioned thoughts originated in the soul (emotion, intellect and will). Because they might not come directly from the demonic like temptation, they are all-the-more subtle.

Good intention is the most deceptive of all camouflages. It can make itself hardly distinguishable from the genuine voice of the Holy Spirit. This is never more true than when suffering impatience in the wilderness. When we act presumptuously, it can sound much like George Otis, Jr. describes:

We become exercised over a given need or opportunity, and pressure God to provide us with more detail. If He fails to comply, we begin to sweat. Our prayers start to sound like a conversation between an entrepreneur and his banker or a beleaguered field commander begging for air support; *God we're facing a critical moment. There is little time to lose. Do you copy!?* If God still does not reply, or if He fails to deliver the response we deem appropriate, our reaction is often to take matters into our own hands...We rationalize our presumption by declaring to anyone who will listen that God *has* expressed His will. He has placed a fire in our bones that cannot be extinguished. Like Jeremiah we can no longer keep silent. We may lack critical details like project timing, the identity of partners of God's means

---

[60]Watchman Nee. *The Release Of The Spirit* (New York: Christian Fellowship Publishers, 2000), 19.

of provision, but further revelation is just a key turn away. We only need to start the engine.[61]

And then—*failure*. Why? Because there are no shortcuts through the wilderness. And because there are no shortcuts, contrived ones do not carry the *divine come* upon them. Because they attempt to move without favor, they end in frustration, and that frustration leads to more time in the wilderness. Dr. Stevens makes an incredible catch as Moses leads the people on the cusp of taking the *Promised Land*. He notes that this was an *unbelieving* people from the beginning that departed Egypt. Now, on the edge of everything they had dreamed of, Deuteronomy 1:22 reveals that the idea to send in spies was not from the Father. Stevens writes:

...the idea originated in the heart of man—They might well have counted on the faithfulness of God to fulfill what remained and gone forward, depending on Him to do it. But instead of their trusting God and believing His word, they demanded that spies be sent to 'see' the land—We cannot accept God's description of the land of Canaan. We must have it confirmed by man.[62]

Yes, God sent the plagues. Yes, God miraculously and conspicuously rescued our firstborn from the angel of death. Yes, God sent us out of Egypt loaded down with treasure. Yes, God parted a sea, allowing us to pass and then drowning our pursuers. Yes, we all witnessed the anger of God at the calf. Yes, we saw the face of Moses when he came down from the mountain. But this matter of taking the land—that's different. This journey has already taken long enough. We need to know what we're walking into.

Even to Moses, it seemed like a good idea at the time. *Yeah...let's send in the spies. Granted, God has spent hours and hours speaking directly to me—but we had better check this one out—it's the wise thing to do. We'll spy out the land and learn the fastest, easiest way to go about this.* Maybe it was Moses taking matters into his own hands and thinking, *Well...if they won't believe me, maybe if they see it for themselves....* Regardless of the motives, some looking for the easy way—others looking for a way out altogether—it resulted in a forty-year extension of their wilderness wandering.

---

[61]George Otis, Jr. *God's Trademarks* (Grand Rapids, MI: Chosen Books, 2000), 129.

[62]Charles H. Stevens. *The Wilderness Journey* (Chicago, IL: Moody Press, 1971), 163-164.

There is no easy nor direct way out. That's how it is when crossing a desert. Once you've crossed a certain distance, you're dead either way. Without help unlooked for, you might as well forge ahead. This becomes especially true when we come to the darkest parts of our desert—those places where every resource of mind and heart are exhausted—those places where you know all of the arguments. You've engaged the heart of God long enough in the journey to *understand* what He's up to. Maybe not all are asked to go to this place.

I have.

You are naked in the dark, crushed under silent waiting. The only thoughts that speed-think through your mind are questions that only God can answer. The silence is deafening. The heart is searching, groaning, reaching out—and you realize in those moments that you are alone. No one can understand. All they can give you are the things you've already considered. Platitudes, clichés, dumb-founded looks. A.W. Tozer speaks of such a time — and so many God-pursuers have experienced it that it has a name: *The Dark Night of the Soul.* He writes:

> Darkness speaks of not knowing. We want God to *do,* but we want Him to do what He does within the scope of our comprehension. The dark night of the soul, however, is a work of the Holy Spirit that exceeds the ability of any man or woman to understand. When we come through the dark night of the soul, we do not know what has really happened to us, but we do know who has made it happen. [63]

These are times we fear and shun. Some have witnessed brothers and sisters who have endured that lonely night and thought them striving and faithless of spirit. The idea that such a time could overtake us can keep us from pressing further in. Tozer again gets to the heart motive that keeps so many at bay, "We surely want God to do His work in our lives, but we want the lights left on. We want God to do in our hearts and lives that which will bring Him honoring glory, but we want to know and understand every step that he takes in our lives." [64] There's something about having the *knowledge* of what is happening to and around us—that can give a false sense of control. The mind is often called the gate of the soul. (Gates can be shut and closed.) Perhaps it's our defense mechanism of controlling what

---

[63] A. W. Tozer. *The Crucified Life* (Ventura, CA: Regal, 2011), 142.

[64] Ibid, 142.

passes in and out to manage our emotion that is so threatened in this type of dark night experience. The mind gate is a stronger, more sure guardian when it can encompass with understanding those things passing in and out —*but mystery clouds everything.* In those clouds, divine Trojan horses have a way of getting in and attacking everything that was once so secure.

And how do these mysteries find their way in? They are introduced in the form of life circumstances. James 1:2-4—walking us into an ocean of life that is over our heads—giving our souls too much to consider, debate, contain, explain, obtain, control. It's why the next few verses give counsel on the seeking of wisdom to deal with such trials. Yet, if we could only internalize the truth that Nee writes of, we could be so *free:*

Oh, we must realize that all life's experiences, troubles, and trials which the Lord sends are for our highest good. We cannot expect the Lord to give anything better, for these constant difficulties are His best. Should one approach the Lord and pray, saying, "O Lord, please let me choose the best thing for my life." I believe the Lord would tell him, "What I have given you is the best—your daily trials are for your greatest profit."[65]

Not long after this, Nee admonishes, "How foolish are those who have murmurings on their tongues and fires of contention and resentment smoldering in their hearts at the very predicaments the Holy Spirit has measured to them for their good."[66]

If you're reading this in a quiet place, you may be pierced to the heart. I would encourage you here and now to put this book down and *let your offense at your Father fall off.* Tell Him you are sorry for your resentment and anger for all that has transpired in your journey thus far. Make confession to Him that He really is a good Father, and receive that which has come from His hand to you. I know for some, this will be no small matter. I'm personally dealing with my delay in my calling. I make no claim to carrying the load of the death of a spouse or child, terminal disease in body or loved one, perhaps even gross injustice—all things God *could have stopped, but didn't—caused*

---

[65]Watchman Nee. *The Release Of The Spirit* (New York: Christian Fellowship Publishers, 2000), 16.

[66]Ibid, 68.

to be averted, but didn't. **If you want to breathe the free air again, you will have to allow your heart to reconcile with Him.**

He is making much of you.

You are, as John Piper writes in *Desiring God,* deep into the endeavor of *the great business of life.* **It's about walking every path, longing after every dream, to find your heart gradually shifted to an aspiration so much higher than the one you set out to claim. Being with God—to be with God—because He is *all satisfying.*** He writes that, "I never tire of saying and savoring the truth that God's passion to be glorified and our passion to be satisfied are *one* experience in the Christ-exalting act of worship."[67]

So much of our dreams are wrapped up in tasks. Tasks, however, have an end. They have a place of accomplishment, and then what??? Another task? The end of this journey is one that walks us into the Infinite Heart that satisfies continually. The pail. The desert journey is likely to show us the futility of celebrating *call* over *being.* It will bring us hard into the battle of the mind that asks, **"Where will we drink? Where will we feast?—Feast on God"**[68] (again from Piper).

WAYS OUT OF THE WILDERNESS

I'm not completely sure about this, but, I think there are only three ways out of the wilderness. (1) You resist so totally, being overcome by hateful grief that God removes your birthday suit prematurely. (2) You quit and settle and—never see the promise but possibly lessen the temporary pain. (3) You come out loving God more than *the promise* and nowhere near where you started from. I resist even mentioning the first two possibilities, yet an honest reading of the scriptures testifies to their veracity. An entire generation of Israelites settled for the wilderness and were never able to leave it (Deut. 1:34-35). Some grumbled and rebelled and were swallowed by the earth (Num. 16). Both of these eventual exits were by death. We won't flesh these out here, hopeful in the confidence "that He who began a good work in you will perfect it until the day of Christ Jesus" (Ph. 1:6)—and that

---

[67]John Piper. *Desiring God* (Sisters, OR: Multnomah Publishers, 2003), 12.

[68] Ibid, 12.

"The Lord will accomplish what concerns *you*" (Ps. 138:8 italics mine) for those who are patient in the wilderness. **More than anything, and more than ever, I am convinced that the *perfected accomplishment* that awaits you is a heart that has grown to *love God more than the promise.* While I certainly believe God will fulfill his promises to us, what will make our hearts happy in the end will be *Him.*** Piper writes:

...in the end the heart longs not for any of God's good gifts, but for God Himself. To see Him and know Him and be in His presence is the soul's final feast. Beyond this there is no quest. Words fail. We call it pleasure, joy, delight. But these are weak pointers to the unspeakable experience: "One thing have I asked of the Lord, that will I seek after: that I may dwell in the house of the Lord all the days of my life, to gaze upon the beauty of the Lord and to inquire in his temple" (Psalm 27:4). "In your presence there is fullness of joy; at your right hand are pleasures forevermore" (Psalm 16:11). "Delight yourself in the Lord" (Psalm 37:4).[69]

Is Piper right that *beyond this, there is no quest*? I would humbly venture yes—and no. Yes, to enjoy God and be enjoyed by Him is the highest and final end. Nowhere in all of scripture are we told that our task or our assignment fills anything permanent in the soul. Only Infinite Essence does that. **Yet, we are made to *do* and *be.*** I would contend that part of enjoying God is being satisfied and content being a thing that is *doing* what it was made to do. If we'll look closely, so much of the *personal promise* that God places before us is related to *becoming that thing that does what it was created to do.* If you're reading these pages, the confusion could be rather disheartening. Are you saying, Scott, that I should cease to care about *the promise*? No! In the end, you will find that being shaped to love God more will be the very thing that births fruit *into your promise.* Nee helps us to grasp the point:

Here is invariably a spiritual fact: Our spirit is released according to the degree of our brokenness. The one who has accepted the most discipline is the one who can best serve. The more one is broken, the more sensitive he can be. The more loss one has suffered, the more he has to give. Wherever we save ourselves, it is at that very place where we become spiritually useless. Wherever we preserve and excuse ourselves, it is at that point where we are deprived of spiritual sensitivity

---

[69]John Piper. *Desiring God* (Sisters, OR: Multnomah Publishers, 2003), 87.

and supply. Let no one imagine he can be effective if he disregards this basic principle.[70]

"the one who has accepted the most discipline is the one who can best serve."[71]

Loving God will not diminish the promise, but rather, fulfill it. "For whoever wishes to save his life will lose it; but whoever loses his life for My sake will find it" (Matt.16:25). It's not one or the other when it comes to loving God and receiving the promise—it's **both/and.** But be warned. God is not mocked, nor is he fooled by any hidden agenda. You will not be able to *use Him* to gain the promise. It will be a subtle endeavor on your part laden with good intentions. Being focused so intently on receiving God's promises (especially when they are Kingdom related), can lead to much presumption and manipulation. The beauty of the wilderness journey is that it is patient until all of our well-intentioned schemes are illuminated and left in the ruin of failed endeavors. This journey will leave the plans *you made soulishly* (designed to manipulate divine favor) in naked abject failure and ruin. God will see to it that those who walk this journey to completion get the proverbial *horse before the cart.*

There is very good reason for it. A.W. Tozer addresses it: "We are more interested in the gift than the giver. God wants to give us Himself. God wants to impart Himself *with* His gift. Separated from God, the gift is dangerous."[72] The Israelites could have gotten their land. But without God, they soon would have devolved into the base lifelessness of the Canaanite cultures, giving their firstborn daughters as temple prostitutes and even burning their firstborn sons in the fires of Molech—becoming a people hopelessly intermingled in satan's dominion. Joseph's brothers could have bowed then and there in his father's tent only to starve years later, if not worse. Peter could have remained a *bull in a china shop* and not seen the day that his inspired epistles were written.

---

[70]Watchman Nee. *The Release Of The Spirit* (New York: Christian Fellowship Publishers, 2000), 50-51.

[71] Ibid, 50-51.

[72]A. W. Tozer. *The Crucified Life* (Ventura, CA: Regal, 2011), 150.

Closer to home, you could receive your promise, but lack the zoe life that the Spirit breathes in communal fellowship, having no power to live it out well or to its fullest, and thus be utterly disappointed and disillusioned fully in the end. Our *purpose and promise* are temporary. They have an end, therefore they cannot fully satisfy. Only the Infinite can do that. Loving God more than *the promise* is **everything.**

IF YOU ARE IN THE WILDERNESS

In your wilderness—if indeed you are in one—let God be God. Tozer refers to it as the key to the entire journey:

I do not believe in keys, per se, but if there ever were a key to unlock the mystery of living the crucified life, it is simply this: Allow God to be Himself...Perhaps the ultimate truth here is that when we allow God to be Himself, we then—and only then—discover who and what we are as men and women.[73]

How ingenious we are at creating a God that somehow fits our worldview and general life circumstance. Some have a harsh, controlling God—others a cheerleading, doting grandparent God—still others, the aloof, distant God. For some, He is the God who presses you down, never allowing your nose more than two inches from the dust. Many serve the God who is holding the *other shoe* prepared to drop it at the most inopportune moments (all for your ultimate good, of course). Whatever the God your mind and experience have created, the same problem exists: YOU CREATED IT.

Allowing God to be God does something so incredibly pure and altogether wonderful. It gives you the unblemished, unclouded, 16:9 ultra HD picture of where He is taking you. In the midst of the journey, isn't that what you want to know?! "Why do you say oh Jacob and assert oh Israel that my way is hidden from the Lord?" (Is. 40:27). **He is taking you full circle, all the way back to what you were created to be—a cherished child breathed into His image.** "God created man in His own image, in the image of God He created him; male and female He created them" (Gen. 1:27).

If you want to know where you're headed and what it will ultimately look like, that's it. "The purpose of God is not to save us from hell; the purpose

---

[73]A. W. Tozer. *The Crucified Life* (Ventura, CA: Regal, 2011), 152.

of God is to save us to make us like Christ and to make us like God."[74] (*tozer once again.*) When we allow God to be God, and we're given eyes that can see God as He is, *we see clearly what we are being disciplined to become.* The desert journey will clear our sight like few things can. We will wander in its circles, eventually coming to that place that is a place of infinite love, majesty, and beauty.

Embrace this journey! I want to share with you a lengthy excerpt from Henri Nouwen's journal. (You may remember the name from earlier in the book as the man who wrote so affectionately about the flying trapeze.) It comes from the last year of his life and represents well the fruit of the journey. I'm hoping you'll make it your own:

The anxiety that has plagued me during the last week shows that a great part of me is not yet 'abiding' in Jesus. My mind and heart keep running away from my true dwelling place, and they explore strange lands where I end up in anger, resentment, lust, fear, and anguish. I know that living a spiritual life means bringing every part of myself home to where it belongs.

Jesus describes the intimacy that he offers as the connectedness between the vine and its branches. I long to be grafted onto Jesus as a branch onto the vine so that all my life comes from the vine. In communion with Jesus, the vine, my little life can grow and bear fruit. I know it, but I do not live it. Somehow I keep living as if there are other sources of life that I must explore, outside Jesus. But Jesus keeps saying, "Come back to me, give me all your burdens, all your worries, fears, and anxieties. Trust that with me you will find rest." I am struggling to listen to that voice of love and to trust in its healing power...

My true spiritual work is to let myself be loved, fully and completely, and to trust that in that love I will come to the fulfillment of my vocation. I keep trying to bring my wandering, restless, anxious self home, so that I can rest there in the embrace of love[75] (italics mine).

i had to find the song below online (and make a bowl of cereal)—and listen to it on repeat for the last chapter. maybe you should make a bowl of cereal and listen too, friend.

---

[74]A. W. Tozer. *The Crucified Life* (Ventura, CA: Regal, 2011), 164.

[75]Henri J. M. Nouwen. *Sabbatical Journey* (New York, NY: The Cross Road Publishing Co. , 1998), 165.

ENOUGH

All of You is more than enough for all of me
For every thirst and every need
You satisfy me with Your love
And all I have in You is more than enough

You are my supply
My breath of life
And still more awesome than I know
You are my reward
worth living for
And still more awesome than I know

All of You is more than enough for all of me
For every thirst and every need
You satisfy me with Your love
And all I have in You is more than enough

You're my sacrifice
Of greatest price
And still more awesome than I know
You're the coming King
You are everything
And still more awesome than I know

More than all I want
More than all I need
You are more than enough for me
More than all I know

More than all I can say
You are more than enough for me
–Chris Tomlin [76]

---

[76] Passion. *Our Love Is Loud.* Sparrow Records, Sixstep Records 7243 8 51923 0
2 / SPD 51923, 2002, compact disc.

i have no idea how to explain how reading this—and writing this—is painfully excruciating and life-givingly freeing all at the same time.

we recently had the dearest of friends (someone very intimately involved in our current ministry assignment) ask us why scott says he is in a wilderness journey now. she sees how God has worked in our church family and in the story of the past few years, and how He has walked this out with us. she is puzzled by the expression and how it seems to include this sweet time and sweet season of church planting in a seventeen-year trial—going on eighteen years of HARD. if she has an opportunity to read this book, it may make a little more sense to her with the understanding of the big picture for us...of falling off and getting back on the bike so many, many times—of holding vision with expectation over and over and over again while carrying the heavy weight and relentless burden of disappointed hope. but. i do see her point (and will never forget the compassionate expression on her face that accompanied the question).

when we talk of a **wilderness journey**, it may sound all completely negative—lost. wandering. lonely possibly. scarce, not abundant. frustrating. joy-stealing. but—and i think jack has done a good job of explaining—it's not all those things. we may FEEL some of those things sometimes, but ultimately, it is a place of living life in the context of seeing one thing and experiencing quite another—time and again—and letting God rewrite hope on our hearts each time. entrusting our souls to His care in the knowledge that He is making something of us in the falling, in the failing...and in the rising. and **most** importantly in it all, He is allowing us to see **Him** as **more than enough** in it all.

CHAPTER 9

THE WAY, THE TRUTH, & THE LIFE
ENCOURAGEMENT! (HE HAS NOT LOST YOUR WAY!)

Perhaps you're looking at these last few chapters and wanting off the world. There was a genuine fear in writing these things that they might depict a journey without life or joy and that somehow, your vision would turn to 4:3 and miss the beauty along the way. I want to be sure that you are left with an encouraging thought—not for *encouragement's* sake and especially not as an anesthetic for your emotion. But what I want to share in this chapter is the promise that you carry in the journey: *He has not lost your way.* (from Is. 40:27). (For Him to lose your way would be for Him to have lost Himself, because He has taken up residence inside of you!) He is with you for the *entire* way—and that's what we want to take a look at over these last few pages.

Jesus says to us, "I am the way, and the truth, and the life; no one comes to the Father but through Me." (Jn. 14:6)

However, before diving into that, let's back up a moment so we can catch the fullness of it.

It begins with an allusion to all that's been said in the course of this book, especially for those of you in walking places or wilderness journeys. Jesus says, "Do not let your heart be troubled." (Jn. 14:1) The mirrored realities then, are things that would trouble the heart. I would remind you that these words in Jn. 14:1-6 were given in the midst of the last meal He would share with them before His trial and crucifixion. He was dropping some heavy stuff. They were not sure how to respond as He washed their feet. He dropped the bomb that one of the twelve was going to betray Him. He let Peter know (right there in front of everybody), that he would deny Him. And—He told them He was going somewhere that they couldn't follow. *Nobody in that room was comfortable.* It was supposed to be a meal of remembrance and celebration—the Passover meal. But it was heavy that night.

A lot of what Jesus was saying in chapters thirteen through seventeen did not sound like the Kingdom they had been expecting—lots of mystery swirling in their midst. Perhaps, these circles and the discipline that inhabits them have you feeling that way.

>>*Let not your heart be troubled; believe in God, believe also in Me.* (Jn. 14:1)<<

Let's say it again. The Father wants to be believed and trusted by His kids. If you can believe it, all is not as hard and bleak as it may appear. It is not *all* battle. (*nor wilderness journeying*) Even when it *is* battle, you will find you have something special that makes you the *happy warrior* (*or the joy-filled wanderer!*) along the way.

Back to Jesus in verse two. He has just told them He's going someplace they can't come...yet. He more than drops the hint now: "In My Father's house are many dwelling places; if it were not so, I would have told you; for I go to prepare a place for you." (Jn. 14:2) I hope you don't think I'm rabbit-trailing here! I'm not, friend.

If we're talking about journey, *we can't miss the final destination!*

PREPARING A PLACE

It carries the theme of *marriage* all through the Gospels, climaxing in Revelation. It's obvious that they didn't catch it in the moment, but clearly, they get it later. Jesus is doing what every Jewish man hopes to do in His lifetime: get the new home ready for His bride. In our western christianized culture, we do *engagement* founded upon Judaic custom, yet miss half of the significance it carried.

Jewish engagement could last for years. They are not, however, idle years. The bride would spend those years in preparation for the wedding. She was trained by her mother in all of the ways that might serve her husband best. She learned duties that would make the home thrive and become a place of rest and beauty. Her father saw to it that it would be a celebration that would be the crowning moment of his parentage. Not only that, he prepared a grand feast—a feast that could go for days! If it was a moderately wealthy Jewish family, the phrase to *rain food and drink* would hardly suffice. The preparation for these days could be lengthy, even years long.

The groom, in this period, does not sit idly by (as we do), dumbfounded by the tornado of extravagance as it blows financial sanity to the far ends of the earth. The only thing I did to get ready for my wedding was to be fitted for my tux. Steph ran the details by me, but I can honestly say I didn't *get* or *hear* any of it. I simply saved up for the honeymoon (most of which was gifted to us). I've officiated a number of weddings since then and don't feel so bad, as I've seen few men do much more. Yet, this is where we miss it.

The Jewish groom sets to work building a home for his bride, and this could mean any number of things for the young Jewish man. It could mean building on to the family dwelling (perhaps an extensive remodel). It may mean obtaining land and building from scratch. It may mean building a financial *nest egg* that would appease the Jewish father to know he wasn't handing his daughter off into abject poverty and so *gaining the son-in-law* he never wanted to mooch off the family assets that are meant for the sons. Whatever the case, *it was a project that required significant finance and time.* During this season, the house—the dwelling—is a mystery to the bride. It was meant to be a surprise ~ a gift to this woman ~ a dream that she would make her own. *He goes to prepare a place for her.*

For long years, I avoided ordination in ministry simply to avoid being asked to officiate a wedding *for the sole reason of evading the pretense of the day.* (I am only half jesting.) Brides scared me. Young girls driving themselves to exhaustion with friends tempted to hide in corners from short tempers and bridezilla panic attacks were things I wanted to avoid. To me, the wedding was about the vows. For crying out loud, make your promises and go live them!!! Save the money and put it in a savings account!

Attending the wedding of a former student in our ministry changed all of that for me. The pastor officiating the wedding did something that had never occurred to me. He complimented the bride for all of her work, connecting the dots to Revelation and the coming of the Groom for the Bride. (Rev. 19:7-9; Matt. 22:1-14; 25:1-13) The picture could not have been more vivid. All that she had done: visits to caterers, visits to venues, dresses, dresses and more dresses!—tuxes, cakes and wines, music and musicians, flowers, table arrangements, invitations (to showers, wedding, and reception), registering for gifts, writing vows, unity candles, toasting glasses, places for out-of-town family to stay, weather contingencies... ahhhhh!!!!!!!—*was all worth it.*

Why? Because it is the perfect symbol for what our birthday suit walking in Jesus is to be all about—getting ready for that glorious day when the Father throws the biggest wedding feast of all time before showing us our new homes he has been preparing since A.D. 33!!! If you're curious, I believe He gives a teaser in Revelation 21 through 22:5. You should spend some time with it. Hint: If this is a literal city that will come down to earth, the earth will have to be enlarged as the city's foundation is simply too large to be accommodated by the planet's current curvature. It's a sizable *wow!*

Friend, let not your heart be troubled. **He has not lost your way.**

We have a date, you and I—a day long-planned, a destination nearing its completion. A time when we will sing the *new song* (Rev. 5:9-10).

Yet, before then, there is great **comfort** *in the here and now.*

Remember the *cutting covenant* with Abraham. Recall that it was a one-way covenant! Something that *God* is doing!! (the comfort!!!!! —>) ***The cross and grace of Jesus have confirmed that covenant in full to us.***

In all of these circles that we will traverse—in every walking season—in every hard place in the desert, He will be getting His bride ready for His wedding!

You are a prized child of God and cherished bride of Christ. Our place in this journey is, as A.W. Tozer said, to *let God be God,* **walking the** *way* **that He has placed before us.**[77]

i have the beautiful privilege of coming back to this second printing/edition to share that a year and a half after its initial publication (and jack's perfect description of Christ's provisions for His bride^^^), we are in the throws of helping to plan our oldest son's wedding, and this is surreal.. .. ..
and very REAL.

and we are helping tsion and his soon-to-be bride fix up an adorable perfect-for-them basement apartment of dear friends in our neighborhood

---

[77]A W. Tozer. *The Crucified Life* (Ventura, CA: Regal, 2011), 152.

from whom they will be renting. (two millennia removed from first century jewish culture and the beautiful, sometimes extravagant preparations that they made, but a fun comparison)..

on a perfect mid-november day—exactly 102 days from today! (but who's counting?), my son and beautiful new daughter will be a picture of Jesus and the Church and will serve communion to their guests as they think of it.. .. ..

and they will go out of town for a few days.. .. ..

and they will come HOME to a perfect place. a place prepared for them.

"if we're talking about journeying, we can't miss the final destination!" .. .. .. and He is the One preparing US as He prepares a place for us. He is the way.. .. ..(back to john 14..)

THE WAY

I totally get Thomas's response to Jesus from verse four. *"...you know the way where I am going."* Uhh...(paraphrasing Thomas) *No, Jesus—we don't have a clue. You're talking mansions and your Father—completely lost on that one* (v.5). We are such earth-bound creatures that when we hear the Spirit speak, we immediately begin to search the physical for touch-and-feel realities. We want facts on the ground. Not often does God offer such *realities.* Remember: He wants His kids to trust Him. Jesus was revealing a vast spiritual truth to Thomas and the disciples. He was taking them to something that would transcend Jerusalem and the Roman world. When we talk about life with Jesus, do you notice that we have to use descriptors like *taking, going, walking, moving,* etc.? Thomas had in mind what we often have in mind: a door to walk through—and you're there. Jesus rarely draws our attention to that kind of conclusion. We're always directed to *a way.*

The theme runs through all of the patriarchal journeys and even to the church fathers. ABRAHAM *walked* a spiritual wilderness of nearly twenty-five years. With God, in total, he *walked* an estimated 1,500 miles. When he passed at age 175 (Gen. 25:7), he was still on the journey. JACOB, having been outmatched for scheming and manipulating, spent fourteen years trying to get the wife of his dreams! He spent twenty years in all in Northern Mesopotamia for fear of Esau's wrath. At Penuel, he had the most ridiculous wrestling match of all time and won by losing (Gen. 32:25-32). The rest of his life, he *walked* with a limp from a broken hip.

JOSEPH received the dream at seventeen as an ambitious teenager, full of life. He spent the next twenty-two years walking where his masters told him to walk. He would be in his forties before his dream would come to fruition, and he would be reunited with his father. MOSES, at age forty, escaped to the wilderness of Midian. It would be another forty years before the Lord would send him back. Back again in Egypt, Pharaoh didn't simply let the Jewish people go. It was an emotional *journey*—start-to-finish— which *walked* Moses out of Egypt into another wilderness that would evolve into an additional forty-one years journeying with God.

DAVID's life is an absolute roller coaster. Perhaps in him, more than any other, we get to see the lowly with the highest of highs—the holy besmirched in the filth, only to be raised and renewed. He's the young shepherd slaying a giant with a sling—the young man of high destiny anointed to be king, hiding in caves and acting as a *crazy man* among the Philistines—the conqueror of Mt. Zion, Philistines, Moab, Zobah, Syria, and Ammon—worshiper and Ark celebrator—adulterer and murderer ~ *repentant one* ~ disobedient census taker—civil war sufferer—father of Solomon and temple preparer ~ and ~ Psalm writer! All of that *walked*, endured, *lived* over a lifetime with God.[78]

If the Old Testament narrates the theme, the New Testament secures it in much of its imagery. "For we **walk** by faith, not by sight..." (2 Cor 5:7) ~ "But I say, **walk** by the Spirit, and you will not carry out the desire of the flesh." (Gal.5:16) ~ "If we live by the Spirit, let us also **walk** by the Spirit." (Gal. 5:25) ~ "but if we **walk** in the Light as He Himself is in the Light, we have fellowship with one another, and the blood of Jesus His Son cleanses us from all sin." (1 Jn 1:7) ~ "Do you not know that those who **run** in a race all run, but *only* one receives the prize? **Run** in such a way that you may win." (1 Cor 9:24)

---

[78] Nelson's. *Nelson's Complete Book of Bible Maps & Charts* (Nashville, TN: Thomas Nelson, 1996), 14-110.

luke records Jesus' words compelling us to count the cost of this
journey/path/race we are walking/running:

For which one of you, when he wants to build a tower, does not first sit down and calculate the cost to see if he has enough to complete it? Otherwise, when he has laid a foundation and is not able to finish, all who observe it begin to ridicule him, saying, 'This man began to build and was not able to finish.' Or what king, when he sets out to meet another king in battle, will not first sit down and consider whether he is strong enough with ten thousand men to encounter the one coming against him with twenty thousand? Or else, while the other is still far away, he sends a delegation and asks for terms of peace. So then, none of you can be My disciple who does not give up all his own possessions. (Lk. 14:28-33)

"Therefore, since we have so great a cloud of witnesses surrounding us, let us also lay aside every encumbrance and the sin which so easily entangles us, and let us *run* with *endurance* the *race* that is set before us..." (Heb. 12:1) ~ "I have fought the good fight, I have finished the *course*, I have kept the faith" (2 Tim 4:7) ~ "And He was saying to them all, 'If anyone wishes to *come after* Me, he must deny himself, and take up his cross daily and *follow Me.*'" (Lk. 9:23)

All of it: the distance, walking, running the race, enduring, consuming of time, journeying—He is the way.

PASTURES & FENCES

Speaking of following, walking back from a break-down session from a discipleship retreat lesson (with students in our ministry), I was in a conversation with my mentor, Larry, who had accompanied us on the retreat. Only an hour before, we had playfully *stormed* the Museum and Spanish American War relic of Fort Desoto. We were remarking how the body (the church body/the body of Christ) takes fortresses—that forts don't go. They sit and hold. Larry recounted a conversation he had with a friend about Jewish shepherding; remarking on the opening verses of John chapter ten, and I had to do a *double-take*. It reads:

Truly, truly, I say to you, he who does not enter by the door into the fold of the sheep, but climbs up some other way, he is a thief and a robber. But he who enters by the door is a shepherd of the sheep. To him the doorkeeper opens, and the sheep hear his voice, and he calls his own sheep by name and leads them out. When

215

he puts forth all his own, he goes ahead of them, and the sheep follow him because they know his voice. (Jn. 10:1-4)

Larry opened my eyes to the cultural barrier that I had, which had been preventing me from understanding the full message of the passage. I have grown up in an agricultural world. Yet, in all of that world, all the pastures have fences. As we drive the North American landscape (especially in the South and Midwest), we pass them by every day. We have no concept of an open range. If a cow or lamb is seen walking along the road or through the neighborhood, it's safe to say, *it got out*. Yet, Jewish shepherding was not so.

The targets of Jesus' symbolism were those Jewish people who had lived their entire lives enslaved in Pharisaical legalisms. The day of Sabbath rest had become a prison to them. The sacrificial system had become a financial burden. The Pharisees themselves had become the *behavior police*. Jesus did warn that there had been some—and would be some—that would attempt to lead them out of this fortress of law, but they would be robbers. These would ultimately reject the Law-*Giver* along with the law itself. Jesus, however, was not one of these. He would come as a Shepherd. He would open the gate, call them by name, and *lead them out*. Where would he lead them?

The Lord is my shepherd, I shall not want. He makes me lie down in green pastures; He leads me beside quiet waters. He restores my soul; He guides me in the paths of righteousness for His name's sake. Even though I walk through the valley of the shadow of death, I fear no evil, for You are with me; Your rod and Your staff, they comfort me. You prepare a table before me in the presence of my enemies; You have anointed my head with oil; my cup overflows. Surely goodness and lovingkindness will follow me all the days of my life, And I will dwell in the house of the Lord forever. (Ps. 23:1-6)

He leads us to good pasture. Yet, good pasture doesn't stay *good pasture* forever. Eventually, it is grazed to the ground. So, the Shepherd is always looking for and taking his sheep to the *next good place*. He takes His sheep to places where the water is calm and clean enough to drink. These are streams which quietly flow (not troughs of stagnant sun-heated pools). The path is a character-building path—a path of righteousness. There will be times when the path to the good pasture land will pass through dangerous places, dry barren places, lonely places. But He is good and will lead you through to the next good place.

You can follow Him and not be afraid—not be anxious about the need. He will bring discipline into your journey. Once you recognize its benefit, you will find comfort in knowing it's there. Because of it, you don't have to worry about veering too far off the path. He will complete the journey with you in tow. **With all of that in mind, you can let a confidence rise into full blossom that sees His goodness as a point of fact and—a confidence that you will experience it *in* and *on* your days.** Jesus, the good Shepherd, walks His sheep *in* and *on* this *way.*

I'm hoping you can hear this as an encouragement. Events can hold so much negative memory and are circumstantial. A *way*—a journey—a *path* can make these seem as blips; small bumps in the rearview mirror as the Shepherd is taking you to the next place. If you're thinking of life in terms of *events*, there is too much pressure in that. *!!!!!!!!!* Mess that up and you're likely to feel finished. You had your chance, and you blew it. **See life as a journey, and you get opportunity day-by-day for redemption. You wake to find His mercies are new every morning (Lam. 3:23). Embrace Jesus as *the way,* and embrace the *way* of Jesus!**

THE TRUTH

A small bit of poetry written by Bilbo Baggins for his friend Strider—Telcontar—Aragorn Elessar the elf stone, heir of Elendil reads, *"Not all who wander are lost..."*[79] (from Tolkien's *Lord of the Rings*). At the very least, it is a subconscious fear that hovers at the foundations of our thought: that He has *lost our way.* The hard parts of life-living can feel that way. Yet, when we can acknowledge the *truth* that these circles we walk are by design and impregnated with purpose and intent, we can begin to see that *we are not lost at all.* The good Shepherd knows exactly where He is taking us. The lands about are new to us, perhaps, **but not to Him.** It is here that we shall see: not only is He the *way,* He is also the *truth.* In its original Greek form, it was *aletheia.* Strong's Dictionary defines it as "signifying the reality lying at the basis of an appearance; the manifested, veritable essence of a matter."[80] Simply said, it is the basement of reality.

[79]J. R R. Tolkien. *The Lord of The Rings* (New York: Houghton Mifflin Co. , 1994), 241.

[80]James Strong. *The New Strong's Dictionary of Bible Words.* (Nashville, TN: Thomas Nelson, 2001), 930.

Jesus is the way and the very rock and foundation of what *is*. Beyond the matrix of our imaginations, the lies of the evil one, and the propaganda of human thought, there lies that which truly *is*. But I think there's more to the idea of what Jesus is saying about Himself in this descriptor. *Aletheia* comes from the root *Alethes,* which has at its very core, the idea of being "unconcealed, manifest."[81] Now, we are getting somewhere. This helps to explain the symbolism which seems to exist between *light* and *truth* in New Testament writings. It can be easily seen in 1 John 1:7-8, "but if we walk in the Light as He Himself is in the Light, we have fellowship with one another, and the blood of Jesus His Son cleanses us from all sin. If we say that we have no sin, we are deceiving ourselves and the truth is not in us."

Light is a revealer. It leaves no place to hide. If we try to say we don't have sin, it is obvious that the truth—the *light of truth* is not operative in us, because **truth reveals** and gets to the basement of reality in our lives. It will show us who we really are. It's why David cries out to the Lord, "*search me and try me and see...*" (Ps. 139:23, italics mine). God is truth. He *searches* and *reveals* the heart of David. James writes, "For if anyone is a hearer of the word and not a doer, he is like a man who looks at his natural face in a mirror..." (James 1:23). Mirrors only work in the light. The word which is *truth* is a light *un-concealing* that which was hidden from you. With this in mind, let's hear it again. Jesus is the *way* and the *truth*—He is light on the path. Walking with God is not walking blindly. We walk with someone Who sees perfectly.

LIGHT FOR THE PATH

On the evening following the day I had finished the previous chapter on wilderness journeys, Steph and I were walking our youngest son, Aiden Journey, back from the beach. The house in which we were staying is roughly three quarters of a mile from Venice Beach. Making our way home through a central park which runs from the beach to the Historic District of Venice, FL, Aiden Journey wanted to experiment. He asked Steph to hold his hand and simply walk him back to the house; he was going to keep his eyes closed for the entire way. (It's a winding path which criss-crosses on itself with three major crosswalks along the way.)

---

[81] James Strong. *The New Strong's Dictionary of Bible Words.* (Nashville, TN: Thomas Nelson, 2001), 931.

With only a few brief peeks (one to stop and look at an amazing banyan tree), we made it safe and sound to our temporary home on Pedro Street. At first, Steph would warn him of impending hills and bumps. Aiden soon asked us to stop with the descriptions altogether. He was supremely confident that we could see well enough for him. We were his light for the walk. And though I am often prone to practical jokes, his mother is not. Every potential tripping spot along the way was foreseen by her careful eye. Aiden Journey would not stumble even once.

It's a beautiful picture, is it not? As profound as it may sound, what Jesus is saying here is more than that. While it is true that along the way, there are places where we trust His keen foresight wholly and step blindly, most of our walking is not that way. Jesus' admonition in Matthew 6:34 does allude to that kind of faith: "So do not worry about tomorrow; for tomorrow will care for itself. Each day has enough trouble of its own." Even the model prayer more than suggests it: "Give us this day our *daily* bread" (Matt. 6:11 italics mine). There is mystery in the journeying.

Yet, James 1 reveals something closer to our current fear and concern. It falls in line and merges the two concepts represented in Matthew 6:34 and 6:11 and in James. He writes, "But if any of you lacks wisdom, let him ask of God, who gives to all generously and without reproach, and it will be given to him." (James 1:5) Remember the context. This is not a verse to pull out during times of general confusion and perplexity. Verses two through four have just told us to consider it a joy when the hard of life comes our way. *When in the midst of the trial, you haven't a clue what to do, where to go, how to feel, ask ME for direction. I am the good Shepherd who has called you out by name, and I have light for this path.*

You can walk this path of Jesus knowing that there is light for it. It is true. It is real, and therefore, discernible. Something unthinkable, perhaps the greatest miracle in all of what is, guarantees it. I quoted this thought earlier from Andrew Murray, and I want to bring it back to mind. HEAR IT!:

The Holy Spirit is the Inmost Self of the Father and the Son. My spirit is my inmost Self. The Holy Spirit renews that inmost self, and then dwells in it, and fills it. And so He becomes to me what He was to Jesus, the very life of my personality. [82]

---

[82]Andrew Murray. *The Spirit of Christ* (Fort Washington, PA: Christian Literature Crusade, 1963), 18-19.

LIGHT THAT SAVES THE SOUL

Let me give you the *elevator version of the book following this one*—within the context of the circles (and this character-sandpaper-process living).

It's nothing new and many theologians have used it. If I could draw you, you would look like this:

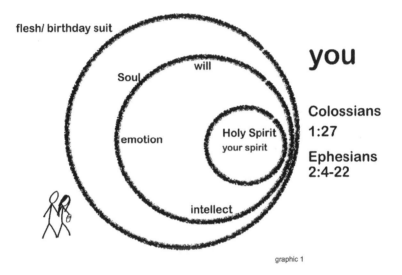

graphic 1

If what we have said thus far about the *purposes* of the seasons is true —especially for those in wilderness journeys—James 1:21 will take on an entirely new meaning for you. He says, "Therefore, putting aside all filthiness and all that remains of wickedness, in humility receive the word implanted, which is able to save your souls."

Understanding that James is writing to Jewish believers who are already "saved," the context needs to focus on the specifics of *what* exactly is *being saved*. It is the soul. The *psuche* (in the Greek)—literally referring to the emotion, intellect, and will. The unity of thought in James chapter one is staggering. Know that the testing and trying of your faith is producing endurance: all of these things—the hard, the mysterious, the frustrating—are coming with great purpose. When in the middle of these you feel stuck —you don't know what to do—*ask for wisdom*. He will put truth and light on your path. But—and don't miss this—understand that you will have to trust His often counterintuitive directions.

Those who continue to walk with Him and not *faint* will receive great reward. He is the *way* and the *information* you will need to walk through all of it. With that in mind—*understanding what this journey is doing in you (making you more like Jesus and stirring your affection for Him!)*— allow the light of truth to shine brightly in you, revealing everything within your emotion, intellect, and will that is hurting you and others. When He does grant you revelation of those things, don't just look at it and walk away.

Let Him remove it from you.

In the end, everything about you will be different. What comes out of your mouth will be wholly different, because what you think and feel will be different. *Your heart will see the hurt in your world, and you will take Him to it.*

All of this hinges on the saving of the soul. The saving of the soul hinges on the receiving of the Word. The Word is truth, and *truth* is a revealer. It's a communication thing. It's the primary way that your Father is going to shine light on your path. While He will give *practical* light on your circumstances when needed—such as to go this way or go that way—He will shed much more light that tells you how to feel and think about your circumstances, so you are being changed as you walk them out.

All decisions and reactions—base and surface—are processed at the level of the soul. From your birth, you've been communicating from the outside in. Your circumstances, the voices of others around you, even the voice of the demonic (that comes in the form of temptation or accusation) has acted upon your flesh with circumstance—and thought upon thought. Based on what was happening around you, you have emoted, thought, and acted accordingly—but now!—*you are in-dwelt with the Spirit of Christ.* Not God little "g," but God big "G." All of the attributes of infinity apply. *God has taken up residence in you!* You are now to live by a communication that flows from the inside out. As you receive *the Word/the Truth*—the Holy Spirit teaches, reveals, and applies that to the *soul* (emotion, will and intellect). "However when He, the Spirit of Truth, is come, He will guide you into all truth" (Jn. 16:13). Also see John 14:26.

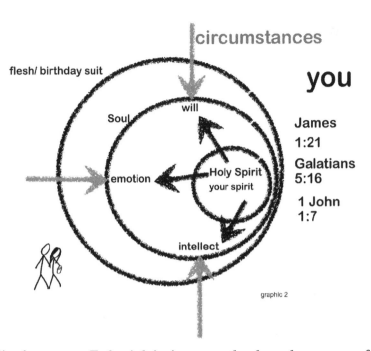

flesh/ birthday suit

circumstances

you

will

Soul

Holy Spirit
your spirit

emotion

intellect

James
1:21
Galatians
5:16
1 John
1:7

graphic 2

Simply put, *your Father is bringing you to the place where you can feel about things the way He feels about them—think about things the way He thinks about them—and act in step with Him.* He is giving you the *mind of Christ!* (1 Cor. 2:16). Ahhhhh!!!!! Who would this help?!!!! I told you it was the unthinkable miracle! That *the personality of Christ*—which never gets it wrong, never is panicked, never is despairing, never eaten by bitterness, never confused on circumstantial decisions nor riddled with angst by them—is becoming *the very life of your personality.*

Why am I sharing this here? I'll try to connect the dots. When we hear that light will be on the path, we immediately turn our attention to *things that we have to deal with*—physical earth-bound tangibles and scenarios with measurable consequence.

A co-worker has been running his mouth about you at work. It's rumored that downsizing is coming down the pipe. It's likely one of you will have to go. You've never been much of a schmoozer, but he seems to excel at it. You're not sure, but your boss doesn't seem to talk to you the same way as before. Maybe you're imagining it, but conversation from across the room seems to have folks sneaking peaks in and out at you. Now, you're having full-on fantasized conversations in your head with this guy, your boss, your

222

co-workers (and hardly any of them are pleasant). In fact, they're ugly. What you are asking for when you're asking for light is: *God—give me a strategy. Show me how to show him up. Show me how to shut him up. I need a way to get the truth to my boss about me. Show me how to DO that.* While there will certainly be moments when God gives specific NOW directions, please know and understand that the light He is most likely to shine will fall upon your reactions to the journey itself—teaching you how to feel about it, and how to think about it, so that when you do act (take a step) it is in the right direction that is blessed with understanding.

That is a much bigger world than simply saying *step here and now there —say this and now say that.* When you feel about it the way He feels about it and think about it the way He thinks about it, your co-worker is blessed, your boss is blessed, everyone in your office blessed—even if they don't know it for themselves. (and there are a hundred different life circumstances we could talk about here...)

What I find in my journey—what I most often need (more than anything) —is to simply know how to feel about things. I am rather confident that much of this is by design so that to ask for their complete removal would be to reject what He has for me. If that is the case, what I need is a divine perspective. *Papa, give me light to see this how You're seeing it. I know You are never emotionally conflicted, confused, panicked, or bitter—show me how to feel about what is happening. Give me your thought on the matter. You are a good Shepherd who knows everything about Your path. Nothing is hidden to You on the path that You are leading me on. Whatever You're thinking about it has to be right. Let me see that!*

Friend, that's what He does on the path. He *illuminates our steps* (Ps. 18:28). *His word is a lamp unto our feet and a light unto our path* (Ps. 119:105), restoring our soul (emotion, will, and intellect) all along the way. So kind of like Aiden Journey—grab His hand (maybe even close your eyes?), and enjoy the path.

THE LIFE

All men seek happiness. This is without exception. Whatever different means they employ, they all tend to this end. The cause of some going to war, and of others avoiding it, is the same desire in both, attended with different views. The will never takes the least step but to this object. This is the motive of every action of every man, even of those who hang themselves. [83]

-Blaise Pascal

Piper, of *Christian hedonism* fame quotes Pascal in his brilliant *Desiring God*. He writes much of being happy in God. That *God is most glorified when we are most satisfied (HAPPY) in Him.*[84] Nothing to quibble about there, it is one of the most astonishing truths in the whole of human existence; a beautiful grace that does the impossible. It fills the *black hole* otherwise known as the heart. Yet, I would like to refine Pascal's statement. All men do seek happiness, but I think it misses something further in. Deeper, if you will.

I think at the base core of man's pursuit is to have *life*. It is the abstract concept of life that, if it can be obtained, will make them happy. Our hearts beat, we breathe—we call these things living—but *in* our hearts (deep in the emotion)—entangled in our subconscious thought, is the nagging emptiness that is the *void*—*the black hole*. In that nothing is lifelessness. There is no movement there. The human heart craves progress, movement, happening—forward or backward—*somewhere*—or we go mad. It's why solitary confinement is the deadliest of measures in maximum security prisons. There is no life in the void. Genesis chapter one affirms this. When there is the abstract *more*—*other*—elusive something else, and we don't have *it*—we feel the *lifelessness* to our core. Pascal is right. We will do anything and everything to obtain it. It's why we're such suckers for satan's advertisements. Desperate people are a con-man's dream! Hear Pascal's thought with a subtle twist again:

All men seek [LIFE]. *This is without exception. Whatever different means they employ, they all tend to this end. The cause of some going to war, and of others avoiding it, is the same desire in both, attended with different views. The will never takes the least step but to this object. This is the motive of every action of every man, even of those who hang themselves.*[85]

---

[83] Pascal, Blaise, *Pascal's Pensees,* trans. W.F. Trotter (New York: E.P. Dutton, 1958), 113, thought #425.

[84] John Piper. *Desiring God* (Sisters, OR: Multnomah Publishers, 2003), 10.

[85] Pascal, Blaise, *Pascal's Pensees,* trans. W.F. Trotter (New York: E.P. Dutton, 1958), 113, thought #425.

If we are honest, what we have been seeking—in all of our *Christian life* and *Christian* endeavors—has been *life* (movement, progress, happening). If you'll notice, none of these attributes we instinctively place on *life* apply to a *person.* They are all circumstantial. Let's go back to our passage and look close at what is offered us.

Jesus says to His disciples in that hour of mystery, "I am the way, and the truth, and the life; no one comes to the Father but through Me" (Jn. 14:6). Jesus is a *way,* a journey that lasts until your birthday suit falls off. Jesus is the light on the path. (It's a path with lots of twists and turns loaded with a good Father's discipline.) If you're going to walk with Him for any length of time, you are going to need *life* to do it.

There is no way for me to know who will read this. There is no way for me to guess what season of life—*flying, running, walking*—you will be in when you begin it. I do speculate, however, that there may be much in this writing that may scare you. If so, that saddens me. Please hear this: *I do not regret or begrudge this journey. It has been the gift of my lifetime. It introduced me to the heart of God. Because of this journey, I get to hear the voice of the God of Genesis and Revelation speak into my very soul! I would not trade it for anything.*

With that said, I want to encourage you with this. If the truth of James 1:2-4 and Hebrews 12 (and how these work out in each of the seasons—especially in wilderness journeys) have you recoiling, please here what Jesus is saying. **He is *life* for the way!** Peter tells us as much: "His divine power has granted to us everything pertaining to life and godliness, through the true knowledge of Him who called us by His own glory and excellence" (2 Pet. 1:3).

Can I ask you a trick question? Is there anything that pertains to life *outside of living* right now? *No!* The context of Peter's statement is that the *entire universe* of your being at present which is entirely wrapped up in the here and now along with whatever tomorrows that will be given. Everything pertaining to *living*—everything pertaining to your chief pursuit—which is the *forming of Christ in you* (Gal. 4:19) and loving God, has been given (*past tense*) to you. The more you know of Jesus (which this journey is designed to make happen), the more of this you can access. If you're looking at the processes of God and thinking, "I can't do this." You're right! *He* can, though, because HE IS THE ONE DOING IT. It's His process over your life, not yours—and He has promised you *life* for the journey!!!!

ZOE LIFE

When the word is used, especially seen in Greek translations of the Old Testament, two forms are typically found. One is *bios*. Keith Kannenberg refers to this as *everyday life*.[86] It's the kind of life referred to in 2 Timothy 2:4, "No soldier in active service entangles himself in the affairs of *everyday life*..." (italics mine). This is not the kind of life we're talking about here. What John 14:6 is referring to is *zoe*—a reminder of this term as referenced in chapter six—here is Strong's definition: "life in the absolute sense—life as God has it, which the Father has in Himself, and which He gave to the Incarnate Son to have in Himself, and which the Son manifested in the world."[87]

Can we go back to Andrew Murray again?—that the Holy Spirit becomes to me the very *life* of my personality! The life that is resident within the Father is the life that now resides within you and is available to you *all along the way*. The essence of this entire journey is the accessing of the *Divine Nature* that is always available to us in getting to know Jesus and *applying* Jesus. "For by these He has granted to us His precious and magnificent promises, so that by them you may become partakers of the Divine nature..." (2 Pet. 1:4)—partakers of a *zoe life* that is inexhaustible. No matter the circumstance of the journey, **He will always be more than enough.**

I mentioned earlier that the Old Testament Judaic culture was very intentional in the naming of their children. Often they selected names that reflected their journey. Steph and I have followed in this tradition in the naming of our own kids. Tsion (alternate spelling of Zion) and Salem are our oldest. They reflect our hopes for them. Psalm 76:2 declares: "His tabernacle is in Salem; His dwelling place also is in Zion." We're watching this become a lived reality in their lives in these days and our hearts are pretty swollen about it. Our daughter was conceived in December. She came to us in a season of our lives when we were wrestling with the hope that I would someday walk out of this wilderness journey. Her full name is Bethlehem

---

[86]Keith Kannenberg. *Soul Talk* (China Grove, NC: 4 a Change, 2010), 23.

[87]James Strong. *The New Strong's Dictionary of Bible Words* (Nashville, TN: Thomas Nelson, 2001), 1128.

Hope Reid. Why? Because *hope* was born in Bethlehem and that Hope is the *light of men* (Jn. 1:4).

Then came Aiden Journey. No, it's not a *Bible* name. Aiden was a complete surprise to Steph and me. I have joked with family and friends that perhaps I should sue the teacher that taught my sex-ed class. Thinking maybe he left something out??? (*hilarious, scottie.*) He is eight years old as of this writing.

While none of my children have known a dad outside of the *wilderness journey,* Aiden was born and raised through the most intense days of it. 2009 was one of those years where if it could go wrong—in terms of vocational pursuit—it did. Right when I was thinking I might be turning the corner into fruitfulness, it all seemed to crash into a humiliating ruin. What I needed more than anything in those days, and have needed to the present day was a *zoe life* to walk these days out. You may have noticed that I'm a bit of an A.W. Tozer fan in the reading of this book. I know I make it sound excruciating at times, but I really do love the journey! *Aiden Wilson Tozer* is an inspiration to Steph and me. That alone, however, was not enough to pass the name to our beloved son. It was the meaning of *Aiden* that did that. It literally means, *little fire.* And—he lives up to it! What I needed—what we sensed *we* might need for the foreseeable future was *fire for the journey.* And so it was that we named the most life-giving of surprises, our beloved Aiden Journey *(little fire = the Holy Spirit!)*

Jesus has been that kind of *life* for me. When I have panicked, flailing for *the catcher*, falling hopelessly through the air, *Papa Eagle* has caught me every time. I won't lie to you. I have some pretty nasty scars—some that I fear may never entirely go away. It's ok. I know He has purpose for them. I've been going in circles for all of my life—*flying, running, and walking* —*flying, running, and walking*—*flying, running, and walking*—and I have seen that *He is good* (Ps. 34:8). I am nowhere near where I started. Even now, in days of vocational mystery, *He has made something of me.*

we need to say—as jack and jill—that we are grateful for the hill, for the journey, and all of the rippling circles of our pail. the God who makes sure our falls are not fatal is **faithful.**

"and God is able to make all grace abound to you, so that having all sufficiency in all things at all times, you may abound in every good work."
—2 corinthians 9:8.

Jesus, my heart is grateful. I haven't said it enough. I am sorry that I haven't. At every turn, You were worthy of hearing it. Thank You for the road and for what You did all along the way. I love You, Jesus. You are my God—so be it with joy!

EPILOGUE

A PRAYER WITH A SONG

(Audrey Assad's *Show Me* & my prayer in bold italics)

You could plant me like a tree beside a river
You could tangle me in soil and let my roots run wild
And I would blossom like a flower in the desert
But for now just let me cry

***You could do this to me, Papa. You could plant me anywhere you wanted.
You could take me out of this wilderness today, rooting me in the very
places where all my hope and desire could blossom like a banyan tree,
consuming it all, becoming a jungle of fruit and glory. But right now, the
hurt is still too deep. Emotion needs to come out of me. All of the feeling
dams in my throat. Simply too much thought, emotion, baggage to come
out all at once. The tears won't start. Maybe if they do, they won't stop.
Somehow it feels like weeping on your chest is all my heart needs.***

You could raise me like a banner in the battle
Put victory like fire behind my shining eyes
And I would drift like falling snow over the embers
But for now, just let me lie

***I would do that, Papa. You could run me at the very front of the battle.
I would carry your banner against all the hosts of hell with your victory
shining in my eyes. I would risk all to march in the company of those
whom you command to such places. You can send all of the fragile me
into the deadliest of places, where my ego and life may be melted away.
But Papa, I've been there before. The wounds of failure, of loyal and
disloyal opposition, have me beaten down. I feel like I have floated over
the embers and not much remains of me. Too raw or sore to move right
now. Papa, I would rise up and do it all, but I hurt right now. I need to
rest.***

Bind up these broken bones
Mercy bend and bring me back to life
But not before you show me how to die

All of it, I would do if I could. But I'm broken. Not blaming You—It was me in the fight and wrestling all along the way. I feel like I'm on life-support now—Mercy, bend and bring me back to life...

Set me like a star before the morning
Like a sun that steals the darkness from a world asleep
And I'll illuminate the path You've laid before me
But for now just let me be

You could do that with me, Papa. You could light me a blaze~~~the glory of Your Spirit burning through the transparent shell of me searing truth and salvation into and through the eyes asleep to You. You could burn straight through—melting all the me of me in ways that give watching men inspired faces and mouths gaped wide open—You can put in me a light so intense that it would be a virtual sun on the twisting path, but right now my heart and hope are nearly spent. My nerves are raw to the touch. The refining fires have left me blistered head to toe. Don't move me right now—don't touch me—let me be....

Bind up these broken bones
Mercy, bend and bring me back to life
But not before You show me how to die
No, not before You show me how to die

Oh my GOD! I would do it all again—ALL OF IT and more...but not until you show me how to die—because I've walked these roads. The bones of emotion and mind are broken. I was alive then. I felt it all. The me in me was pierced by the arrows, burnt from the flames, bruised from the blows, and I can't do that again. You can take me to all of these places, but I'm not going until You show me how to die. Because if I'm dead—If I'm really dead, the arrows, the flames, the blows—they won't hurt me anymore. Your victory will shine behind my eyes and I will bear no hurt—because dead men don't feel with the lives of mortal men. I'll be of another kind. A living child of the firstfruits who walk these places in resurrection power! Fill the dead me, Lord Jesus, and I'll walk impervious enveloped in the glory/other of You.
(galatians 2:20).

So let me go **like a leaf upon the water**
Let me brave the wild currents flowing to the sea
And I will disappear into a deeper beauty

But for now just stay with me
God, for now just stay with me

In that place—in resurrection power—in soul-healed knowing, lay me
on the fast moving waters. I'll go with joy over every rock, swirl, and fall.
Further up and further in, [88] **until all of me is lost in the infinite**
companionship of You. *In the meantime Papa, between here and there*
—in the journey and along the way, please stay with Me. [89]

-from *Show Me* by Audrey Assad **(italics and bold mine)**

---

[88]C. S. Lewis. *Chronicles of Narnia* (New York, NY: Harper Collins, 2001), 753.

[89] Assad, Audrey. *The House You're Building.* Sparrow 5099945707520, 2010,
compact disc.

BIBLIOGRAPHY

Bruce, F.F. *Paul Apostle of the Heart Set Free.* Grand Rapids, MI: William B. Eerdmans Publishing, 1977.

Davis, John J. *Paradise to Prison.* Grand Rapids, MI: Baker Book House, 1975.

Dictionary.com Unabridged. Random House, Inc. 6 Feb. 2018. *<Dictionary.com>.*

Friedberg, Arther L. & Ira S. *A Guide Book of United States Paper Money.* Atlanta, GA: Whitman Publishing, 2016.

Hill, Craig. *Living On the Third River.* Littleton, CO: Family Foundation International, 2002.

Hurnard, Hannah. *Hinds Feet on High Places.* Uhrichsville, OH: Barbour, 1987.

Kannenberg, Keith. *Soul Talk.* China Grove, NC: 4 a Change, 2010.

Lasor, William Sanford, David Allen Hubbard, and Frederic W. M. Bush. *Old Testament Survey.* Grand Rapids, MI: William B. Eerdmans Publishing, 1996.

Lewis, C.S. *Chronicles of Narnia.* New York, NY: Harper Collins, 2001.

Lewis, C.S. *Mere Christianity.* SanFrancisco, CA: Harper, 1952.

Martindale, Wayne & Jerry Root. *The Quotable Lewis.* Carol Stream, IL: Tyndale House Publishers, 1990.

Murray, Andrew. *The Spirit of Christ.* Fort Washington, PA: Christian Literature Crusade, 1963.

Nee, Watchman. *Secrets to Spiritual Power.* New Kensington, PA: Whitaker House, 1999.

Nee, Watchman. *The Release Of The Spirit.* New York: Christian Fellowship Publishers, 2000.

Nelson's. *Nelson's Complete Book of Bible Maps & Charts.* Nashville, TN: Thomas Nelson, 1996.

233

Nouwen, Henri J.M. *Sabbatical Journey.* New York, NY: The Cross Road Publishing Co., 1998.

Otis, George Jr. *God's Trademarks.* Grand Rapids, MI: Chosen Books, 2000.

Pascal, Blaise. *Pascal's Pensees,* trans. W.F. Trotter, New York: E.P. Dutton, 1958.

Peterson, Eugene H. *The Message.* Colorado Springs, CO: Navpress, 1993.

Piper, John. *Desiring God.* Sisters, OR: Multnomah Publishers, 2003.

Schultz, Samuel J. *The Old Testament Speaks.* San Francisco, CA: Harper, 1990.

Spangler, Ann. *The Names of God Bible.* Grand Rapids, MI: Revell, 2011.

Stevens, Charles H. *The Wilderness Journey.* Chicago, IL: Moody Press, 1971.

Strong, James. *The New Strong's Dictionary of Bible Words.* Nashville, TN: Thomas Nelson, 2001.

Strong, James. *The Strongest NASB Exhaustive Concordance.* Grand Rapids, MI: Zondervan, 2000.

Thayer, Joseph H. *Greek-English Lexicon Of The New Testament.* Peabody, MA: Hendrickson Publishers,1999.

Tolkien, J.R.R. *The Lord of The Rings.* New York: Houghton Mifflin Co., 1994.

Tozer, A.W. *The Crucified Life.* Ventura, CA: Regal, 2011.

Voskamp, Ann. *One Thousand Gifts.* Grand Rapids, MI: Zondervan, 2010.

Walton, John H. *Ancient Near Eastern Thought and the Old Testament.* Grand Rapids, MI: Baker Academic, 2006.

Warren, Rick. *The Purpose Driven Life.* Grand Rapids, MI: Zondervan, 2012.

WebMD Medical Reference Reviewed by Dan Brennan, MD on December 22, 2015. http://teens.webmd.com/boys/circumcision-faq#1.

Webster's. *Webster's New Encyclopedic Dictionary.* New York, NY: BD&L, 1993.

DISCOGRAPHY

Assad, Audrey. *The House You're Building.* Sparrow 5099945707520, 2010, compact disc.
Copyright © 2010 Spiritandsong.Com Pub (BMI) River Oaks Music Company (BMI) (adm. at CapitolCMGPublishing.com) All rights reserved. Used by permission.

Corts, Dr. Mark. *From Filling to Power.* Sharelife, Calvary Baptist Church. 0038-1B. 1999. cassette tape.

Corts, Dr. Mark. *Looking for Strength.* Share life, Calvary Baptist Church. 2000, cassette tape.

David Crowder Band. *The Lime CD.* Sparrow Records, Sixstep Records B0001KL4VS, 2004, compact disc.
Copyright © 1998 worshiptogether.com Songs (ASCAP) (adm. at CapitolCMGPublishing.com) All rights reserved. Used by permission.

Forrest Gump. Directed by Robert Zemeckis, Steve Starkey and Rick Carter. Paramount Pictures, 1994.

Hall, Charlie. *The Bright Sadness.* Sparrow Records, Sixstep Records 5099952222221, 2008, compact disc.
Copyright © 2008 worshiptogether.com Songs (ASCAP) sixsteps Music (ASCAP) (adm. at CapitolCMGPublishing.com) All rights reserved. Used by permission.

Hillsong. *The Peace Project.* Hillsong Music Publishing, 2017.
Copyright © 2017 Hillsong Music Publishing (APRA) (adm. in the US and Canada at CapitolCMGPublishing.com) All rights reserved. Used by permission.

Newton, John. *Amazing Grace. Best Loved Songs And Hymns.* Edited by Ruth W. Shelton. Kendallville, IN: Ellis J. Crum, 1961.

Passion. *Our Love Is Loud.* Sparrow Records, Sixstep Records 7243 8 51923 0 2 / SPD 51923, 2002, compact disc.

Return of Jafar. Directed by Toby Shelton, Tad Stones & Alan Zaslove, Walt Disney Pictures, 1994.

CURRENT PROJECTS FROM SCOTT & STEPHANIE FOR 121 RESOURCES:

Still Going in Circles and Getting Somewhere
Sequel to *Going in Circles and Actually Getting Somewhere*

A Hosea Christmas: UnF**king The World

Yahweh Remembered
A Word to the Church in the West

Yahweh Remembered—Making it Right
A Conclusion of the Word to the Church in the West

Jack and Jill Series
Case study series that will address specific topics and life circumstances
using the tools given in *Still Going in Circles and Getting Somewhere.*

Learn more about 121 resources and ministries at www.one21.life.

Printed in Great Britain
by Amazon

45304737R00136